Lecture Notes of the Institute for Computer Sciences, Social Informatics and Telecommunications Engineering 177

More information about this series at http://www.springer.com/series/8197

Song Guo · Guiyi Wei
Yang Xiang · Xiaodong Lin
Pascal Lorenz (Eds.)

Testbeds and Research Infrastructures for the Development of Networks and Communities

11th International Conference, TRIDENTCOM 2016
Hangzhou, China, June 14–15, 2016
Revised Selected Papers

 Springer

Editors

Song Guo
Hong Kong Polytechnic University
Kowloon
Hong Kong

Guiyi Wei
Computer and Information Engineering
Zhejiang Gongshang University
Hangzhou
China

Yang Xiang
School of Information Technology
Deakin University
Burwood, VIC
Australia

Xiaodong Lin
Faculty of Business and Information
University of Ontario Institute of
 Technology
Oshawa, ON
Canada

Pascal Lorenz
IUT
University of Haute Alsace
Colmar
France

ISSN 1867-8211   ISSN 1867-822X   (electronic)
Lecture Notes of the Institute for Computer Sciences, Social Informatics
and Telecommunications Engineering
ISBN 978-3-319-49579-8   ISBN 978-3-319-49580-4   (eBook)
DOI 10.1007/978-3-319-49580-4

Library of Congress Control Number: 2016957481

Printed on acid-free paper

This Springer imprint is published by Springer Nature
The registered company is Springer International Publishing AG
The registered company address is: Gewerbestrasse 11, 6330 Cham, Switzerland

Preface

The 11th International Conference on Testbeds and Research Infrastructures for the Development of Networks and Communities (TRIDENTCOM 2016) provided a successful forum for practitioners and researchers from diverse backgrounds from all over the world to interact and exchange experiences about the emerging technologies of big data, cyber-physical systems, and computer communications.

It is our distinct honor to acknowledge two keynote speeches: "D2D: Research Trend and Future Perspective" by Prof. Nei Kato from Tohoku University and "Testbeds, Test Points and Measurements in an IPTV Network" by Prof. Jaime Lloret from the Polytechnic University of Valencia. The technical program was highly selective with 16 regular papers in four sessions: Future Internet and Software Defined Network, Network Testbed Design and Implementation, Testbed for Network Applications, and QoS/QoE on Networks. The conference successfully inspired many innovative directions in the fields of big data science and applications, cyber-physical systems and applications, networking and communications, all with a special focus on testbeds for these emerging technologies and applications.

The technical program was the result of the hard work of many individuals. We would like to thank all the authors for submitting their outstanding work to TRIDENTCOM 2016. We offer our sincere gratitude to the Technical Program Committee members and reviewers, who worked hard to provide thorough and constructive reviews in a timely manner. We are grateful to the Steering Committee of TRIDENTCOM 2016 for their invaluable guidance and support. Finally, we are grateful to all the participants in TRIDENTCOM 2016.

October 2016

Song Guo
Guiyi Wei
Yang Xiang
Xiaodong Lin
Pascal Lorenz

Organization

Steering Committee

Imrich Chlamtac	CREATE-NET, Italy (Chair)
Victor C.M. Leung	The University of British Columbia, Canada
Athanasios V. Vasilakos	National Technical University of Athens, Greece

Organizing Committee

General Chairs

Song Guo	Hong Kong Polytechnic University, Hong Kong
Guiyi Wei	Zhejiang Gongshang University, China

Honorary General Chair

Wenzhan Dai	Zhejiang Gongshang University, China

Technical Program Chairs

Yang Xiang	Deakin University, Australia
Xiaodong Lin	University of Ontario Institute of Technology, Canada
Pascal Lorenz	University of Haute Alsace, France

Web Chair

Jun Shao	Zhejiang Gongshang University, China

Workshops Chair

Shibo He	Zhejiang University, China

Tutorials Chair

Lei Liu	Shandong University, China

Sponsorship and Exhibits Chair

Mande Xie	Zhejiang Gongshang University, China

Local Chair

Zhiguo Shi	Zhejiang University, China

Publicity and Social Media Chair

Kaimin Wei	Jinan University, China

Conference Manager

Barbara Fertalova   EAI (European Alliance for Innovation)

Technical Program Committee

Yang Xiang   Deakin University, Australia
Xiaodong Lin   University of Ontario Institute of Technology, Canada
Pascal Lorenz   University of Haute Alsace, France
Marin Litoiu   York University, Canada
Andy Bavier   Princeton University, USA
Weibin Sun   University of Utah, USA
Maher Elshakankiri   Umm Al-Qura University, Saudi Arabia
Abdelmajid Khelil   Science and Technology Unit, UQU University, KSA
Marc St-Hilaire   Carleton University, Canada
Vicraj Thomas   BBN Technologies, USA
Jason Liu   Florida International University, USA
Mike Wittie   Montana State University, USA
Jeannie Albrecht   Williams College, USA
Geoffrey Challen   University at Buffalo, USA
Chip Elliott   GENI Project Office, USA
Mohamed El-Darieby   University of Regina, Canada
Justin Cappos   New York University, USA

Contents

Future Internet and Software
Defined Network

Loose Management for Multi-controller in SDN

Ligang Dong$^{(\boxtimes)}$, Jing Zhou, Tijie Xu, Dandan Yang, Ying Li,
and Weiming Wang

School of Information and Electronic Engineering,
Zhejiang Gongshang University, No. 18, Xuezheng Street,
Xiasha University Town, Hangzhou 310018, China
donglg@zjgsu.edu.cn

Abstract. Centralized network control plane in SDN brings scalability and reliability problem to the network, therefore, the research of multi-controller is appeared. For improving the communication efficiency between the controller and the network device, this paper proposes a loose management strategy to dynamically adjust the frequency of interaction between controllers and network devices. Based on the above idea, firstly, this paper designed the scheme and algorithm of multi-controller loose management. Secondly, this paper quantitatively analyzed the advantages of multi-controller loose management algorithm by mathematically modeling the virtual network deployment success ratio and the management revenue between controllers and network devices. Finally, experiment results show that the multi-controller loose management idea can improve the communication efficiency between the controller and the network device and the controller management efficiency. Simulation results also show that mathematical model accurately predict the performance of loose management algorithm.

Keywords: Distributed control · Multi-controller · Loose management · SDN

1 Introduction

Software Defined Network (SDN) as a new network architecture [1, 2], realizes the centralized, dynamic, and programmable control of the entire network by the virtualization and the separation of application layer, control layer, and data layer.

Like other centralized systems, centralized control in SDN also causes problems of scalability and reliability. Therefore, it is necessary to establish a logical centralized control platform to management the entire network.

In the multi-controller structure of SDN, the controller may not know the status of the network device resources, so a heavy-load network device will probably repeatedly refuse requests from controllers. For improving the communication efficiency between the controller and the network device, this paper proposes a loose management strategy to dynamically adjust the frequency of interaction between controllers and network devices. We consider Virtual Networks (VNs) deployment in SDN as an example. When the number of VNs not deployed by a network device reaches a threshold, the

© ICST Institute for Computer Sciences, Social Informatics and Telecommunications Engineering 2017
S. Guo et al. (Eds.): TridentCom 2016, LNICST 177, pp. 3–13, 2017.
DOI: 10.1007/978-3-319-49580-4_1

controller will temporarily stop the communication with the network device. After a period of time, the communication between the controller and the network device is resumed. It will improve the management and communication efficiency between controllers and network devices. That is the first contribution of this paper. The second contribution of paper is mathematically modeling of the Virtual Network (VN) deployment success ratio, and the communication benefits between controllers and network devices. Both of the model and simulation results confirm the advantages of loose management.

The remainder of the paper is organized as follows. Section 2 introduces the related work, including the classification of the multi-controller. Section 3 proposes the scheme and algorithm of loose management. Section 4 evaluates the model using simulations. Finally, Sect. 5 concludes the paper.

2   Related Work

Currently, the implementation for SDN [4] architecture is reliant upon a single controller to push flow rules to all SDN-enabled switches in the network, which creates a performance bottleneck and single point of failure in large networks [5]. Therefore, many scholars have attracted to the research of multi-controller. Multi-controller in SDN can be classified from four viewpoints.

(1) Whole network view controller and local network view controller. The former controllers have a complete information about the entire networks, e.g., HyperFlow [3] and D-ZENIC [7]. While the latter controller have not, e.g., Devolved [8].

(2) Multi-management controller and no multi-management controller. The former means that a single network device may be managed by more than one controller, e.g., Devolved [8], ElastiCon [9], and the literatures [10–12]. The latter refers to that every controller manages part of the network, and a single network device is managed only by one controller, e.g., HyperFlow [3].

(3) Single-level controller and multi-level controller. The latter controllers have a root controller as management operations coordinator of local controllers, e.g., Kandoo [13], D-ZENIC [7]. The former controllers locate on the same level of managing the network devices, e.g., Devolved [8], HyperFlow [3], ONOS [18], and the literature [10, 11].

(4) Static management controller and dynamic management controller. Their difference is whether or not the management relationship between network devices and controllers will change the controller with time on. In other words, a network device probably has different controllers in different situations. The typical examples of the former are Onix [14], HyperFlow [3], the literature [15], while the examples of the latter are literature [12, 16] and ElastiCon [9].

Based on the multi-controller multi-management, this paper proposes the loose management idea to improve communication efficiency between devices and controllers. There are some researches of improving communication efficiency between devices and controllers, e.g., the literature [17].

3   Scheme and Algorithm of Loose Management for Multi-controller

Control plane and data plane are physically separated in SDN network architecture, which makes centralized configuration and management of the network possible. Based on this, we propose a loose management scheme on network device for multi-controller multi-management, as shown in Fig. 1.

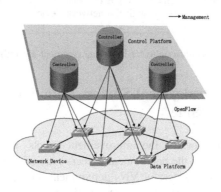

Fig. 1. Multi-controller multi-management

We assume that required resources of deploying a VN is R_{VN}. Here, the "resource" is a generic concept and can be referred to memory, bandwidth, CPU, etc., or the composite of various resource types, which depends on users' applications. We assume that the life cycle of a VN is T, the amount of resources in a network device is R_{sub}, the average time between two adjacent request of deploying a VN is Δ, the VN deployment requests arrive according to a Poisson process. When $(T/\Delta)R_{VN} \leq R_{sub}$, the amount of resources in a network device is adequate to deploy VN. When $(T/\Delta)R_{VN} > R_{sub}$, the amount of resources in a network device is insufficient to deploy VN. The later will cause that the network device is not able to participate in the deployment of VNs, and refuses requests from controllers, which wastes communication and management overheads (including receiving, handling, and replying the request, maintaining the communication state) in both controllers and network devices. Meanwhile, the success ratio of VN deployment is low since more requests are refused.

When the resources of network device are not enough to deploy VNs, the controller will suspend the communication with the network device for some time. When the resources in the network device are released, the controller will restore communication with the network device. Based on the above scheme, we propose an multi-controller loose management algorithm, shown as follows:

> **Step 1.** Network devices send connection requests and establish connections with the controllers.
> **Step 2.** A controller (i.e., any controller in the multi-controller structure) waits for network application requests.
> **Step 3.** The controller selects appropriate network devices to deploy the VN, and sends the deployment message to related network devices.
> **Step 4.** If each network device deploys the VN successfully, then go to Step 2, otherwise, the network device of deployment failure sends a failure message to the controller.
> **Step 5.** The controller suspend to communicate with the network device, in which the number of deployment failure reach r (r is a positive integer). (After a preset period of time, the controller restores communication with the network device. The number of failures is reset to zero.) Go to Step 3.

Fig. 2. Multi-controller loose management algorithm.

4   Analysis of the Deployment Success Ratio and the Loose Management Revenue

We use two metrics to measure the improvement effects of the strategy of loose management. The first one is the deployment success ratio of VNs, which is defined as the ratio of the number of successful VNs deployment on a network device and the number of VNs deployment request on the network device. The second one is the net revenue of deploying a VN, which is defined as the difference between the revenue of a successful deployment and the cost of communication.

In this section, firstly, we conduct simulations to compare loose with non-loose management algorithms in terms of the above two metrics. Secondly, in order to better predict the performance of loose management algorithm, we establish the mathematical model and verified it by simulations.

The independent and dependent variables used in this section are defined in Tables 1 and 2 respectively.

Table 1. Independent variables

Parameters	Definition
R_{sub}	The resource capacity of a network device
R_{VN}	The resource requirement for deploying a VN
λ	The number of VNs deployment requests per unit time
r	The threshold number of VNs that the network device doesn't participate in before the communication is suspended
t_1	The duration of communication suspension
T	The lifecycle of VN
x	The communication cost of a VN deployment
s	The net income of deploying a VN
M	The total number of requests for deploying VNs

Table 2. Dependent Variables

Parameters	Definitions
m_0	The average number of VNs that one network device can participate in in unit time
y	The proportion of communication time in unit time
t_2	The average duration of a communication cycle
R_0	The net income of VN deployment in unit time
η	The success ratio of VN deployment requests
R_{ev}	The total net income of VN deployment

4.1 Comparison Between the Loose and Non-loose Management Algorithms

Based on the algorithm in Fig. 2, we use discrete event simulation to simulate multiple controllers communication with a single network device. It is worth explaining that our simulation scenario can represent the general case containing multi-controllers and multiple network devices, as every network device is independent. Our simulation platform is Eclipse IDE for C/C ++ Developers. The simulation of VNs request generated using a Poisson process.

By default, the number of VNs deployment requests per unit time is 0.04. The life cycle of each VN request is distributed with a mean of $T = 1000$ exponential distribution; the resource requirement for deploying a VN obeys [0, 25] uniform distribution; the resource capacity of a network device is 100; the total number of requests for deploying VNs is 2000.

During the experiment we generate VN deployment requests in accordance with the above parameters configuration. We conducted simulation experiments to compare the non-loose and the loose management algorithm. The simulation process of non-loose management algorithm is shown in Fig. 3 below. The simulation process of loose management algorithm is shown in Fig. 4 below.

In the simulation, default parameters are: $r = 3$, $t_1 = 300$, $T = 1000$, $\lambda = 0.04$, $M = 2000$.

Figures 5 and 6 show the performance of η and R_{ev} with the change of λ (from 0.04 to 0.08), respectively.

Figures 7 and 8 show the performance of η and R_{ev} with the change of T (from 500 to 2000), respectively.

Figures 9 and 10 show the performance of η and R_{ev} with the change of M (from 500 to 2500), respectively.

From the simulation results, we concluded that:

(a) Compared with the non-loose management algorithm, the loose management algorithm has higher success ratio of deployment of VN requests and higher net income of VN deployment. The simulation result is consistent with the analysis in Sect. 3.

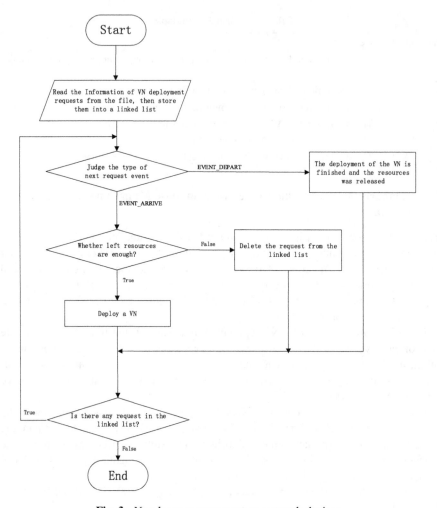

Fig. 3. Non-loose management on network devices

(b) The more number of VNs deployment requests per unit time causes the more number of VNs deployment that the network device doesn't participate in because of limited network device resources, so that the net income is lower.

(c) The longer life cycle of VNs means the longer occupation of network device resources by the VN. It causes the network device participate in a less number of VNs deployment, so that the net income of VN deployment is lower.

(d) The more number of VNs deployment requests causes the more net income of VN deployment. The success ratio of deployment of VN requests have little change vary with the number of VNs deployment requests.

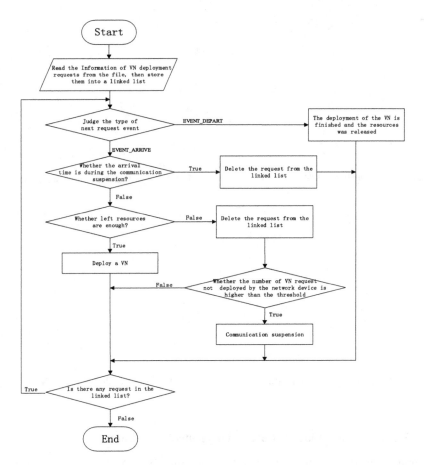

Fig. 4. Loose management on network devices

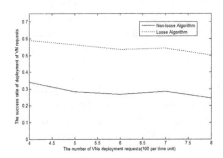

Fig. 5. Relationship between λ and η

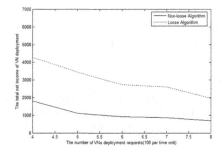

Fig. 6. Relationship between λ and R_{ev}

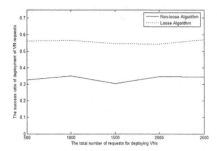

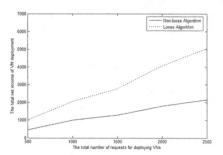

Fig. 7. Relationship between T and η

Fig. 8. Relationship between T and R_{ev}

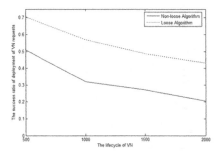

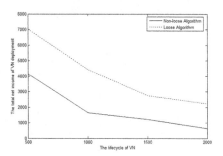

Fig. 9. Relationship between M and η

Fig. 10. Relationship between M and R_{ev}

4.2   Mathematical Model of Loose Management Algorithm

To simplify the derivation, we assume that the request of VNs are uniform arrived in our mathematical modeling.

The maximum number of virtual nodes that a single network device can support at the same time is defined as R_{sub}/R_{VN}, $(R_{sub}/R_{VN}) + r$ is the number of requests for deploying VNs from the beginning to the suspension of communication. $((R_{sub}/R_{VN}) + r)/\lambda$ is the average duration of a communication cycle. Next, we will discuss two cases.

(1) $t_1 < (T - ((R_{sub}/R_{VN}) + r)/\lambda)$ means the duration of communication suspension is shorter. Assume the proportion of communication time in unit time is y, the duration of communication time during the lifecycle of a VN is yT. So the average number of VNs that a network device can participate in unit time is

$$m_0 = (R_{sub}/R_{VN})/(yT). \tag{1}$$

During a period of communication between network devices and controllers, when the number of failed VN deployment reaches k, the network device will suspend the communication with the controller, therefore the average duration of a communication cycle is

$$t_2 = r/(\lambda - m_0). \tag{2}$$

Since y is the proportion of communication time in unit time, then,

$$t_1 + t_2 = t_2/y. \tag{3}$$

According to formula (1), (2), and (3), we can obtain

$$y = (r + \frac{R_{Sub}/R_{VN}}{T} t_1)/(r + \lambda t_1). \tag{4}$$

(2) $t_1 \geq (T - ((R_{sub}/R_{VN}) + r)/\lambda)$ means the duration of communication suspension is longer, so that the network device restores communication with the controller after the VNs are already finished. Therefore, the average duration of a communication cycle is

$$t_2 = (R_{Sub}/R_{VN} + r)/\lambda. \tag{5}$$

So the average number of VNs that a network device can participate in in unit time is

$$m_0 = (R_{Sub}/R_{VN})/((R_{Sub}/R_{VN} + r)/\lambda). \tag{6}$$

According to formula (2) and (6), we can obtain

$$y = r/(r + (\lambda - m_0)t_1) \tag{7}$$

For both cases, the net income of VN deployment in unit time is,

$$R_0 = (m_0 \cdot s - \lambda \cdot x)y \tag{8}$$

The success ratio of VN deployment requests is:

$$\eta = m_0/\lambda \tag{9}$$

Next we will contrast mathematical models and simulation of the loose management.

In the simulation, default parameters are: $r = 3$, $T = 1000$, $\lambda = 0.04$, $M = 2000$, $R_{sub} = 100$, $R_{VN} = 12.5$. The simulation results are shown in Figs. 11 and 12 below.

From Figs. 11 and 12 we can see that the mathematical model can accurately reflect the performance of the loose management.

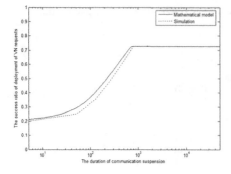
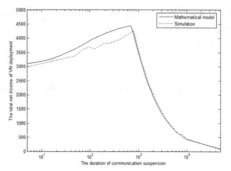

Fig. 11. Relationship between t_1 and η **Fig. 12.** Relationship between t_1 and R_{ev}

When the duration of communication suspension is much shorter. The number of communication suspension will decrease with the increasing of the duration of the communication suspension, therefore the number of VNs that the network device doesn't participate is fewer, so the success ratio of VN deployment requests and the total net income of VN deployment will increase.

When the communication suspension is much greater. Therefore, each communication cycle has almost the same number of VN deployment requests and the same number of successful VN deployment. Consequently, the success ratio of VN deployment requests will remain unchanged. However the total number of requests for deploying VNs will decrease with the increasing of the duration of the communication suspension, so the number of successfully deployment VNs will decrease, therefore the net income of VN deployment will decrease.

5 Conclusion

This paper proposes a novel loose management strategy to dynamically adjust the frequency of interaction between controllers and network devices. In detail, When the number of not deploy VNs in a network device reaches a threshold, the controller will temporarily stop the communication with the network device. After a period of time, the communication between the controller and the network device is resumed. It will improve the management and communication efficiency between controllers and network devices.

Based on the above idea, firstly, we designed the scheme and algorithm of controller loose management. Secondly, we quantitatively analyzed the advantages of controller loose management algorithm by mathematically modeling the VN deployment success rate and the communication revenue between controllers and network devices. Finally, simulation results show that the controller loose management idea can improve the communication efficiency between the controller and the network device and the controller management efficiency. Simulation results also show that mathematical model accurately predict the performance of loose management algorithm.

References

1. O.M.E. Committee.: Software-defined networking: the new norm for networks. In: ONF White Paper, Palo Alto, US. Open Networking Foundation (2012)
2. Agarwal, S., Kodialam, M., Lakshman, T.V.: Traffic engineering in software defined networks. In: Proceedings of IEEE INFOCOM, pp. 2211–2219 (2013)
3. Tootoonchian, A., Ganjali, Y.: Hyperflow: a distributed control plane for OpenFlow. In: Proceedings of the 2010 Internet Network Management Conference on Research on Enterprise Networking USENIX Association, p. 3 (2010)
4. OpenFlow Swtich Specification v1.5.0. Open Networking Foundation (2014)
5. Dan Marconett, S., Yoo, J.B.: FlowBroker: a software-defined network controller architecture for multi-domain brokering and reputation, pp. 328–359 (2014)
6. Casado, M., Freedman, M.J., Pettit, J.: Ethane: taking control of the enterprise. In: Proceedings of the 2007 Conference on Applications, Technologies, Architectures, and Protocols for Computer Communications. ACM, pp. 1–12, New York (2007)
7. Hu, Y., Tian, T., Wang, J.: D-ZENIC: a scalable distributed SDN controller architecture. ZTE Technology, pp. 23–27 (2014)
8. Tam, A.S.W., Xi, K., Chao, H.J.: Use of devolved controllers in data center networks. In: Proceedings of 2011 IEEE Conference on Computer Communications Workshops, pp. 596–601 (2011)
9. Dixit, A., Hao, F., Mukherjee, S.: Towards an elastic distributed sdn controller. In: Proceedings of The Second ACM SIGCOMM Workshop on Hot Topics in Software Defined Networking. ACM, pp. 7–12 (2013)
10. Canini, M., Kuznetsov, P., Levin, D.: A Distributed SDN Control Plane for Consistent Policy Updates. arXiv preprint arXiv (2014)
11. Canini, M., Kuznetsov, P., Levin, D.D.: Software transactional networking: concurrent and consistent policy composition. In: Proceedings of the Second ACM SIGCOMM Workshop on Hot Topics in Software Defined Networking. ACM, pp. 1–6 (2013)
12. Fu, Y.H., Bi, J., Wu, J.P.: A dormant multi-controller model for software defined networking. In: Proceedings of Communications System Design, pp. 45–55, China (2014)
13. Yeganeh, S.H., Ganjali, Y.: Kandoo: a framework for efficient and scalable offloading of control applications. In: Proceedings of the First Workshop on Hot Topics in Software Defined Networks. ACM, pp. 19–24 (2012)
14. Koponen, T., Casado, M., Gude, N.: Onix:. A distributed control platform for large-scale production networks. In: Proceedings of the 9th USENIX OSDI Conference, pp. 1–6 (2010)
15. Macapuna, C.A.B., Rothenberg, C.E., Magalh, F.: In-Packet bloom filter based data center networking with distributed openflow controllers. In: Proceedings of 2010 IEEE International Workshop on Management of Emerging Networks and Services. IEEE, pp. 584–588 (2010)
16. Bari, M.F., Roy, A.R., Chowdhury, S.R.: Dynamic controller provisioning in software defined networks. In: Proceedings of the 9th International Conference on Network and Service Management (CNSM 2013), pp. 18–25 (2013)
17. Xin, J., Jennifer, R., David, W.: Incremental update for a compositional SDN hypervisor. In: Proceedings of the Third Workshop on Hot Topics in Software Defined Networking, HotSDN 2014, pp. 187–192, New York (2014)
18. ONOS Team. Open network operating system (2012). http://onosproject.org/

On Designing SDN Services for Energy-Aware Traffic Engineering

Marcos Dias de Assunção[✉], Radu Carpa, Laurent Lefèvre, and Olivier Glück

Inria Avalon, LIP Laboratory, École Normale Supérieure de Lyon,
University of Lyon, Lyon, France
{marcos.dias.de.assuncao,radu.carpa,laurent.lefevre,
olivier.gluck}@ens-lyon.fr

Abstract. As experimenting with energy-aware techniques on large-scale production infrastructure is prohibitive, several traffic-engineering strategies have been evaluated using discrete-event simulation. The present work discusses (i) challenges towards building testbeds that allow researchers and practitioners to validate and evaluate the performance of energy-aware traffic-engineering strategies and (ii) requirements when porting simulations to testbeds. We discuss a proof-of-concept platform and an application that use and provide Software-Defined Network (SDN) services created on the Open Network Operating System (ONOS) to validate previously proposed energy-aware traffic engineering strategies. We detail the platform and illustrate how it has been used for performance evaluation.

1 Introduction

Advances in network and computing technologies have enabled a multitude of services — *e.g.* those used for big-data analysis, stream processing, video streaming, and Internet of Things (IoT) [1] — that are hosted at one or multiple data centres often interconnected by high-speed optical networks. Many of these services follow business models such as cloud computing [2], which allows a customer to rent resources from a cloud and pay only for what is consumed. Although these models are flexible and benefit from economies of scale, the increasing amount of data transferred over the network requires continuous expansion of installed capacity in order to handle peak demands. Existing work argues that the amount of electricity consumed by network infrastructure can become a bottleneck and further limit the Internet growth [3].

Given that high performance wired networks are seldom fully utilised, many organisations attempt to curb their energy consumption by reducing the number of resources that are made available during off-peak periods. Several technologies have been employed generally resulting in overall lower energy use; *e.g.* putting resources into low power consumption modes [4], adapting links' data transmission rates [5,6], and grouping and transferring packets in bursts [7]. Traffic engineering [8], initially conceived to enable quality of service and service differentiation, has been investigated as a network-wide approach to improve energy efficiency by, for instance, redirecting traffic and freeing network links that are

S. Guo et al. (Eds.): TridentCom 2016, LNICST 177, pp. 14–23, 2017.
DOI: 10.1007/978-3-319-49580-4_2

henceforth put into low power consumption modes [9,10]. The already difficult traffic-engineering problem of optimising the use of network resources becomes even more challenging when considering energy efficiency.

To simplify configuration and management operations, traffic-engineering schemes are increasingly relying on SDN as it separates control and data planes thus providing a centralised view of (i) the network topology, (ii) running applications and, (iii) traffic demands; which are important requirements to program a network and change its topology according to traffic conditions. In previous work [10,11], we investigated SDN enabled traffic engineering to redirect data flows and reduce energy consumption. The proposed techniques have been evaluated using a discrete-event simulation tool [12] since experimenting with production networks is rarely possible. Although very promising results have been obtained, there is always a need for designing proofs of concept that help evaluating the performance of energy-aware traffic-engineering techniques that support findings of simulations and eliminate undesired biases that may have resulted from simplifying the evaluated scenario.

This work describes challenges and requirements towards building testbeds for evaluating energy-aware traffic engineering strategies and porting simulations to such testbeds as SDN services. We discuss the design and implementation of an SDN application that uses segment-routing and energy-aware algorithms to redirect flows in backbone networks and free certain links [10]. We describe how a custom platform termed as GrEen Traffic engineering testBed (GETB) is used for evaluating the proposed strategies.

The rest of this paper is organised as follows. Section 2 discusses energy-aware traffic engineering, requirements for platforms used for evaluation and SDNs. The testbed used for building proofs of concept is presented in Sect. 3. The SDN application developed for validating and evaluating the performance of the traffic-engineering strategies, its life cycle and results are described in Sect. 4. Section 5 discusses related work and Sect. 6 concludes the paper.

2   Energy-Aware Traffic Engineering and SDNs

Internet traffic engineering deals with issues of performance evaluation, optimisation, and deployment of technology for measuring, characterising, modelling and controlling network traffic. One of its goals is to control and optimise the routing function, to steer traffic through the network in an effective way [8], generally to provide Quality of Service (QoS) and efficient use of network resources. Over the years, interest has grown on applying traffic engineering as a network-wide technique to improve the energy efficiency of network resources [9,13,14]; such efforts are hereafter termed simply as Green Traffic Engineering (GreenTE). Although obtained results are promising, much of the work remains based on numerical analyses and simulation. By attempting to validate our findings using a real testbed, we identified certain GreenTE requirements that experimental platforms should provide, some of which are summarised in Table 1.

The requirements are grouped in hardware resources, information about traffic, energy-optimisation mechanisms, protocols for enabling traffic engineering,

Table 1. GreenTE requirements and commonly adopted approaches.

GreenTE requirements	How requirements are tackled by solutions	
	Simulation	Testbeds
Hardware resources	Simplified and approximate software abstractions of hardware, energy consumption, access time to resources	Often real equipments running in a controlled environment
Traffic information	Commonly assumed that information about flows can be gathered without perturbing the network; centrally available	Monitoring protocols coexist with other network functions, excessive monitoring can impact normal traffic when sharing network resources
Energy-optimisation mechanisms (*e.g.* Link/port switch on/off, Adaptive Link Rate (ALR), Low Power Idle (LPI))	Simplified models, assumptions made when implementing support on simulators, parameter details not always available	Actual ALR and LPI, simulated or actual link/port switch off/on
Network protocols (*e.g.* MPLS-TE, RSVP, SPRING, OpenFlow)	Partial implementation of evaluated schemes, often relying on lower-level protocols that present already approximate behaviour	Normally complete protocol stack, presence of side-effects that may be neglected by simulation tools
Management and control	Commonly assumed that the overhead of configuration and control is negligible	Either dedicated infrastructure allocated to management or it shares resources used by normal traffic; overhead can be measured
Monitoring of power consumption and performance evaluation	Monitoring is performed by gathering stats derived from consumption models	Use of managed PDUs, wattmeters for measuring the consumption of power lines, infrastructure for gathering energy consumption stats

management and control, and measurement of power consumption and performance evaluation. Ideally, modelling and simulation should reflect the behaviour of a real system, but Table 1 provides some assumptions and simplifications found in literature and how they could be circumvented by using an actual testbed. Whilst some elements may look obvious, it is important to notice that testbeds and actual measurements of performance and energy-consumption can eliminate undesirable biases introduced during modelling and can reveal side-effects of solutions not captured during simulations.

Moreover, one of the important requirements of traffic-engineering comprises the ability to gather information about the state of the network, the needs of applications, and configure the behaviour of network resources to steer flows accordingly. Such functions, embedded into data and control planes, were traditionally performed in a decentralised manner, but more recently many traffic-engineering schemes have considered the centralisation of control functions enabled by technologies such as SDNs. SDN separates control and data planes, which in practical terms means that network devices can perform tasks

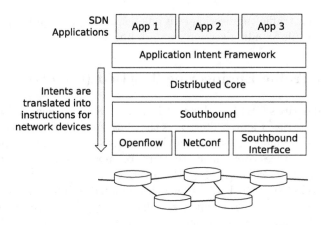

Fig. 1. ONOS intent framework.

that ensure data forwarding (*i.e.* the data plane) whereas management activities (*i.e.* the control plane) are factored out and placed at a central entity termed as SDN controller. SDN has evolved from several technologies, such as OpenFlow, which aim to provide a remote controller with the power to modify the behaviour of network devices via well-defined *forwarding instructions*. Effort has been made towards standardising the interface between controller and the data plane, generally termed as *southbound* API, and the manner the controller exposes network programmability features to applications, commonly called *northbound* API.

SDNs simplify many of the traffic-engineering requirements on gathering traffic information, performing management and control. As described in the next section, we use ONOS, an initiative to build an SDN controller that relies on open-source software components, provides northbound abstractions, and has southbound interfaces to handle OpenFlow capable and legacy devices [15]. In addition to a distributed core that enables control functions to be executed by a cluster of servers, ONOS provides two interesting northbound abstractions, namely the *Intent Framework* and the *Global Network View*. The intent framework, depicted in Fig. 1, allows an application to request a network service without knowledge of how the service is performed. An intent manifested by an application is converted into a series of rules and actions that are applied to network equipments. An example of intent is setting up an optical path between switches A and B with amount C of bandwidth. The global network view, as the name implies, provides an application with a view of the network and APIs to program it. The application can treat the view as a graph and perform several tasks such as finding shortest paths that are crucial to traffic engineering. ONOS provides an application that partially implements SPRING, a framework to enable segment routing currently being standardised by IETF[1]. SPRING pro-

---

[1] Source Packet Routing in Networking – Working Group
https://tools.ietf.org/wg/spring/.

vides features for traffic engineering as it enables an application to specify paths for data flows while avoiding certain network links.

3   GrEen Traffic Engineering TestBed (GETB)

This section describes GETB and how it is used to evaluate energy-aware traffic engineering strategies. Figure 2 illustrates the platform and its main components, depicting the deployment of a set of switches, an SDN controller and applications. The platform comprises components that are common to other infrastructure set up for networking research [16–18]. Moreover, we attempt to employ software used at the Grid5000 testbed [19][2] to which we intend to integrate the platform.

To use the platform, a user requests: a slice or set of cluster nodes to be used by an application, as virtual switches, or serving as traffic sources and sinks; the OS image to be deployed; and the network topology to be used (step 1). We crafted several OS images so that nodes can be configured as SDN controllers and OpenFlow software switches, as discussed later. A bare-metal deployment system copies the OS images to the nodes and configures them accordingly [20], whereas a Python application sets up VLANs and ports of the optical switches in order to form the user-specified network topology.

Once the nodes and network topology are configured, a user deploys her application (step 2 in Fig. 2). All cluster nodes are connected to enclosure Power Distribution Units (ePDUs)[3] that monitor the power consumption of individual sockets [21]. The information on power consumption can be used to evaluate the efficiency of an SDN technique (step 3). The data plane comprises two types of OpenFlow switches, namely software-based and hardware-assisted. The former

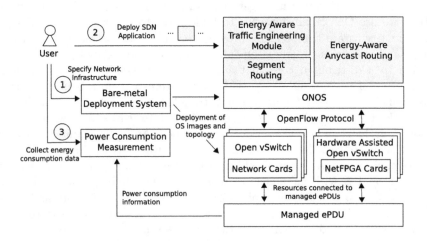

Fig. 2. Overview of the GETB platform.

[2] https://www.grid5000.fr.
[3] http://www.eaton.com/Eaton/index.htm.

consists of vanilla Open vSwitch (OVS) [22], whereas the latter OVS offloads certain OpenFlow functionalities to NetFPGA cards [23] [4]. We use a custom OpenFlow implementation for NetFPGAs initially provided by the Universität Paderborn (UPB) [24] that performs certain OpenFlow functions in the card; *e.g.* flow tables, packet matching against tables, and forwarding.

A NetFPGA card, programmed by default to assist the custom OVS, can allow for other implementations. The current platform comprises ten servers, of which five are equipped with NetFPGA cards and the rest have 10Gbps Ethernet cards with 2 SPF+ ports each and multiple 1Gbps Ethernet ports. The servers are interconnected by both a Dell N4032F optical switch and a Dell N2024 Ethernet switch, which enable testing multiple network topologies.

The infrastructure and the use of ONOS satisfy some requirements of energy-aware traffic engineering namely providing actual hardware, allowing for traffic information to be gathered, using actual network protocols, enabling the overhead of control and management to be measured, and monitoring the power consumption of equipments. Some energy-optimisation mechanisms, however, are still emulated, such as switching off/on individual switch ports. Although the IP cores of the Ethernet hardware used in the NetFPGA cards enable changing the state of certain components, such as switching off transceivers, that would require a complete redesign of the employed OpenFlow implementation. It has been therefore left for future work.

4   Segment-Routing Service

Our strategies for routing data flows so that underutilised links can be freed and powered off [10] stem from the observation that networks are seldom highly utilised, and that most traffic often follows diurnal and weekly patterns. The SPRING framework is used because unlike MultiProtocol Label Switching (MPLS)-TE, link and switch IDs, called Segment Identifiers (SIDs) under SPRING, are global within an autonomous domain, hence allowing for source-routing. At an ingress router a flow can be classified and steered through a given path. This section describes the service life cycle and discusses issues that the testbed enables us to identify and investigate.

4.1   Service Life Cycle

The service, which is a custom version of ONOS segment-routing application, uses a series of ONOS components, including its topology information, flow-rule services, and traffic flow objectives. As shown in Fig. 3, when first launched, a service *Manager* triggers the creation of remaining components. The energy-aware module, which comprises the proposed traffic-engineering algorithms, registers a flow-rule listener in order to measure flow and link utilisations. The configuration component loads a file that specifies how switches are connected

---

[4] http://netfpga.org/site/#/systems/3netfpga-10g/details/.

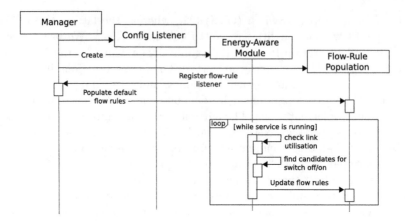

Fig. 3. Start phase of the segment-routing application.

to local networks; information which is then augmented by a topology discovery process. Once the topology is updated, default shortest-path rules are created to guarantee that hosts from a network connected to a switch can reach hosts linked to another switch. A rule consists of a forwarding objective comprising a traffic selector and a treatment. Selectors and treatments result in sets of Open-Flow instructions that are passed to the switches. MPLS push/pop forwarding objectives are created for switches that do not have ports in the source and destination segments — *i.e.* are neither ingress nor egress switches — and normal IP forwarding objectives are built otherwise. While the service is running, the energy-aware module is notified about changes in topology as well as link utilisation, and periodically evaluates whether there are links to switch off/on. If changes in the link availability are required, the energy-aware module requests a flow-rule update to the Flow-Rule Population module.

4.2   GreenTE Issues

Although switching off underused links can be effective from an energy efficiency perspective, sudden bursts in traffic can lead to congestion, hence requiring off links to be made available. In our previous work [11], we proposed algorithms that can react rapidly to traffic bursts by switching links back on when traffic increases. Performance evaluation using discrete-event simulation and UDP-like traffic has shown that the approach can react to traffic bursts without incurring considerable packet loss. It is assumed, however, that the SDN controller can gather the information on link utilisation from switches every second and that a decision on switching a link on can be made and enforced quickly.

We performed a simple test and measured the time taken for a controller to decide on switching on a link. A small network topology was considered as depicted in Fig. 4, which also shows the ONOS graphical interface and a data flow (green lines). The network starts with only a spanning tree turned on and

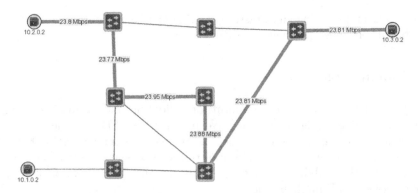

Fig. 4. ONOS GUI showing a data flow avoiding the shortest path.

a TCP flow is injected nearly exceeding the utilisation threshold, above which the controller decides to turn on more links to handle congestion. A second flow is injected, thus exceeding the threshold and forcing the controller to switch links on; we measure the time from flow injection to a switch-on decision. In the simulation, the decision takes on average 1.075 s, with most of the time spent gathering information on link utilisation. In the testbed, the time is on average 20% higher than on simulation.

Other issues that we are investigating concern the stability of the algorithms and the impact of traffic re-routing on TCP flows. Unlike traditional networks where changes in link availability are sporadic, under GreenTE frequent changes can become the rule. Re-routing TCP flows, however, can lead to serious performance degradation due to segments arriving out of order, which can in turn result in multiple duplicate ACKs and trigger the TCP congestion algorithms at the source. We are evaluating how often such conditions can emerge and investigating mechanisms to handle them.

5   Related Work

Several solutions have been proposed to make networks more energy efficient, comprising improvements in used materials, encoding and decoding techniques, power efficient transceivers and other network equipments. Whilst our algorithms can benefit from improvements in hardware and transmission, we focus on techniques that operate at the routing level. In this area, solutions range from putting network interfaces into sleep mode [4] to increasing idle periods of certain links by changing flow paths [9]. A detailed review of the state of the art on this topic is presented in previous work [10].

In the present work, we focused on describing the importance of a platform to evaluate energy-aware traffic-engineering algorithms. Infrastructure for research and development of distributed systems have been established over the years [19,25,26], including platforms for SDN solutions [27] and SDN testbeds [16–18,28]. Our approach has many similarities with previously described platforms, but we focus on providing an infrastructure that can be used for evaluating both SDN-based solutions and their energy efficiency.

6   Conclusions

This paper discussed an SDN platform for validating and evaluating energy-aware traffic-engineering algorithms. We presented an SDN application that uses segment routing to reroute traffic, and free certain network links that can be switched off. We illustrated the use of the testbed and discussed challenges on improving the stability of routing algorithms and TCP flows on networks employing GreenTE mechanisms.

Acknowledgments. This work is financially supported by the CHIST-ERA STAR project [29].

References

1. Atzori, L., et al.: The internet of things: a survey. Comput. Netw. **54**(15), 2787–2805 (2010)
2. Armbrust, M., et al.: Above the clouds: a Berkeley view of cloud computing. Electrical Engineering and Computer Sciences, University of California at Berkeley, Berkeley, USA, Technical report UCB/EECS-2009-28, February 2009
3. Kilper, D.: Energy challenges in access, aggregation networks. In: Symposium on Communication Networks Beyond the Capacity Crunch. The Royal Society, London, UK, May 2015. https://royalsociety.org/events/2015/05/communication-networks/
4. Gupta, M., Singh, S.: Greening of the internet. In: ACM Conference on Applications, Technologies, Architectures, Protocols for Computer Communications, ser. SIGCOMM 2003, pp. 19–26. ACM, New York (2003)
5. Gunaratne, C., et al.: Reducing the energy consumption of ethernet with adaptive link rate (ALR). IEEE Trans. Comput. **57**(4), 448–461 (2008)
6. Miyazaki, T., et al.: High speed 100GE adaptive link rate switching for energy consumption reduction. In: International Conference on Optical Network Design and Modeling (ONDM 2015), pp. 227–232, May 2015
7. Nedevschi, S., et al.: Reducing network energy consumption via sleeping, rate-adaptation. In: 5th USENIX Symposium on Networked Systems Design, Implementation, ser. NSDI 2008, pp. 323–336. USENIX Association, Berkeley (2008)
8. Awduche, D., et al.: Overview, principles of internet traffic engineering. RFC 3272 (Informational), Internet Engineering Task Force, May 2002. http://www.ietf.org/rfc/rfc3272.txt
9. Vasić, N., Kostić, D.: Energy-aware traffic engineering. In: 1st International Conference on Energy-Efficient Computing, Networking, ser. e-Energy 2010, pp. 169–178. ACM, New York (2010)
10. Carpa, R., et al.: Segment routing based traffic engineering for energy efficient backbone networks. In: IEEE International Conference on Advanced Networks and Telecommunications Systems (ANTS 2014), pp. 1–6, December 2014

11. Carpa, R., de Assuncao, M.D., Glück, O., Lefevre, L., Mignot, J.-C.: Responsive algorithms for handling load surges and switching links on in green networks. In: IEEE International Conference on Communications (ICC 2016), Kuala Lumpur, Malaysia, May 2016
12. OMNeT++ Discrete Event Simulator. https://omnetpp.org/
13. Zhang, M., et al.: GreenTE: power-aware traffic engineering. In: 18th IEEE International Conference on Network Protocols (ICNP 2010), pp. 21–30, October 2010
14. Borylo, P., et al.: Anycast routing for carbon footprint reduction in WDM hybrid power networks with data centers. In: IEEE International Conference on Communications (ICC 2014), pp. 3714–3720. IEEE (2014)
15. Introducing ONOS: a SDN network operating system for service providers. Open Networking Lab ON.Lab, Whitepaper, November 2014. http://onosproject.org/wp-content/uploads/2014/11/Whitepaper-ONOS-final.pdf
16. Kim, J., et al.: Proceedings of the Asia-Pacific advanced network. In: OF@TEIN: An OpenFlow-Enabled SDN Testbed over International SmartX Rack Sites, vol. 36, pp. 17–22 (2013)
17. Melazzi, N., et al.: An openflow-based testbed for information centric networking. In: Future Network Mobile Summit (FutureNetw 2012), pp. 1–9, July 2012
18. Sallent, S., Abelém, A., Machado, I., Bergesio, L., Fdida, S., Rezende, J., Azodolmolky, S., Salvador, M., Ciuffo, L., Tassiulas, L.: FIBRE project: Brazil and Europe unite forces and testbeds for the internet of the future. In: Korakis, T., Zink, M., Ott, M. (eds.) TridentCom 2012. LNICSSITE, vol. 44, pp. 372–372. Springer, Heidelberg (2012). doi:10.1007/978-3-642-35576-9_33
19. Bolze, R., et al.: Grid'5000: a large scale and highly reconfigurable experimental Grid testbed. Int. J. High Perform. Comput. Appl. **20**(4), 481–494 (2006)
20. Jeanvoine, E., et al.: Kadeploy3: efficient and scalable operating system provisioning. USENIX Login **38**(1), 38–44 (2013)
21. Rossigneux, F., et al.: A generic and extensible framework for monitoring energy consumption of OpenStack clouds. In: SustainCom, pp. 696–702, December 2014
22. Pfaff, B., et al.: The design and implementation of open vSwitch. In: 12th USENIX Symposium on Networked Systems Design and Implementation (NSDI 2015) (2015)
23. Netfpga 10g. http://netfpga.org
24. The netfpga-10g upb openflow switch. https://github.com/pc2/NetFPGA-10G-UPB-OpenFlow
25. Peterson, L., et al.: PlanetLab architecture: an overview. In: PlanetLab Consortium, Princeton, USA, Technical report PDN-06-031, May 2006
26. GENI: Exploring networks of the future. http://www.geni.net
27. Banikazemi, M., et al.: Meridian: an SDN platform for cloud network services. IEEE Commun. Mag. **51**(2), 120–127 (2013)
28. Ooteghem, J.V., et al.: Sustaining a federation of future internet experimental facilities. International Telecommunications Society (ITS). Technical report 101436 (2014)
29. CHIST-ERA SwiTching And tRansmission (STAR) Project. http://www.chistera.eu/projects/star

Research on Network Policy Combination and Conflict Detection in SDN

Bohan He, Ligang Dong[⊠], Tijie Xu, Shuocheng Fei, Huafei Zhang, and Weiming Wang

School of Information and Electronic Engineering,
Zhejiang Gongshang University, No. 18, Xuezheng Street,
Xiasha University Town, Hangzhou 310018, China
donglg@zjgsu.edu.cn

Abstract. Since the current SDN southbound interface level is low and programming situation is complex, it requires a high-level abstract programming language to simplify programming. First, this paper improves the NetCore programming language to generate NetCore-M language, so that it can support deployment of multi-policies combination including packet drop action. This paper describes in detail the syntax, semanteme, and implementation of NetCore-M language. Secondly, this paper describes the network policy conflict systematically and solves it. Finally, this paper shows that the modified multi-policies combination algorithm can effectively detect and prompt policies conflicts based on the implementation of the Pyretic project.

Keywords: Policy combination · Conflict detection · SDN · Pyretic

1 Introduction

Compared with the traditional network [1–3], Software Defined Network (SDN) [6] is a new type of network architecture whose goal is to simplify network control and management with the programmability of the network leading innovation. Despite SDN uses open, standard interfaces such as ForCES [4], OpenFlow [5] to replace the private configuration commands of different equipment suppliers to simplify the network configuration task. A high-level programming language for SDN is very necessary.

There are several kinds of high-level programming languages for SDN, such as Frenetic [12], Pyretic [9], NetCore [7], Procera [13]. NetCore is a programming policy language based on Frenetic. Our study is based on NetCore.

NetCore policy combination algorithm only takes the forwarding operation into consideration. The conflict between policies hasn't been solved yet. Therefore, this paper modifies NetCore language to support forwarding and packet drop, and then proposes NetCore-M policy combination algorithm to achieve the conflict detection of policies combination in order to make the algorithm adapt to more complex programming environment.

The main part of this paper is divided into seven sections: The Sect. 2 analyzes the related research of network programming language in SDN. The Sect. 3 introduces the

© ICST Institute for Computer Sciences, Social Informatics and Telecommunications Engineering 2017
S. Guo et al. (Eds.): TridentCom 2016, LNICST 177, pp. 24–34, 2017.
DOI: 10.1007/978-3-319-49580-4_3

improved NetCore-M programming language, syntax and forms. The Sect. 4 introduces the policy conflict problems in policy combination algorithm. In the Sect. 5, we give a verification experiment to show the results of the policy combination and the policy conflict. The Sect. 6 summarizes the paper.

2 Related Work

Researchers have developed a number of high-level network programming languages for SDN to hide the complexity of SDN programming (Table 1).

Table 1. High-level network programming languages

Languages	Controllers	Actions	The Operation model
Frenetic	NOX	Forwarding	Parallel model
Pyretic	POX	Forwarding, Packet Drop	Parallel model, Serial model
Kinetic	POX	Forwarding, Packet Drop	Parallel model, Serial model
NetCore	NOX	Forwarding, Packet Drop	Parallel model, Serial model

Frenetic is a policy language based on the Ocaml [14] programming language. Frenetic languages can be classified into two sub-language, one is network policy management library which process packet forwarding based on FRP [15] and the other is a declarative SQL language for the network status inquiry.

Pyretic language uses the policy as a function and packets as input and output variables. Packets can be processed in the form of the parallel or sequential combination. Later versions of Pyretic is Kinetic [8] which supports combinations of several consecutive service functions in series and parallel connections. It achieves the function of simple static service chains.

NetCore is a policy language developed on the basis of Frenetic with more expressive syntax than that of Frenetic. Besides, NetCore can use arbitrary functions to process packets with more flexibilities. In addition, NetCore contains a minimalist inquiry formula language which can be used to analyze the flow.

These four languages have a common feature which is transforming a few abstract high-level policies into numerous and complicated OpenFlow [10] commands with the cooperation of the NOX/POX controllers.

3 NetCore-M Programming Language

This paper modifies the NetCore policy combination algorithm and, adds the action of packet drop and detects the policy conflict. It also proposes the policy conflict detection mechanism and the policy option scheme based on the priority compromise policy options.

3.1 Formal Syntax and Semantics of NetCore-M Programming Language

In this section, we will modify the NetCore language [7] as NetCore-M, to describe the policy services including language syntax, semanteme, and the description of the achievement.

We continue to use the basic syntax and semanteme [7] of NetCore and extend the packet drop action D to the original syntax of the action set A, so that the policy can support packet drop. Thus the following syntactic definition is added.

Drop action d
Packet drop set $D ::= \{d\}$
Action set $A ::= D \mid S$

Fig. 1. The improved formal syntax

NetCore-M contains two parts including predicate and policy. The predicate describes a set of packets that policy is interested in, and the policy specifies the way to handle packet sets. Figure 1 shows the improved formal syntax of predicate and policy.

Two types of action sets can't work together in the same packet, so the current policy contains two basic forms, namely, e → S and e → D. When the packet is matching predicate policy in the policy, the packet will implement the attached action.

3.2 The Description of Policy Semanteme

Policy is a priority list composed of priority, mode and action list [11]. The Policy Compiler is the core component of network policy service. Policy combination and policy conflict detection will be implemented in the Policy Compiler.

The classification table $\vec{r}$ is composed of sequence rules $r(r_1, \ldots, r_i, \ldots, r_n)$. Switches process packets based on the information provided by the rules. Each rule consists of a mode Z and an action list α. The order of the rule in the sequence represents the priority while the priority of the rule is lower than the rules on the left side and higher than the rules on the right side.

Functions of rule model are that if the packet p can match the z model of the rule r_i, packet will implement action α according to the description of rule.

The operation semanteme of the policy compiler and switch is shown in action list which can be expressed as the three cases in the Table 2.

Table 2. The actions of rules

Symbol	Meaning
S	Forward packets to each switch of set S
Ω	Forward packets to controllers
__(Empty)	Drop packets

We will describe operation semanteme of the compiler and the switch by the molecular machine [16] as same as NetCore used to. The definition of the relevant symbols of the molecular machine is shown in Fig. 2.

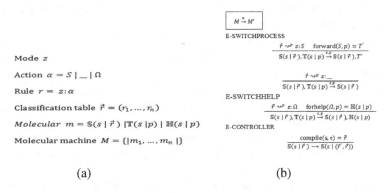

$$M \xrightarrow{o} M'$$

E-SWITCHPROCESS

Mode z

Action $\alpha = S \mid \_ \mid \Omega$

Rule $r = z : \alpha$

Classification table $\vec{r} = (r_1, \dots, r_n)$

Molecular $m = \mathbb{S}(s \mid \vec{r}) \mid \mathbb{T}(s \mid p) \mid \mathbb{H}(s \mid p)$

Molecular machine $M = \{|m_1, \dots, m_n|\}$

$$\frac{\vec{r} \rightsquigarrow^{p} z : S \quad forward(S, p) = T'}{\mathbb{S}(s \mid \vec{r}), \mathbb{T}(s \mid p) \xrightarrow{z, p} \mathbb{S}(s \mid \vec{r}), T'}$$

$$\frac{\vec{r} \rightsquigarrow^{p} z : \_}{\mathbb{S}(s \mid \vec{r}), \mathbb{T}(s \mid p) \xrightarrow{z, p} \mathbb{S}(s \mid \vec{r})}$$

E-SWITCHHELP

$$\frac{\vec{r} \rightsquigarrow^{p} z : \Omega \quad forhelp(\Omega, p) = \mathbb{H}(s \mid p)}{\mathbb{S}(s \mid \vec{r}), \mathbb{T}(s \mid p) \xrightarrow{z, p} \mathbb{S}(s \mid \vec{r}), \mathbb{H}(s \mid p)}$$

E-CONTROLLER

$$\frac{compile(s, \tau) = \vec{r}}{\mathbb{S}(s \mid \vec{r}) \rightarrow \mathbb{S}(s \mid (\vec{r}', \vec{r}))}$$

(a)   (b)

Fig. 2. The molecular machine, (a) & (b)

As shown in Fig. 2(b), the operational semanteme is given in the form of derivation rules. The switch molecules $\mathbb{S}(s \mid \vec{r})$ in the figure contain switch s in classification table r. The transport molecules $\mathbb{T}(s \mid p)$ represent packet p on the way to switch s; the assistant molecules $\mathbb{H}(s \mid p)$ indicate switch s send a requests to the controller for help on how to process the packet p.

E-SWITCHPROCESS is utilized when matching rules of packets have no "sent to the controller" action $\mathbb{T}(s \mid p)forward(S, p)$. The molecular machine will remove and then it will determine whether use the function according to the rules of the specific action list. If matching rules of the packet contain "sent to the controller" action, then E-SWITCHHELP is utilized and a help request of switch structure is sent to the controller. In this process, the molecular machine will remove processed transport molecules, and then use function $forhelp(\Omega, p)$ to generate assistant molecules.

The derivation rule E-CONTROLLER describes the way controllers use compiler to compile policy classification table and the means to issue and update switch.

3.3 Compilation Process of Forwarding Policy Services

The compilation process of the policies can be divided into two steps, namely, the policy intermediate form and the classification tablet of policy intermediate form. The previous step can be further subdivided into the following steps:

(1) Detection and resolution of policy combination.
(2) Detection and resolution of predicate combination.
(3) Predicate compiles to predicate intermediate form.
(4) The combination of predicate intermediate form.
(5) Predicate intermediate form compiles to policy intermediate form.

(6) Policy conflict detection.
(7) The combination of policy intermediate form.

The whole procedure is carried out in sequence, and the result of the last step is the input of the next step.

We define the intermediate form of syntax as follows in order to discuss policy conflicts in an easier way.

Boolean value b ::= True |False

Switch level matching mode $z ::= (h_1 : \vec{w}) \wedge \ldots \wedge (h_n : \vec{w})$

Predicate intermediate form $\pi ::= \langle e : z : b \rangle$

Policy intermediate form $\rho :: = \langle e : z : A \rangle$

Predicate intermediate form contains three values: sequence predicate e, sequence mode z (i.e., regular mode), and Boolean value b.

The sequence predicate e and the sequence model z have different expression form, but they contain the same semanteme. The sequence predicate is patterned with header h and vector $\vec{w}$.

In the same tuple of intermediate forms, sequence model z is representation of bit vector of predicate sequences e. When the model z_1 can match the packet set is a subset of sets which z_2 matches, it is denoted as $z_1 \sqsubseteq z_2$. We can give a slight extension of the symbol $\sqsubseteq$ which makes $p \sqsubseteq z_2$ mean that packet p can match the mode z.

Boolean value b represents the way to process packet set defined by the ordinary predicates. Policy intermediate form $\langle e : z : A \rangle$ is similar to predicate intermediate form, among them, A represents the action set.

3.4 Compilation and Combination Algorithm of Predicate and Policy

Figure 3(a) shows the formal description of predicate compilation and combination algorithm.

$$\mathrm{T}(s, e) = \vec{\pi}$$

$$\mathrm{T}(s, h : \vec{w}) = \langle (h : \vec{w}) : \mathrm{O}(h : \vec{w}) : \mathrm{True} \rangle, \quad \langle * : \top : \mathrm{False} \rangle.$$

$$\mathrm{T}(s, \text{switch } s') = \begin{cases} \langle * : \top : \mathrm{True} \rangle, & \text{if } s = s' \\ \langle * : \top : \mathrm{False} \rangle, & \text{if } s \neq s' \end{cases}$$

$$\mathrm{T}(s, \neg e) = \prod_i \langle e_i : z_i : \neg b_i \rangle, \quad (\mathrm{T}(s, e))_i = \langle e_i : z_i : b_i \rangle.$$

$$\mathrm{T}(s, e \cap e') = \prod_i \prod_j \langle e_i \cap e_j' : z_i \sqcap z_j' : b_i \wedge b_j' \rangle, \quad (\mathrm{T}(s, e))_i = \langle e_i : z_i : b_i \rangle, \ (\mathrm{T}(s, e'))_j = \langle e'_j : z'_j : b'_j \rangle.$$

$$\mathrm{T}(s, e \cup e') = \prod_i \prod_j \langle e_i \cap e_j' : z_i \sqcap z_j' : b_i \vee b_j' \rangle, \quad (\mathrm{T}(s, e))_i = \langle e_i : z_i : b_i \rangle, \ (\mathrm{T}(s, e'))_j = \langle e'_j : z'_j : b'_j \rangle.$$

(a)

$$\mathrm{T}(s, \tau) = \vec{\rho}$$

$$\mathrm{T}(s, e \to A) = \prod_i \begin{cases} \langle e_i : z_i : A \rangle, & \text{if } b_i = \mathrm{True} \\ \langle e_i : z_i : \emptyset \rangle, & \text{if } b_i = \mathrm{False} \end{cases}, \quad (\mathrm{T}(s, e))_i = \langle e_i : z_i : b_i \rangle.$$

$$\mathrm{T}(s, \tau \cup \tau') = \prod_i \prod_j \langle e_i \cap e_j' : z_i \sqcap z_j' : A_i \cup A_j' \rangle, \quad (\mathrm{T}(s, \tau))_i = \langle e_i : z_i : A_i \rangle, \ (\mathrm{T}(s, \tau'))_j = \langle e'_j : z'_j : A'_j \rangle.$$

$$\mathrm{C}(s, \tau) = \vec{r}$$

$$\mathrm{C}(s, \tau) = \prod_i \begin{cases} z_i : S, & \text{if } A_i = S \\ z_i : _, & \text{if } A_i = D \\ z_i : \Omega, & \text{if } A_i = \emptyset \end{cases}, \quad \mathrm{T}(s, \tau) = \vec{\rho}, \ (\vec{\rho})_i = \langle e_i : z_i : A_i \rangle.$$

(b)

Fig. 3. The compilation and combination algorithm

$T(s, e) = \prod_i e_i : z_i : b_i$ indicates the sequence of predicate intermediate form is compiled by original predicate e. Among the sequences, the i-th tuple is marked as $(T(s, e))_i = e_i : z_i : b_i$. The first equation in Fig. 3(a) shows that the compiler will compile original predicate $h : \vec{w}$ into a sequence of intermediate form tuple containing with two predicates. The first tuple in the sequence $\langle (h : \vec{w}) : O(h : \vec{w}) : \text{True} \rangle$ contains model which is generated by compilation oracle.

For intersection operation of predicates, predicates should be compiled in advance. And we have tuple members of the predicate e and tuple members of e' intersection combination operation. All of the operation results such as $\langle e_i \cap e_j' : z_i \sqcap z_j' : b_i \wedge b_j' \rangle$ constitute of $e \cap e'$. If a packet match z_i which comes from e, as well as z_j' which comes from e', and finally the packet will match the sequence model is $z_i \sqcap z_j'$.

For the predicate "and" operation $e \cup e'$, the compilation process is similar to the compilation process of $e \cap e'$. What we should focus on is the combination of sequence predicates and sequence model also remains intersection operation.

For the predicate "not" operation $\neg e$, the compilation results is the negation of Boolean values of the intermediate form.

Figure 3(b) resents a description of policy compilation and combination algorithm.

Function $T(s, \tau)$ describes the process of policy compiling to the policy intermediate form, and $C(s, \tau)$ corresponds to the process of policy intermediate form generating classification table.

If we want to compile a basic policy $e \rightarrow A$, firstly the compiler need to compile predicate e to generate predicates intermediate sequence, and then add actions for each predicate intermediate tuple in order to generate policy intermediate forms tuples which additional actions are determined by the values b_i of $\langle e_i : z_i : b_i \rangle$. There are two kinds of situations, if b_i is true, the additional action is A, as $\langle e_i : z_i : A \rangle$; if b_i is false, the additional action is $\emptyset$, as $\langle e_i : z_i : \emptyset \rangle$. There is different between the action of predicate intermediate tuples and the action of the classification table, so it requires function $C(s, \tau)$ for further conversion.

For policy combination $\tau \cup \tau'$, the compilation process is similar to it of predicate "and" operation. The difference is the operation $b_i \wedge b_j'$ of the Boolean value is replaced by action set operation $A_i \cup A_j'$.

Because of policy conflicts, we must conduct conflict detection after packets processing action is added to predicate intermediate form and before the action combine into policy intermediate form. The specific issues of policy conflict will be introduced in Sect. 4.

4   Policy Conflicts

This section gives further discussions in the policy conflicts.

We divided policy action into two categories including the set of forwarding and set of packet drop. A packet will never implement packet drop and forwarding operations at the same time. Therefore, policy conflicts can be defined as following:

Define 1 (policy conflict). There is intersection in the packet sets of different policy predicate definitions and the actions of forwarding and packet drop exist in the intersection.

We obtained five cases which are shown in Fig. 4.

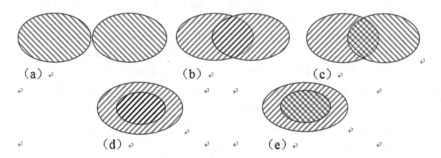

Fig. 4. Relationship between policies

As shown in Fig. 4(c) and (e) describe the existence of policy conflicts, Fig. 4(a) (b) and (d) describe cases of no conflict.

As mentioned above, if there is a conflict, you can choose the appropriate conflict policy considering the functions of the policy and the scope of the intersection in order to implement the maximization of the semantics of the policy.

If the conflict in case of Fig. 4(c) occurs, it indicates that the conflict occurs in the local scope of the two policies. It is the time we further analyze the influence of the scope of the conflict to compromise policy. If the scope of conflicts have little impact on compromise policy, we can make compromise policy valid outside the scope of the conflicts. If the scope of conflicts have much impact on compromise policy, then the compromise policy must be completely removed.

If a conflict in Fig. 4(e) occurs, it indicates there is a comprehensive conflict policy. At this point, if the local conflict policy is chosen as a compromise policy, we do further analysis by the above method. If comprehensive conflict policy is chosen as a compromise policy, it can be completely removed.

The method is to set the conflict scope set C during the policy combination process and make the operation under the following conditions:

if $e_i \cap e_j' \neq \emptyset$ and $A_i \cup A_j' = \{S, D\}$ then C $\cup \left(e_i \cap e_j'\right) \overset{assign}{\rightarrow}$ C

if C $= \emptyset$, no conflict

if C $= e$, completely conflict in τ

if C $= e'$, completely conflict in τ'

if C$\subseteq e$, partly conflict in τ

if C$\subseteq e'$, partly conflict in τ'

Obviously, the necessary and sufficient conditions for conflicts in form can be expressed as $C \neq \emptyset$.

If the local conflicts compromise policy is required to be valid outside the scope of the conflict in the process of policy combination, we can replace D or S to $\emptyset$ in accordance with the priority policy. Therefore, we get the following forms.

$$A_i \cup A'_j = \begin{cases} A_i, & \text{if } C \neq \emptyset \text{ 且} P(A_i) > P(A'_j) \\ A'_j, & \text{if } C \neq \emptyset \text{ 且} P(A_i) < P(A'_j) \end{cases}$$

Among them, $P(A_i)$ represents the priority of the corresponding actions attached in policies.

5 Experiments of Policy Combination Algorithm

Pyretic project and NetCore project share similarities in contents, Therefore, this section chooses the Pyretic project as the experimental platform to test the policy combination algorithm.

5.1 Experimental Environment

In order to test the effects of policy combination, this study builds an OpenFlow (OpenFlow version 1.1. 0) & SDN network test platform based on Mininet and POX controller, and the test platform runs under Linux.

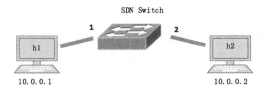

Fig. 5. The experimental topology

At the beginning of the experiment, firstly we need to implement the shell script / pyretic/mininet.sh to start up Mininet and build the network topology as shown in Fig. 5.

The topology uses two Mininet simulation hosts (h1 and h2) as well as an OpenFlow switch, and IP of the two hosts are 10.0.0.1 and 10.0.0.2, respectively.

Then Pyretic project is inputted into integrated development environment PyCharm.

In the condition without any policy applications, host h1 and host h2 are connected physically but they are logically disconnected. Set the host h1 and h2 connected with the policies as follow, Fig. 6.

```
from pyretic.lib.corelib import *
from pyretic.lib.std import *

link = (match(dstip='10.0.0.1')>>fwd(1)) + (match(dstip='10.0.0.2')>>fwd(2))

def main():
    return link
```

Fig. 6. The policy of connection

The function of this policy is to forward the packet of destination IP address 10.0.0.1 to interface 1 and to forward the packet of destination IP address 10.0.0.2 to interface 2. After the application of the policy, the result was shown in Fig. 7. It shows that the two hosts have been successfully connected physically and logically so that the experimental environment has been successfully completed.

```
From 10.0.0.2 icmp_seq=97 Destination Host Unreachable
From 10.0.0.2 icmp_seq=98 Destination Host Unreachable
From 10.0.0.2 icmp_seq=99 Destination Host Unreachable
64 bytes from 10.0.0.1: icmp_req=100 ttl=64 time=0.191 ms
64 bytes from 10.0.0.1: icmp_req=101 ttl=64 time=0.243 ms
64 bytes from 10.0.0.1: icmp_req=102 ttl=64 time=0.038 ms
64 bytes from 10.0.0.1: icmp_req=103 ttl=64 time=0.041 ms
```

Fig. 7. Connected policy application results

5.2   The Experiment of Policy Conflict

The result of policy conflict as following Fig. 8.

```
from pyretic.lib.corelib import *
from pyretic.lib.std import *

conflict = (match(dstip='10.0.0.1')>>fwd(1)) + (match(dstip='10.0.0.2')>>fwd(2)) + (match(dstip='10.0.0.1')>>drop)

def main():
    return conflict
```

Fig. 8. Policy conflict sample

The policy adds actions of forwarding and packet dropping to packets of destination IP address 10.0.0.1. According to the definition of conflict in Sect. 4, the modified policy generates to policy conflicts. After the policy is implemented, the result was shown in Fig. 9.

```
64 bytes from 10.0.0.1: icmp_req=34 ttl=64 time=0.033 ms
64 bytes from 10.0.0.1: icmp_req=35 ttl=64 time=0.227 ms
64 bytes from 10.0.0.1: icmp_req=36 ttl=64 time=0.037 ms
64 bytes from 10.0.0.1: icmp_req=37 ttl=64 time=0.136 ms
```

Fig. 9. The result of conflict policy application results

The results indicates that the function of sub-policy "match (dstip = '10.0.0.1') >> drop" was not achieved and has no prompt.

According to the discussion of the policy conflict in Sect. 4, policy conflicts can not be resolved but can be detected. Therefore, this study adds the detection of policy conflict and prompt mechanism to the policy combination algorithm in Pyretic projects. After the policy is utilized in the modified Pyretic project, the results was shown in Fig. 10.

```
Warning: policy confilct
Involved policy:
    match(dstip='10.0.0.1')>>fwd(1)
    match(dstip='10.0.0.1')>>drop
Range:
    dstip = '10.0.0.1'

Please check the policies
```

Fig. 10. Policy conflict prompt

5.3 Summary

This part carries out a policy conflict test. The policy conflict test shows that the modified policy combination algorithm can effectively detect the conflict as well as prompt.

6 The Summary and Prospect

This paper improves the original NetCore programming language. The design of policy combination algorithm in this paper mainly refers to the policy combination algorithm in the operation of NetCore system. And on this basis, we added the action of packet drop to switches. We propose the detection and resolution project after occurrences of the policy conflict. Finally in order to verify whether the policy combination algorithm can effectively detect and prompt policy conflict, we implement relevant experiences to testify the effect of the algorithm based on the Pyretic project.

This paper studies and analyzes on the policy management of the controller, but due to the limited time and proficiency, the following aspects need to be improved.

(1) We neglect the analysis and comparison of the algorithm performance which will be completed after the work of forwarding management subsystem is finished.
(2) The algorithm need to be experienced several complex situations and to find the defects of it. We will finish these tasks in the future.

References

1. Ballani, H., Francis, P.: CONMan: a step towards network manageability. J. ACM SIGCOMM Comput. Commun. Rev. **37**(4), 205–216 (2007)
2. Chen, X., Mao, Y., Mao, Z.M., et al.: Declarative configuration management for complex and dynamic networks. In: International Conference. ACM, pp. 1–12 (2010)
3. Loo, B.T., Hellerstein, J.M., Stoica, I., et al.: Declarative routing: extensible routing with declarative queries. J. ACM SIGCOMM Comput. Commun. Rev. **35**(4), 289–300 (2005)
4. Doria, A., Salim, J.H., Haas, R., et al.: Forwarding and Control Element Separation (ForCES) Protocol Specification. In: IETF RFC 5810 (Proposed Standard) (2010)
5. Mckeown, N., Andemon, T., Balakrishnan, H., et al.: OpenFlow: enabling innovation in campus networks. J. ACM SIGCOMM Comput. Commun. Rev. **38**(2), 69–74 (2008)
6. Yi, Z., Yiqiang, H., Xiaofeng, H.: Characteristics, development and future of SDN. J. Telecommun. Sci. **29**(9), 102–107 (2013). (in Chinese)
7. Monsanto, C., Foster, N., Harrison, R., et al.: A compiler and run-time system for network programming languages. J. ACM SIGPLAN Not. **47**(1), 217–230 (2012)
8. Kim, H., Reich, J., Gupta, A., et al.: Kinetic: verifiable dynamic network control. In: USENIX NSDI 2015 (2015)
9. Reich, J., Monsanto, C., Foster, N., et al.: Modular SDN programming with Pyretic. USENIX; login **38**(5), 128–134 (2013)
10. OpenFlow Switch Specification Version 1.0. 0. OpenFlow Switch Consortium (2009)
11. Jin, X., Rexford, J., Walker, D.: Incremental update for a compositional SDN hypervisor. In: Third Workshop on Hot Topics in Software Defined Networking. ACM, pp. 187–192 (2014)
12. Foster, N., Harrison, R., Freedman, M.J., et al.: Frenetic: a network programming language. ACM SIGPLAN Not. **46**(9), 279–291 (2011). ACM
13. Voellmy, A., Kim, H., Feamster, N.: Procera: a language for high-level reactive network control. In: Proceedings of the First Workshop on Hot Topics in Software Defined Networks. ACM, pp. 43–48 (2012)
14. Hickey, J.: Introduction to the Objective Caml programming language. Verfügbar unter. http://docs.happycoders.org/html/dev/ocaml/index.php
15. Nilsson, H., Courtney, A., Peterson, J.: Functional reactive programming, continued. In: Proceedings of the 2002 ACM SIGPLAN Workshop on Haskell. ACM, pp. 51–64 (2002)
16. Berry, G., Boudol, G.: The chemical abstract machine. In: Proceedings of the 17th ACM SIGPLAN-SIGACT Symposium on Principles of Programming Languages. ACM, pp. 81–94 (1989)

Towards an Experimental LegoLand: Slice Modification and Recovery in ExoGENI Testbed

Yufeng Xin[1]([✉]), Ilya Baldin[1], Anirban Mandal[1], Paul Ruth[1], and Jeff Chase[2]

[1] RENCI, University of North Carolina at Chapel Hill, Chapel Hill, NC 27517, USA
yxin@renci.org
[2] Department of Computer Science, Duke University, Durham, NC 27708, USA

Abstract. This paper describes advanced capabilities that were deployed recently in the ExoGENI testbed to offer increased flexibility in provisioning, modifying, and recovering the topologies and the configuration settings of the virtual systems, or *slices*, in which experiments are run. Using the analogy of building complex structures with LEGO blocks, we envision an environment in which users arbitrarily scale out, scale in, scale up, and scale down their topologies using various modular constructs of compute, storage, and network resources. Portions of topologies can be shut down and brought back up to support resiliency, repeatability, migration, and other needs of the control software or application. Distributed applications running inside of slices can require programmatic control over the evolution of the topology as the execution progresses. The introduced capabilities, *slice modification* and *slice recovery*, are used either with the user GUI or through the programmable APIs. These new features expand the range and ease of options available to cloud-control software and to application developers as they test their designs at scale.

1 Introduction

The work that we present here endows researchers in networking and in distributed computing with flexible, efficient control over the scaling and configuration of network topologies in real time. It represents a substantive improvement in their ability to test the performance, scalability, and resiliency of the systems under investigation. Our work equips networked applications that are deployed inside and between data centers and clouds to operate more nimbly and robustly, optimizing available compute, storage, and networking resources. These types of requirements have been studied extensively as distributed application technologies and their uses have evolved [6,9,10].

Modern testbeds in networking and in distributed systems support virtual machines (VM) and other virtualization mechanisms [12,13] not only to improve usability and configurability but also to optimize resource utilization. Thus, they

This work is supported by the US National Science Foundation through the GENI initiative and NSF awards ACI-1245926, ACI-1440715, and CNS-1329745.

© ICST Institute for Computer Sciences, Social Informatics and Telecommunications Engineering 2017
S. Guo et al. (Eds.): TridentCom 2016, LNICST 177, pp. 35–45, 2017.
DOI: 10.1007/978-3-319-49580-4_4

resemble the public clouds deployed by Amazon, RackSpace, and other commercial providers. GENI, the federation of multiple testbeds, is consequently evolving into a cloud-based infrastructure-as-a-service (IaaS) system suited to real-world deployments of innovative distributed services and Future-Internet architectures as well as to experimentation [5].

Individual virtual machines provide a great deal of flexibility in configuring the performance attributes of individual compute nodes [14]. Allowing generalized manipulation of the topology interconnecting them, however, remains an open challenge. The only exceptions are a few typical data-intensive or web-service applications within a cloud in which the size of the worker server pool is allowed to be adjusted [10]. The challenge is greater in the case of a large-scale federated testbed system such as GENI, which includes multiple cloud sites connected by multi-domain networks. Each topology-modification action may involve modifying, provisioning, or releasing resources across multiple providers and may require provisioning of inter-site networking.

GENI creates virtual topologies for users. Each topology is called a *slice*. Individually configurable indivisible elements of slice topology are called *slivers*. Slivers can be individual virtual machines, bare-metal nodes, or links acquired from transit providers. Throughout this paper, we will use the term "slice"; however, instead of "sliver", we prefer *reservation* because we always associate a start and an end time with each sliver.

In this paper, we address four types of *topology-scaling*, defined as follows: (1) *Scale up*: increasing the size of a virtual cluster by adding more homogeneous nodes, or by raising the bandwidth of the network link in a slice; (2) *Scale down*: decreasing the size of a virtual cluster by removing nodes, or by reducing the bandwidth of reserved network links in a slice; (3) *Scale out*: adding new links, nodes, clusters, or third-party resources and linking them to existing reservations; (4) *Scale in*: deleting existing links, nodes, clusters, or third-party resources. We further define *slice modification* to be some form of *topology scaling* associated with reservation *term extension*. Reservation extension is required to ensure that the topology continues to exist after slice modification and to prevent older reservations from expiring. *Slice recovery* allows the system to stop, and then to restart, a slice while preserving its topology and resource accounting in the IaaS control system.

We focus on the implementation of generalized slice-modification capabilities in the ExoGENI testbed [3,7]. Since its inception seven years ago, ExoGENI has become an ambitious multi-domain IaaS system that has evolved well beyond the original design goal of a built-to-order virtual networking testbed. It is powered by a suite of information models, topology abstractions, and embedding algorithms, with resource-orchestration and -control software. It includes experimental tools that orchestrate a federation of independent cloud sites and networking providers through their native IaaS interfaces [1,3]. Due to the architectural flexibility of the ORCA [8,11] control software, ExoGENI continues to evolve. It now possesses the comprehensive generalized topology-scaling capabilities described here, which distinguish it from other similar testbeds.

The remainder of the paper presents our major contributions in three parts. In Sect. 2, we review the key components of ORCA, including system information models, topology abstraction, inter-domain orchestration, and end-to-end provisioning. We also describe the details of slice modification and recovery functions. In Sect. 3, we demonstrate several use cases that benefit from these new capabilities. Section 4 briefly states conclusions and ongoing work.

2 Slice Modification and Control Framework Design

In this section, we first motivate the slice-topology scaling with two typical use cases in cloud application and networking experiments. We then explain the technical challenges and the software enhancements that we added to the ORCA control framework to enable the slice modification. Due to the modular nature and flexible resource-description mechanisms of ORCA, most of the modifications were done outside of the ORCA core code, which handles such basic functions as agent communication, state maintenance, and recovery. We did modify the ORCA state machines, however, to support the sliver-modify cycle, which is discussed later in this section.

2.1 Motivating Examples

Figure 1 shows two types of virtual clusters that are commonly requested by big-data or tiered web-service applications. A virtual cluster request abstraction can be represented as N (virtual) nodes connecting to a virtual root R via links with bandwidth B as shown in Fig. 1(a). A more general representation is a virtual oversubscribed cluster [4] as shown in Fig. 1(c). Here, N VMs are grouped in a two-layered structure, where V_i is the virtual switch for connecting VMs in the group C_i with intra-group and inter-group bandwidths B_i' and B_i, respectively. A cluster is expressed by *NodeGroup* abstraction in ExoGENI, which specifies a group of VMs of identical configuration and connectivity.

The sizes and locations of the node groups are the most important scaling factors affecting the performance. A simple virtual cluster can be *scaled up* by

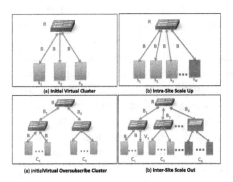

Fig. 1. Virtual cluster topology scaling

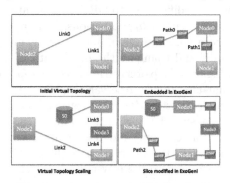

Fig. 2. General topology scaling

adding more nodes, or *scaled down* by deleting the existing nodes, as shown in Fig. 1(b). In this case, the entire cluster is embedded in a single cloud site. The modification action reduces to attaching/deleting the NICs of the newly added/deleted VMs to/from the broadcast link, which is a VLAN that is instantiated in the site switch. The case becomes much more complex when an over-subscribed virtual cluster consists of multiple sub-clusters that are embedded in different cloud sites. As shown in Fig. 1(d), we call this type of modification a *scale-out*, since the new sub-clusters are added from other sites. This mechanism is enabled by an *Exchange Domain* [15] deployed in ExoGENI. It can create multi-site broadcast domains to support large-scale distributed virtual clusters.

Figure 2 shows a sequence of modifications in a generic slice. The initial request is for a simple bus topology of three network nodes, as shown in Fig. 2(a). The topology is created in the testbed on an inter-site path (Link0 in Path0) and on an intra-site path (Link1 in Path1); the manifest topology is shown in Fig. 2(b). Next, modifications are made to the virtual topology, as shown in Fig. 2(c). In the example, the system deleted both Path0 and Path1 (*scale-in*), added a storage device to Node0, created a new link between Node2 and Node1, and created another new path between Node0 and Node1 via a new node, Node3 (*e.g.*, a router) (scale-out). The resulting topology is depicted in Fig. 2(d).

In addition to the basic topology-scaling performance, we can easily see the value of topology modification in other important system studies. For example, the option of adding or deleting arbitrary links in the virtual topology would be very useful in studying fault tolerance or congestion-avoidance performance. Link and node deletion can emulate network link or node failures and can be used to exercise backup and rerouting strategies. The ability to add new components to the topology, especially new types of resources (*e.g.*, storage nodes on demand), would yield significant benefits for distributed or big-data system designs.

2.2   Control Framework Support

We implemented slice modification in the ORCA control framework using extensions to resource-control policies and substrate drivers, all pluggable components in ORCA architecture. These modifications consisted of two parts. First, there were modifications to ORCA core-state machines to support a variety of atomic *reservation modify* operations. Examples of these include inserting new SSH keys into a compute node, adding or removing network interfaces from a compute node, and changing the bandwidth of a link. Second, we modified the control plugins to help orchestrate *slice modify* operations as sequenced sets of operations that *created* new reservations, *removed* or *modified* existing ones. This function required reservation modifications to accommodate stitching or unstitching parts of the slice. For instance, linking a new node to an existing node in the topology (*i.e.*, a scale-out) requires creating new link and node reservations as well as modifying the reservation of the existing node to add a new network interface attaching it to the new link, as shown in Fig. 2(d).

In this paper, we focus on the enhancements to ORCA that were created to support slice modification. The sequencing of provisioning operations in ORCA is part of its core functionality and is described more fully in [2,3], while further details of ExoGENI architecture and ORCA implementation can be found in [1] and on the project website [7].

A critical design principle in ORCA is that of maintaining provider autonomy, in which substrate providers advertise topology information and resource counts at the desired level of granularity and commitment. This feature allows providers to decide whether to under - or oversubscribe their resources and enables them to maintain the privacy of their internal topologies. The abstract representations of provider topology and resource levels are delegated to a broker in the form of resource pools of different types (VLAN, VM, etc.) with associated constraints on total bandwidth, core counts, available memory, and storage space.

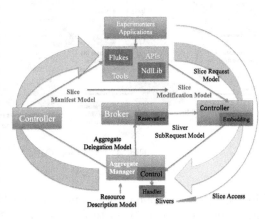

Fig. 3. ORCA information model and slice lifecycle

An ORCA user agent called *controller* queries the broker in real time for available resources, then constructs the inter-site topology from individual abstractions. Next, it embeds the user topology request and generates individual resource reservations for different aggregate managers (AMs) representing resource providers. These reservations are sent to the AMs to be redeemed for actual resources, which are provisioned by the respective AMs.

Each AM has its own resource-control policy to account for available resources. Each uses customized drivers to invoke APIs, which then provision the resources, *e.g.*, OpenStack nova for VM, or AL2S OSCARS for the dynamic circuits over Internet2. The operation of ORCA actors is depicted in Fig. 3, with red boxes showing the enhancements that were added to support the generalized slice-modification capability.

Reservation Modify Support. The core of ORCA consists of three types of distributed, autonomous ORCA actors that interact with each other to maintain reservation states. Each reservation passes through different states using well defined state machine actions for each actor. Reservations are associated with dictionaries of properties that describe their configurations according to the type of each reservation. Providing support for slice modification required that we first enable changes to slivers/reservations, allowing the controller logic to combine such modifications with other reservation operations. We extended the internal reservation-state machine to support new states for reservations and introduced new inter-actor calls to communicate modification actions.

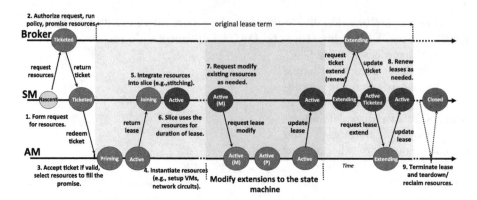

Fig. 4. Extended ORCA state machine.

Modifying a reservation involves updating the dictionary of properties and invoking a substrate-update task to implement those changes. For example, adding a new network interface involves adding new properties that specify, *e.g.*, its MAC and IP addresses along with the VLAN tag to which it attaches. Then, a substrate update task can be invoked, *e.g.*, on OpenStack, to equip an existing VM with a new interface that possesses the desired properties.

The new reservation states for each actor were designed to support progressive modification of stored reservation properties, and had to be reconciled with the existing state transitions. The state machine transitions on each of the three types of ORCA actors are shown in Fig. 4. The area of the figure that is shaded in green shows the extra states and transitions that were introduced to support modification of reservations. We added a new "pending" reservation state called *ModifyingLease*, shown as (M) in the figure. We also extended the ORCA management API, *i.e.*, the API used by external entities to interface with the ORCA core, to support calls from the controller for reservation modifications.

Stateful Slice Control. Conceptually, a slice is a resource container. It holds a set of resource reservations (slivers) that are granted by the providers for a specific term. We implemented the ORCA controller to maintain the current state of the slice, including individual reservations and their respective topologies. The controller also sequences the generation of new reservations, removes old reservations, and modifies existing reservations, all of which are steps in a single slice modification. Each slice-modification request consists of a subgraph that is either added or removed from the existing topology graph. Based on this slice-modification request, the controller computes sets of reservations to be added and to be removed, along with modification operations for existing affected reservations. It sequences them properly using dependency tracking and submits them to the ORCA core for execution. The standard ORCA core mechanisms communicate among the various relevant actors, making sure that resources are instantiated, deleted, or modified to reflect the new topology of the slice.

Slice-modification requests are not idempotent. They are always based on the latest slice-manifest document, reflecting the latest topology. Elements of the slice have unique URL names in the manifest. To stitch new elements of the slice these names are included in slice-modification requests as reference points to be used in the attachment of new reservations to existing ones and in the removal of existing reservations. Replaying a scale-up/out modification request results in the generation of duplicate subgraphs that are added to the slice.

The dependency-tracking mechanism builds on previously described work [2]. To support slice modifications, we extended this mechanism to include a new type of dependency. It is used in the initiation of reservation modifications only after prerequisites have been fulfilled, *e.g.*, after creating or removing a reservation. The prerequisites may provide information that is needed to invoke the reservation modification, such as the tag of a VLAN from which a node needs to be disconnected because the associated link was removed. Originally, the tracking of dependencies supported only the sequencing of new reservation events.

Persistent Resource Models. ORCA is a complex distributed system with many actors. Thus, it can experience a variety of failure modes. Recovery of state is critical; the affected portion of the system must be able to resume its state correctly and to proceed with its operation after a failure. ORCA recovery is based on two different approaches, *i.e.*, recovery of slice - or substrate topologies and recovery of reservation states in other actors such as brokers and AMs. The topology information models in ORCA are represented in Semantic Web RDF and OWL models, which are implemented using the popular RDF library Jena. Jena has a TDB component for persistent storage and query from the disk. We implemented our slice-recovery function by using TDB to save all the substrate information models at each actor and the slice models in the controller. When an actor crashes or is shut down and restarted, it can invoke the recovery function to restore its models from the latest committed state in the TDB store. The recovery function automatically reconciles the actor's information with the available resource information acquired from the ORCA core, which has its own recovery capability based on storing resource-accounting information in a relational database. Once the recovery is complete, the actor resumes its operation.

2.3   Aggregate Manager Control

ExoGENI AMs control the physical substrate and instantiate resources requested by the user via a controller. Addition and removal of network links require, respectively, addition and removal of network interfaces to existing virtual machines. This modification is handled by the AM.

Most compute aggregates in ExoGENI are individual hybrid Open-Stack/xCAT clouds. ExoGENI uses a custom plugin to OpenStack networking that supports dynamic addition and removal of Layer-2 networks as well as of the corresponding network interfaces on existing virtual machines.

2.4   User Tool and API

The Flukes GUI and the NDLLIB library are the two user interfaces to Exo-GENI that support the new slice-modification features. The Flukes GUI has been enhanced to support the different types of scaling behaviors described earlier.

The NDLLIB library provides a programmable interface to ExoGENI providing procedural interface to the controller API. The library consists of Java classes and methods that simplify the generation and parsing of NDL requests and manifests. The library uses an abstraction of Java objects to model slices and resources within slice topologies, *e.g.*, compute nodes, network links, and storage nodes. Users can add, remove, and modify resources in this slice model. Then, they can programmatically generate a NDL request and submit to ExoGENI controller to instantiate new resources or to change existing resources.

3   Use Cases and Evaluation

Today, the ExoGENI testbed has some twenty cloud sites across the world, the highest concentration of which is located in the U.S. Dynamic circuits must be provisioned over, *e.g.*, AL2S, the Exchange Domain, and regional networks to provision slices over multiple sites. With this in mind, we first studied the scaling performance of ExoGENI in provisioning virtual clusters scaling out to various sites. Figure 5 shows a screenshot of the user interface in Flukes from this work. The background view is the request for five sub-clusters of size 12 at different sites, expressed in the simple virtual-cluster (VC) abstraction using the *node group*. The front view is the *manifest* that shows the result, which is a slice with the instantiated VMs interconnected to the virtual broadcast link in the Exchange domain via five multi-domain dynamic paths.

Figure 6 shows the provisioning time of a VC with different numbers of nodes in three scenarios. The VC is embedded, respectively, in one cloud site, in three different sites, and in five different sites. The most important observation is that the time increases with the number of sites involved. Examination of the provisioning stages in more detail yields further insights: (1) There may be limited

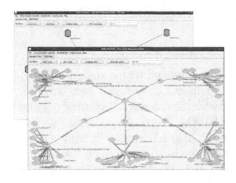

Fig. 5. VC seen in Flukes

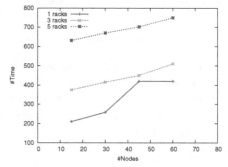

Fig. 6. VC scaling performance

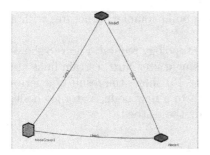

Fig. 7. Original topology

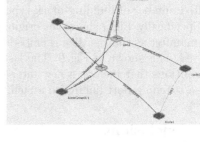

Fig. 8. Original manifest

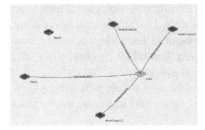

Fig. 9. Delete links

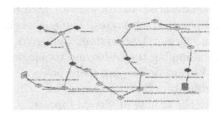

Fig. 10. Add links and nodes

resources available at a site, which affects results. For example, at the time of the experiment, if only 52 cores (standard VM resources) are available at many sites, VC size cannot be increased to 60. (2) If the entire VC is embedded in a single site, the majority of provisioning time is spent in creating the VMs. For example, when the VC size is 45, 75% of the time is used in VM creation in the OpenStack rack, and most of the rest is spent by ORCA to generate the 45 ORCA reservations. (3) In the multiple-site case, the majority of provisioning time is spent in configuring the network circuits, including the point-to-point circuits in AL2S and the multi-point circuits in the Exchange domain. Due the highly parallel configuration process in ORCA, VM creation occurs in parallel with the creation of the circuits. In the 60-node five-site case, about 35% of the time is spent on AL2S and 35% on exchange-domain configuration, whereas the remaining 30% is spent in ORCA. Circuit-creation times increase in proportion with the number of sites used, as more path computation and configuration are needed. (4) ORCA computation time also rises in proportion with the number of sites involved, as more path- and stitching computations are needed and as the reservation-management load increases.

Next, we demonstrate the modification sequence for a general topology slice with live screenshots from Flukes. The time-performance results (not shown) are dominated by the path-provisioning time. Screenshots show that a slice can be modified arbitrarily in unlimited steps, an example of the kind of capabilities inherent in the use of LEGO-like constructs to build complex structures with a limited number of building-block types.

Specifically, Fig. 7 shows the original virtual topology request. Figure 8 shows the manifest as the the slice is embedded in a single site. Next, certain links are deleted, as is shown in Fig. 9. The last one (Fig. 10) shows the result of a series of additions that include a new inter-rack path to a new node, a storage node, and a stitching port linking to a facility outside the testbed.

4   Conclusions

The present paper describes the newly developed slice-modification capabilities in the ExoGENI testbed with emphasis on the scaling of topologies. The underlying advanced control software architecture is focused on the federation of cloud and network substrates. The enhancements presented here yield a comprehensive, efficient IaaS system that gives users great flexibility in controlling and programming the scales and topologies of virtual systems.

We are developing more powerful APIs and libraries that will utilize slice-modification functions more fully, thus allowing users and applications to automate the scaling of virtual topologies.

References

1. Baldin, I., Chase, J., Xin, Y., Mandal, A., Ruth, P., Castillo, C., Orlikowski, V., Heermann, C., Mills, J.: Exogeni: a multi-domain infrastructure-as-a-service testbed. In: McGeer, R., Berman, M., Elliott, C., Ricci, R. (eds.) GENI: Prototype of the Next Internet. Springer-Verlag, New York (2016)
2. Baldine, I., Xin, Y., Mandal, A., Heermann, C., Chase, J., Marupadi, V., Yumerefendi, A., Irwin, D.: Orchestration, autonomic cloud network: a GENI perspective. In: 2nd International Workshop on Management of Emerging Networks and Services (IEEE MENS 2010), Co-Located with GLOBECOM 2010, December 2010
3. Baldine, I., Xin, Y., Mandal, A., Ruth, P., Yumerefendi, A., Chase, J.: Exogeni: a multi-domain infrastructure-as-a-service testbed. In: TridentCom: International Conference on Testbeds and Research Infrastructures for the Development of Networks and Communities, June 2012
4. Ballani, H., Costa, P., Karagiannis, T., Rowstron, A.: Towards predictable datacenter networks. In: Proceedings of the ACM SIGCOMM 2011 Conference, SIGCOMM 2011, pp. 242–253. ACM, New York (2011)
5. Berman, M., Chase, J.S., Landweber, L., Nakao, A., Ott, M., Raychaudhuri, D., Ricci, R., Seskar, I.: GENI: a federated testbed for innovative network experiments. Comput. Netw. **61**, 5–23 (2014)
6. Chard, R., Bubendorfer, K., Ng, B.: Network health and e-science in commercial clouds. Future Gener. Comput. Syst. **56**, 595–604 (2016)
7. ExoGENI websites. http://www.exogeni.net, http://wiki.exogeni.net
8. Fu, Y., Chase, J., Chun, B., Schwab, S., Vahdat, A.: SHARP: an architecture for secure resource peering. In: Proceedings of the 19th ACM Symposium on Operating System Principles, October 2003

9. Gibbons, P.B.: Big data: scale down, scale up, scale out. In: Keynote Talk at the 29th IEEE International Parallel and Distributed Processing Symposium (IPDPS 2015), Hyderabad, India, May 2015

10. Hwang, K., Bai, X., Shi, Y., Li, M., Chen, W.-G., Wu, Y.: Cloud performance modeling with benchmark evaluation of elastic scaling strategies. IEEE Trans. Parallel Distrib. Syst. **27**(1), 130–143 (2016)

11. Irwin, D., Chase, J.S., Grit, L., Yumerefendi, A., Becker, D., Yocum, K.G.: Sharing networked resources with brokered leases. In: Proceedings of the USENIX Technical Conference, June 2006

12. Kang, J.-M., Lin, T., Bannazadeh, H., Leon-Garcia, A.: Software-defined infrastructure and the SAVI testbed. In: Leung, C.V., Chen, M., Wan, J., Zhang, Y. (eds.) Testbeds and Research Infrastructure: Development of Networks and Communities: 9th International ICST Conference, pp. 3–13. Springer International Publishing, Cham (2014)

13. McGeer, R., Berman, M., Elliott, C., Ricci, R. (eds.): GENI: Prototype of the Next Internet. Springer-Verlag, New York (2016). In production for publication, July 2016

14. Shen, Z., Subbiah, S., Gu, X., Wilkes, J.: Cloudscale: elastic resource scaling for multi-tenant cloud systems. In: Proceedings of the 2Nd ACM Symposium on Cloud Computing, SOCC 2011, pp. 5:1–5:14. ACM, New York (2011)

15. Xin, Y., Baldin, I., Heerman, C., Mandal, A., Ruth, P.: Scaling up applications over distributed clouds with dynamic layer-2 exchange and broadcast service. In: ITC'26 Workshop on Federated Future Internet and Distributed Cloud Testbeds (FIDC 2014), Karlskrona, Sweden, September 2014

Network Testbed Design
and Implementation

MobiLab: A Testbed for Evaluating Mobility Management Protocols in WSN

Jianjun Wen, Zeeshan Ansar, and Waltenegus Dargie$^{(\boxtimes)}$

Technical University of Dresden, 01062 Dresden, Germany
{jianjun.wen,zeeshan.ansar,waltenegus.dargie}@tu-dresden.de

Abstract. Wireless sensor networks that support the mobility of nodes are finding applications in different areas such as healthcare, elderly care, and rehabilitation from total knee and hip replacement. However, these application areas also require reliable and high throughput networks. Considering the high fluctuation of link quality during mobility, protocols supporting mobile wireless sensor nodes should be rigorously tested to ensure that they produce predictable outcomes. In this paper we present a wireless sensor network testbed for carrying out repeated and reproducible experiments, independent of the application or protocol types which should be tested. The testbed consists of, among others, a server side control station and a client side traffic flow controller which coordinate inter- and intra-experiment activities. We fully implemented the testbed for the TinyOS and TelosB platforms. We employed Diddyborg robots for emulating different types of movements in indoor and outdoor environments. The paper includes also an extensive evaluation of the testbed.

Keywords: Testbed · Mobility management · Experiment management · Wireless sensor networks

1 Introduction

Wireless sensor networks which support the mobility of nodes are useful for different applications. For example, in the healthcare domain, they have been proposed to monitor patients with Parkinson Disease [9], gastroparesis [6], and asthma [8]. As a result, there is an endeavour to integrate medical devices and make them interact with existing wireless sensor platforms. For instance, the wireless mobility capsule integrating pH, pressure, and temperature sensors for the diagnosis of gastroparesis has officially been approved by the US drug and food administration since 2006; it has produced promising results and may replace existing invasive and painful procedures (such as endoscopy) [4]. Similarly, there are commercially available wireless electrocardiograms which can be integrated with existing sensor platforms.

There are, however, some challenges associated with mobility, one of the most significant challenges being the difficulty of maintaining link quality during mobility. Independent experiments show that link quality quickly deteriorates when nodes are mobile while communicating, resulting in high packet loss, drift,

© ICST Institute for Computer Sciences, Social Informatics and Telecommunications Engineering 2017
S. Guo et al. (Eds.): TridentCom 2016, LNICST 177, pp. 49–58, 2017.
DOI: 10.1007/978-3-319-49580-4_5

and jitter. This aspect particularly affects applications which require relatively high throughput. Devices such as wireless electrocardiograms typically generate data at tens of kilobits per second rate. While this in itself may not be high, if other sensors such as 3D accelerometers and gyroscopes have to be sampled at comparatively the same rate, then the aggregate data rate from a single node can be high. Whereas the effect of mobility on link quality fluctuation has been extensively studied in the context of cellular communications (owing, luckily, to the ability of collecting ample statistics from a large number of users in different settings and locations), investigation of link quality fluctuation in mobile wireless sensor networks is a work in progress.

In this paper we propose a testbed for evaluating the effect of mobility in wireless sensor networks. The testbed separates the concern of application development from the evaluation of the application in different mobile scenarios. By doing so, complex and reproducible experiments can be carried out to ensure that the behaviors of applications are both reproducible and predictable. We fully implemented the testbed for the TinyOS and TelosB platforms. Our mobile nodes are carried by Diddyborg robots[1], each of which is controlled by 6 powerful gear motors, so that the robots can be tasked to emulate different types of movements in indoor as well as outdoor environments.

The remaining part of this paper is organized as follows: In Sect. 2, we review related work and position our own work. In Sect. 3, we present the system architecture of our testbed. In Sect. 4, the performance of MobiLab is evaluated from different perspectives. Finally, in Sect. 5, we give concluding remarks and outline future work.

2   Related Work

Testbeds are intended to efficiently test wireless sensor networks before they are actually deployed in real-world environments. Compared to the area or volume an actual deployment occupies, testbeds are considerably compact, so that they can be installed in labs or in areas which are easily accessible. This means, some communication parameters are intentionally scaled and events can be deliberately injected into the network to suit the test setting and to emulate actual events. There are online testbeds which are available to the WSN research community, most of them establishing two types of networks. One of the networks is the actual wireless link the characteristic of which is investigated and the other network serves as a backbone, reliable network for collecting performance indicator metrics. This network can be wireless (for example, a WLAN) or wired (using USB hubs or serial interfaces). As far as the software architecture is concerned, the existing testbeds also share similar aspects such as: (a) provision of web-based infrastructure and experiment management services; and (b) functionalities for dynamic reprogramming, specification, configuration, and execution of experiments. Some of the testbeds employ robots [2,5,7] while others employ toy trains [10] as mobile platforms, to which wireless sensor nodes are attached.

---

[1] https://www.piborg.org/diddyborg.

Besides providing mobility, the mobile platforms also serve as power suppliers and node managers, through which new program images can be installed and experiment procedures are controlled and managed.

Emulab [5] is perhaps the first publicly reachable mobility-enabled testbed for WSNs experimentation. The testbed is deployed in an L-shaped area and consists of (1) 25 Mica2 static nodes installed on the walls and ceiling of a building to form a grid-like topology, (2) 6 mobile nodes attached to robotic platforms, which can perform user-specific and accurate way-point walking models (according to the authors, the position of the robots can be determined within 1 cm error, the worst-case), (3) 6 cameras which are installed on the ceiling to track the robots, and (4) additional 3 web-cams to provide live-monitoring. One of the limitations of the testbed is the difficulty of influencing the movements of the robots during experiment execution, because their movement pattern is predetermined and is not accessible at runtime.

Kansei [3] is a testbed employing the same types of robots like Emulab to support mobility, but it does not provide any positioning system. The testbed uses five robots integrating TMote Sky nodes and Extreme Scale Mote (XSM). These robots are deployed on top of a Plexiglas plane in which 210 XSMs and TMote Sky nodes are arranged in a 15 × 14 grid bench-work. In addition to the common functionalities the previous testbed provides, Kansei provides a mechanism to inject events into individual nodes and gateways. Sensei-UU [7] employs a Lego NXT robot as the mobile platform, on which a TelosB node and a smartphone are attached. Its unique feature is employing WL-500GP wireless access point as a control station to provide programming, experiment monitoring, and data logging functionalities via a wireless channel. While it is relatively easy to reproduce and repeat experiments with this testbed, it has some drawbacks: (1) the robot requires the installation of tapes on the floor, which limits the types of movement that can be imitated by the mobile platform (i.e., undertaking different random movements is difficult); and 2) it is difficult to support multiple mobile nodes at the same time.

SensLAB [2] and TrainSense [10] are two recently proposed testbeds for mobile platforms. Both utilize toy trains as mobile platforms. Since the trains run on tracks, which physically limit their motion, the testbeds are difficult to extend. It is also difficult to introduce random walks into experiments. One of the merits of these testbeds is their ability to provide better accuracy of localization and control of mobility compared with the other mobile platforms.

3   Architecture of MobiLab

The main purpose and, therefore, contribution of our testbed is the flexible but reproducible execution of complex experiments with wireless sensor networks in which some of the nodes are mobile. The testbed enables users to upload their own program image onto individual nodes and to specify experiment procedures and the movement pattern of mobile robots independent of the types of applications the wireless sensor networks are supporting. To achieve these goals, our testbed separates resource management into different concerns.

3.1   Hardware Architecture

The hardware architecture consists of four modules: a control station, a wireless sensor network, a node manager, and a backbone wireless channel. The control station serves as the main interface between the user and the testbed. A group of dedicated software services run in the control station to manage the testbed resources and to control experiments. In the next subsection we provide a detail description of the software architecture of the control station.

The wireless sensor network consists of three types of nodes: static relay nodes, mobile nodes, and sniffer nodes. The sniffer nodes are special stationary nodes used for monitoring the state of the wireless channel to obtain complementary information about experiment execution during debugging. By changing the firmware, they can also serve as interference source. A node manager interfaces a node with the control station. Each node manager (for our implementation we use the raspberry Pi 2) is connected to a sensor node via a USB port. We use a Wi-Fi *ad hoc* network as our backbone network because of its scalability and flexibility.

3.2   Software Architecture

The control station is the most important module in MobiLab. It ensures that the testbed as a whole functions as a unified system. It is through the control station every program image or command is propagated to the wireless sensor network. Figure 1 displays its software architecture, which consists of a user interface, a resource management service, an experiment management service, a data management service, and a data analysis service.

User Interface. MobiLab provides both a web-based and a command-line-interface through which users can access the testbed and conduct experiments

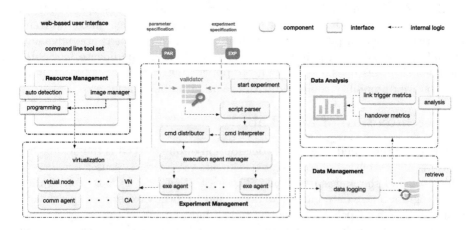

Fig. 1. The software architecture of the control station.

Table 1. Traffic flow control primitives.

Primitive	Description
Configure	Setup the application dependent parameters
Start	Initiate the test round
Stop	Notify finish of test round
Pause	Suspend execution
Continue	Resume execution
Terminate	Stop execution permanently

remotely. Users can browse active nodes and their status, upload program images into the wireless sensor network, and specify and manage experiment procedures using experiment execution primitives we defined (to be discussed below).

Resource Management. MobiLab does not require a fixed infrastructure (a specific network size or topology) to run experiments. The resource management service is responsible for authorizing nodes to join the network and users to access individual nodes; for managing binary images, and for ensuring proper program installation. Moreover, the resource management service uploads and deletes program images to and from nodes and controls versions. In it, a synchronization daemon runs in the background to ensure that program images in the control station and the node managers are consistent.

Experiment Management Service. The experiment management service enables users to define and manage inter- and intra-experiment activities. As regards management, users can initiate, interrupt, suspend, modify, and end experiments at runtime by using experiment execution primitives (see Table 1). The primitives enable users to configure interaction (transmission power, channel, partner nodes) and to specify communication durations, among others. When an experiment procedure is submitted to it, the experiment management service validates the procedure to ensure that it is executable, parse the procedure to extract experiment parameters, translates the parameters into binary, creates a control flow (execution sequence), and passes the control flow to the execution manager. The execution manager is responsible for coordinating the execution of an experiment procedure until it terminates. A virtual node manager within the control station's architecture creates a virtual representation for each physical node. The aim is to hide differences in hardware architecture between nodes from users and to provide common interfaces for accessing and interacting with them.

Data Management and Analysis. Data management or logging is one of the useful features of testbed frameworks. When an experiment is launched, MobiLab creates an instance of a data logging module which is then associated with the communication agents of the corresponding virtual nodes. During experiment execution, the physical nodes log the desired data locally and forward them to their virtual node managers at the control station, which then stores the data in a database. Alternatively performance indicators can be directly streamed to virtual node managers as they are generated.

3.3   Node Manager

The software aspect of a node manager has three components, which are the local server, a resource manager, and a traffic flow controller. A robot node manager includes an extra module for managing mobility.

Local Server. Its main responsibility is managing the physical node and controlling the proper execution of experiments. The server is logically connected with the resource management service at the control station, thus it is able to provide the functionalities for probing the sensor node, updating firmware; it is also responsible for coordinating experiment control flows and commands pertaining to the motion of a robot.

Traffic Flow Controller. The procedure of an experiment is first encoded using the traffic primitives we specified in Table 1. By the time it reaches the traffic flow controller at the node manager, it is translated into a sequence of commands and parameters. The traffic flow controller is responsible for creating a channel between the node manager and the physical node and for transmitting the commands and parameters in their sequence and appropriate delay to the physical node. It also channels the logged data from the physical node to the node manager. The node managers are time synchronized with the control station at the beginning of each run of an experiment. For a detailed description of the Traffic Control Flow protocol, we refer the reader to [11].

Robot Controller. Different mobility models can be implemented and integrated into the node manager a priori and an instance of a model can be loaded when the robot controller is first instantiated. The parameters of this model can be modified at runtime by using the experiment primitives in Table 1. Currently, we are experimenting with straight line walking and the random waypoint model [1].

3.4   Sensor Node

Figure 2 (right side) illustrates the software architecture of a wireless sensor node. Most relevant to this paper is the traffic flow control protocol middleware (TFCP). The TFCP middleware is an application independent layer for managing inter and intra-experiment activities. It is loosely coupled with the OS layer, interacting with communication drivers by send and receive interfaces

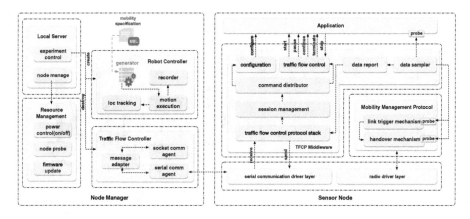

Fig. 2. An overview of the software architecture of the testbed from a single node perspective: (Left) The software architecture of the node manager. (Right) The software architecture of a sensor node.

Fig. 3. MobiLab deployment: A MobiLab robot carrying a wireless sensor node.

and exposing six interfaces to the higher layers (MAC, network and application layers), so that users can setup experiment and application specific parameters and control the execution steps of experiments. The data sampler and report module locally collects and aggregates performance indicator metrics from relevant layers and communicates them with the control station via the TFCP middleware. The TFCP middleware running on each sensor node is built on top of TinyOS and has a footprint of 1058 bytes of ROM and 84 bytes of RAM.

The mobility management protocol does not belong to the MobiLab testbed. We integrated it to investigate the performance of different mobility management protocols under the same setting.

4   Evaluation

One of the features of MobiLab is the simplicity with which it can be deployed in different places, since it does not rely on any fixed infrastructure. It takes

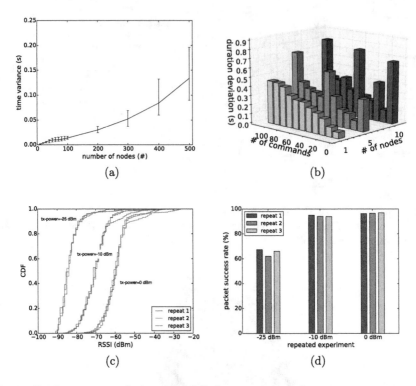

Fig. 4. Performance analysis of MobiLab as an experiment management tool: (a) The time variance of synchronized starting time for networks of different sizes; (b) The deviation in the duration of arbitrary control commands in a single experiment. (c) cdf of RSSI fluctuation of repeated experiments; (d) packet success rate of repeated experiments

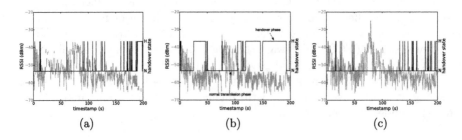

Fig. 5. RSSI fluctuation of incoming acknowledgement packets and handover oscillation. (a) Single threshold scheme. (b) Dual threshold scheme. (c) LMS.

less than 10 min to setup the environment and start to perform the experiment. In order to carry out repeatable experiments, the detail of the experiment procedures are scripted, i.e., the beginning, end, and duration of every activity is specified. When the control station dispatches experiment procedures, they may not be executed by the individual nodes at precisely the same time. Consequently, nodes may not begin and end the execution of experiments at the same time. This phenomenon is an aspect of both the size of the network and the complexity of the experiments. To investigate this phenomenon, we launched a set of simple experiments with variable number of physical nodes (from 5 to 20) and emulated nodes (up to 500). We recorded the starting time of each node and calculated the maximum variance (time difference between the earliest starting node and the latest staring node). We observed that the maximum variance of experiment beginning time was 200 ms. Secondly, we inserted arbitrary number of control commands (*pause* and *continue* commands) in the experiments lasting up to 600 seconds, and varied the number of nodes from 1 to 10. We did not observe significant increments of experiment completion times when the number of commands increased (shown in Fig. 4(b)). To show the repeatability of an experiment using MobiLab, we evaluated the RSSI fluctuation and packet reception rate under different configurations. We conducted a series of experiments and repeated each one three times. As Fig. 4(c) and (d) shown, the CDF of RSSI values are almost the same for the experiment with the same configuration (transmission power, motion pattern, walking path etc.) and the packet reception rates are consistent for each repetition.

Figure 5 shows how we evaluated the performance of three handover supporting MAC protocols using our testbed. The protocols evaluated the RSSI fluctuation of incoming ACK packets and determined the appropriate time to change a relay node with which a mobile robot (refer to Fig. 3) should communicate.

5   Conclusion

In this paper we introduced MobiLab, a testbed we developed to experiment with wireless sensor networks supporting mobile nodes. MobiLab separates the concerns of application and protocol developments from their testing phase. Our main motivation was performing repeated and reproducible experiments independent of the types of network topology, communication protocols, and communication parameters involved in the experiments. From the software perspective, besides sharing the same design principles with existing testbeds, MobiLab provides several novel contributions such as supporting both inter- and intra-experiment management, TFCP middleware in a sensor node, and a robot motion management. Except for the sensor node architecture, which is implemented in C for the TelosB platform, all the remaining software components are implemented in python, which is relatively easy to port to other platforms.

Acknowledgment. This work is funded by the DFG under project agreement: DA 1211/5-2.

References

1. Camp, T., Boleng, J., Davies, V.: A survey of mobility models for ad hoc network research. Wireless Commun. Mob. Comput. **2**(5), 483–502 (2002)
2. Des Rosiers, C.B., Chelius, G., Fleury, E., Fraboulet, A., Gallais, A., Mitton, N., Noël, T.: Senslab very large scale open wireless sensor network testbed. In: Proceedings of the 7th International ICST Conference on Testbeds and Research Infrastructures for the Development of Networks and Communities (TridentCOM) (2011)
3. Ertin, E., Arora, A., Ramnath, R., Naik, V., Bapat, S., Kulathumani, V., Sridharan, M., Zhang, H., Cao, H., Nesterenko, M.: Kansei: a testbed for sensing at scale. In: Proceedings of the 5th International Conference on Information Processing in Sensor Networks, pp. 399–406. ACM (2006)
4. Farmer, A.D., Scott, S.M., Hobson, A.R.: Gastrointestinal motility revisited: the wireless motility capsule. United Eur. Gastroenterol. J., 2050640613510161 (2013)
5. Fish, R., Flickinger, M., Lepreau, J.: Mobile emulab: a robotic wireless and sensor network testbed. In: IEEE INFOCOM (2006)
6. Grimes, C.A., Ong, K.G., Varghese, O.K., Yang, X., Mor, G., Paulose, M., Dickey, E.C., Ruan, C., Pishko, M.V., Kendig, J.W., et al.: A sentinel sensor network for hydrogen sensing. Sensors **3**(3), 69–82 (2003)
7. Rensfelt, O., Hermans, F., Larzon, L., Gunningberg, P.: Sensei-UU: a relocatable sensor network testbed. In: Proceedings of the Fifth ACM International Workshop on Wireless Network Testbeds, Experimental Evaluation and Characterization, pp. 63–70. ACM (2010)
8. Seto, E.Y., Giani, A., Shia, V., Wang, C., Yan, P., Yang, A.Y., Jerrett, M., Bajcsy, R.: A wireless body sensor network for the prevention and management of asthma. In: 2009 IEEE International Symposium on Industrial Embedded Systems, SIES 2009, pp. 120–123. IEEE (2009)
9. Sha, D.L., Xie, W.C., Fan, X.L., Li, Y.: Based on wireless sensor network (NWK) of non-contact tremor monitoring equipment improvement for Parkinson's disease. In: Applied Mechanics and Materials, vol. 713, pp. 491–494. Trans Tech Publications (2015)
10. Smeets, H., Shih, C.-Y., Zuniga, M., Hagemeier, T., Marrón, P.J.: TrainSense: a novel infrastructure to support mobility in wireless sensor networks. In: Demeester, P., Moerman, I., Terzis, A. (eds.) EWSN 2013. LNCS, vol. 7772, pp. 18–33. Springer, Heidelberg (2013). doi:10.1007/978-3-642-36672-7_2
11. Wen, J., Ansar, Z., Dargie, W.: A system architecture for managing complex experiments in wireless sensor networks. In: The 25th International Conference on Computer Communication and Networks (ICCCN 2016), Waikoloa, Hawaii, USA, 1–4 August 2016

Alfons: A Mimetic Network Environment Construction System

Shingo Yasuda[✉], Ryosuke Miura, Satoshi Ohta, Yuuki Takano,
and Toshiyuki Miyachi

Hokuriku StarBED Technology Center, National Institute of Information
and Communications Technology, 2-12, Nomi, Ishikawa 923-1211, Japan
s-yasuda@nict.go.jp
http://starbed.nict.go.jp/en/

Abstract. Mimetic environments, which mimic actual networks including personal computers, network assets, etc., are required for cyber range or malware analysis. However, constructing various mimetic environments is costly and tedious because each environment has different network assets. Thus, we propose a building block system for constructing mimetic network environments for cyber security experiments. These building blocks provides a fine-grained way to manage disk images and files to reduce the construction cost. In this paper, we describe the design and implementation of the building block system called Alfons.

Keywords: Network testbed · Cyber range environment · Testbed construction system · Building block method

1 Introduction

The target of malware attacks is changing from an unspecified number of computers to a particular company or individual. Such attacks are called "targeted attacks." Malware that is utilized in targeted attacks has become increasingly sophisticated over time. Hence, the research and development of countermeasure technology are urgently needed.

The analysis of malware utilizes not only a static analysis but also a dynamic analysis because most malware that is captured at the first intrusion stage is a dropper that obtains the next malware from a command and control server (C&C server); therefore, it is not possible to ascertain its purpose without running the malware. Furthermore, some targeted-attack malware utilizes internal (private) information such as a proxy address or an account ID/PASSWORD. Such malware does not run as expected without these services or that configuration in an analysis environment. Accordingly, the analysis environment should be a mimetic environment with the same services and configuration that are configured for the targeted domain network.

In addition, there is a shortage of security personnel in Japan. In order to foster the knowledge of the security personnel, hands-on practice is effective.

© ICST Institute for Computer Sciences, Social Informatics and Telecommunications Engineering 2017
S. Guo et al. (Eds.): TridentCom 2016, LNICST 177, pp. 59–69, 2017.
DOI: 10.1007/978-3-319-49580-4_6

Thus, we have cooperated with some event or security curricula that utilize tools including SecCap [1], the Hardening Project [2], and so on. Such a cyber range needs various network services and mimetic contents in their environments. For example, these services and content include generic and domestic network service applications within a targeted organization and their configurations and business content such as office documents, mail, and so on. We have researched and developed some tools for network testbed orchestration such as SpringOS [3]. These tools can construct a network environment for network software validation. However, an operator must manually install these data when constructing an event environment because SpringOS does not enough functionality for these requirements. This work is costly and tedious.

To address this, we proposed a mimetic environment construction system called "Alfons" for the dynamic analysis and cyber range [4]. Alfons allows for the configuration of applications and has an installation mechanism for content to reduce these costs. Alfons also can configure the applications without trace in the instance; moreover, it also can insert the content files into instance without trace. In this paper, we describe the design and implementation of Alfons. Moreover, we describe a basic performance evaluation based on a conceptual implementation.

2   Related Work

Dynamic Analysis System for Malware: Cuckoo [5] is a dynamic analysis tool for malware. Cuckoo builds a sandbox environment that can run an exe file and utilizes a Kernel-based Virtual Machine (KVM) as virtualization technology.

Christopher Kruegel [6] proposed a dynamic analysis approach that utilizes full virtualization. According to Kruegel, full virtualization such as KVM is more suitable than para-virtualization techniques, because of its affinity for the instruction level and the possibility of observation on Windows.

Miwa proposed a malware analysis platform called MIMI/MAT [7]. This is a full automatic dynamic malware analysis platform that utilizes the network domain, which has some virtual nodes including network services.

These tools usually utilize a clean node that is not used because they do not have the functionality for customizing the internal data of the node.

Virtual Environment Configuration Tools: A cloud controller such as OpenStack [8], VMWare vSphere [9] can create a network service node on demand. SpringOS [3] can manage a physical node on StarBED. Moreover, SpringOS can control the network topology such as the VLAN connectivity between physical nodes, even though other cloud orchestrators cannot. In addition, these orchestrator tools do not have functions that imitate content and configurations.

Vagrant [10], Ansible [11] and Chef [12] are management tools that configure a virtual environment. These tools enable users to configure the virtual node including the configuration of applications, the installation of content, and so on with recipes. A recipe is useful for customizing a virtual node on the basis of the template node image. However, many recipes are necessary when an operator creates many environments or a large environment with various nodes.

Cyber Range Environment Construction: We have cooperated with some events that partially apply these StarBED achievements [1, 2]. ENCS,ICS-CERT, and Boeing have other types of cyber ranges, such as Red TEAM - Blue TEAM [13–15]. However, providing many various environments requires a high cost if we utilize these tools or achievements.

3   Definition of Requirements

In this section, we discuss the functionality that the orchestrator tools should have in each step of the network environment construction process. Current network orchestrators have the functions listed in Table 1. Although it appears that the functional coverage area is exhaustive, there is a lack of functionality caused as the premise mismatch of the individual functions. In addition, there is no tool that can transparently control the entire environment. We describe the individual functional requirements in the following.

Table 1. Support coverage of orchestrator tools

	Facility management	Network parameter configuration	Contents installation	Virtual/Physical node support
SpringOS	○	○(Agent)	○(Agent)	Physical
Cloud controller	×	○	×	Virtual
Vagrant	○	○	×	Virtual

Facility Management and Virtual/Physical Node Support: SpringOS has a function related to network topology management that utilizes a bare metal network switch configuration with a VLAN. A cloud controller such as VMWare vSphere and Vagrant can configure the network connection on a hypervisor utilizing a bridge or virtual switch devices instead of not supporting the management of these facilities. It is sufficient if one cyber range or dynamic analysis environment can run on a hypervisor. However, some malware samples have a function for sandbox detection, such as virtualization node detection [16]. There are some techniques for evading sandbox detection [17]; nevertheless, in some cases, we should run such malware on a bare metal machine. Hence, the orchestrator should support virtual and physical nodes; moreover, it should manage integrated with bare metal and virtual switch.

Network Parameter Configuration: All orchestrators can configure network parameters such as the IP address of a node. Moreover, there are some approaches that perform this configuration. SpringOS configures the network parameters by utilizing an agent program. The agent program configures the parameters on an experimental node. Owing to this, all experimental nodes have a management network connection to manage the agents. It is a simple solution for generic network system software or application validation; however, this is bad for malware analysis and a cyber range. This is because the management connection has the risk of malware traffic leakage outside the environment; moreover, a specific daemon program will interfere with the cyber range and analysis. Vagrant needs a specific account in the construction node to configure the nodes and is also subject to interference. Hence, the orchestrator tool should configure or customize the experimental nodes without a trace.

Installation of Content: Some malware abuses the target internal proxy server to connect to the outside. Other malware explores contents such as office documents or mail. Malware such as this will not run as expected without those network services, configurations, and content in the environment. Hence, to analyze advanced malware, the software should have a function for configuring the network parameters and a function for inserting content. In addition, these functions should perform without a trace.

Environment Separation on a Network Testbed: In a generic network testbed such as StarBED, the bare metal nodes have a management network interface that can be found and used by an OS. In case of generic network software validation, this is useful for managing the environment. On the other hand, this has the risk of traffic leakage outside the environment for a malware analysis or cyber range; moreover, it will be a feature of the analysis environment. Thus, this feature will be the target of sandbox detection. Hence, the orchestrator tool should have environment separation mechanism.

4   Design and Implementation of Alfons

In this section, we describe the design and implementation of "Alfons," which is a mimetic environment construction system for dynamic analysis and cyber range construction. Alfons is assumed to operate on StarBED. Hence, Alfons utilizes the API provided by SpringOS to control the bare metal switches, power control, and OS installation of bare metal servers in StarBED. The other part of the SpringOS API on Alfons is written in Ruby.

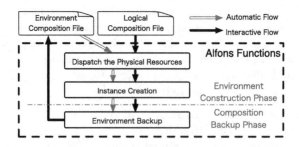

Fig. 1. Construction flow of Alfons

```
nbs:
  nb1:
  nb2:
vlans:
  vl1: {nb1: {eth0: ut}, nb2: {eth0: ut}}
  vl2: {nb2: {eth1: tg}}
```

Fig. 2. Sample logical composition file

4.1 Construction Flow

Alfons has two construction flows based on the CLI shown in Fig. 1. The first
is an interactive and sequential construction flow with a logical composition
file as seed information. We define the physical server resource as a "Nodebox"
in Alfons. Although all networks are defined on a VLAN (802.1q), it is managed by the logical resource names in Alfons because the dynamic analysis and
cyber range environments are usually created iteratively. On the other hand,
the physical resources that can be used are not always the same in an experimental environment such as StarBED. Hence, in order to obtain environmental
portability, it is necessary to separate the logical resource name and the physical
resources. A sample of the logical composition is shown in Fig. 2. The logical
composition file has adopted the YAML format. This logical composition file
defines two Nodeboxes and two VLANs; moreover, two VLANs are connected to
each Nodebox as an untagged or tagged VLAN.

First, a user writes and registers a logical composition file to Alfons in this
flow. The user then defines the physical resource id, VLAN id to a Nodebox, and
the VLANs name by a CLI command in the next step. Next, the user creates
an experimental node that utilizes template disk images with content files. In
addition, Alfons can save the environment as an environment composition file
after the construction of an experimental environment.

The other construction flow is a fully automatic construction flow with an
environmental composition file. A sample of the environmental composition file
is shown in Fig. 3, which adopts the XML format. This file is created by Alfons
as result of an interactive construction or the user who creates it. In addition,
this file includes the physical resource and logical resource binding. Hence, the
user can easily change a physical resource to construct a copy environment.

4.2 Instance Creation

In Alfons, a physical or virtual node in the environment is called an "instance";
moreover, the template instance dataset is called a "component." Basically, all
modern OSs are collection of files on a file system. In other words, an original
node is a clean OS disk image with uniquely polluted data files. Hence, we can
create the original node image by inserting specified files into the template node
image. Alfons adopts this method. A component is preliminarily registered and
shared in Alfons by an operator. Alfons creates an instance with its component
and the specified files that identify the instance. We call this creation method
a "building block system." Figure 4 shows an image of this instance creation

```
<?xml version='1.0' encoding='UTF-8'?>
<NEED ID='Sample-2016-02-22' MiID='SAMPLE01' >
 <node ID='root' nodetype='root'/>
 <node ID='nb1' parentID='root' nodetype='actant'>
  <parameters> <network> <hostname> k001 </hostname>
   <interface name='eth0' bindvlan='731' vlanmode='untagged'/>
  </network> </parameters>
 </node>
 <node ID='ubuntu1404' componentID='ubuntu1404' parentID='nb1' nodetype='emulant'>
  <parameters>
   <hardware name='kvm'/>
   <network type='emulated'> <hostname> ubuntu01 </hostname>
    <interface name='eth0' bindvlan='eth0.731' vlanmode='untagged' ipaddr='192.168.1.1'\
    netmask='255.255.255.0' gateway='192.168.1.254' dns1='192.168.1.241' dns2=''\
    macaddr='AA:BB:CC:DD:EE:FF' media='e1000'/>
   </network>
  </parameters>
 </node>
</NEED>
```

Fig. 3. Sample environmental composition file

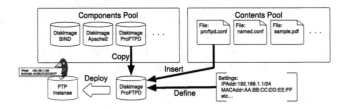

Fig. 4. Instance creation by a building block system

method. A user creates an instance with identifying information such as the
hostname, IP address, MAC address, bound VLAN name, and inserted content
after determining the component as a base node image. For example, a user can
create an FTP service instance with the specified proftpd.conf file if Alfons has
the CentOS component that includes the ProFTPD package. To do this, Alfons
customizes the instance image file on the Alfons server through a file system
mount before transporting the instance image file to a Nodebox; therefore, Alfons
can customize without leaving unwanted traces.

4.3 Configuration File Generation

Alfons has the functionality for simple file insertion as well as file string replacement of inserted files. With this function, a user can replace the strings in the
configuration files of a component. There are two types of replacement mechanisms. The first mechanism is simple replacement utilizing a format such as
__STRING__. For example, this mechanism is utilized for hostname replacement.
The user must define the hostname when creating an instance. If a component has configuration files including the replace string "__hostname__," Alfons
replaces this when customizing the component image, etc. /etc/hosts,...

The other mechanism is replacement with a specific script. This mechanism
utilizes "__(SCRIPT,ARG)__" as a replacement string. "SCRIPT" is a script
name that is registered with a component by an operator. The operator can
register any language script if it can run on the Alfons server, e.g., a shell script,

Perl, Python, and Ruby. The next column of the script name is the argument, which can be specified as zero or with more arguments delimited by commas. Nesting descriptions are also possible with these formats. For these reasons, it is also possible to define the processing results through multiple stages.

They are very simple instance customization solutions for generating distinctive instance from a component. Ansible or Vagrant and SpringOS can customize the instance images by a specific user account or specific agent program with a specific language such as a recipe. In contrast, these solutions are combination of general regular expressions and scripting language; additionally, they do not need a specific user account or an agent program. This solution should be easily understood by the user.

4.4   Physical and Virtual Node Support

The user can choose either a virtual node instance or a physical node instance based on a component. Thus, the user can construct an optimum environment for analysis or cyber range depending on the type of malware. Alfons automatically installs a hypervisor into a Nodebox if the instance type is a virtual node. In addition, Alfons directly installs an instance into the Nodebox if the operator chooses a physical node as the type of instance. Altogether, the operator does not need to manage the installation of the hypervisor. The current version of Alfons supports the Linux KVM and ESXi as a hypervisor. In addition, Alfons controls the bridge devices in a hypervisor to attach physical network devices to instance tap devices since SpringOS can control only bare metal switches.

5   Evaluation of Conceptual Implementation

In this section, we describe the evaluation of a conceptual implementation utilizing a small cyber-range environment.

5.1   Evaluation Environment

We defined a cyber-range environment that assumes the CTF shown in Fig. 5 for evaluation. This environment has five Nodeboxes in total, including a global router Nodebox and four team Nodeboxes. The team environment has three internal segments: the client, internal-server, and DMZ segments. There are five instances in total for each segment: the firewall, Windows 7 client, file server, database, and DNS/mail instances. Basically, most of the configuration is the same in each team environment, but the IP tables (NAT policy) and global IP address of the firewall instance and the BIND/Postfix/Dovecot configuration of the DNS/mail instance are different. We utilize the six servers listed in Table 2 for this evaluation. These servers connect to a bare metal switch. Only the Alfons server has flash disk storage because the Alfons server copies the component disk image to customize it. The servers for the Nodebox have only HDD drives.

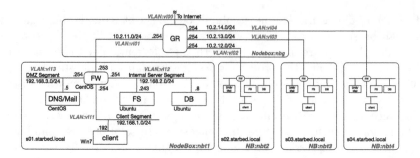

Fig. 5. Network topology for evaluation

Table 2. Hardware specifications of the evaluation environment

Server	CPU	Memory	DISK	Network IF
Alfons server	Intel Xeon®E5-2620 v3 x 2	64 GB	FusionIO SX300 x 2	10 Gbps
Nodebox server	Intel Xeon®X5670 x 2	48 GB	SATA HDD x 2	1 Gbps
Experimental switch	D-Link®DGS-3427	-	-	-

5.2 Performance Evaluation

We constructed the environment ten times for evaluation. In this evaluation, all instances are virtual nodes utilizing the Ubuntu 14.04 Linux KVM as a hypervisor. Table 3 lists the processing times and disk image sizes. Alfons installs the hypervisor only once when creating a new Nodebox. In addition, the current version of Alfons runs all processes sequentially. Alfons took about 1624 s to construct a TEAM environment and about 6754 s to finish the entire construction. Alfons generated the configuration files (BIND files, Postfix files, and so on) on the basis of the template configuration files.

We measured the relationship between the inserted data size and the processing time. In this experiment, we created the firewall instance utilized in the previous experiment with five dummy datas which is different data sizes. Figure 6 shows the results. The results show that the time required for the process depends on the template disk image size and the size of the inserted content.

5.3 System Evaluation

Table 4 summarizes a system evaluation based on a comparison of the conceptual implementation of Alfons and recent tools. Alfons can control the physical facilities and can create a virtual instance on a hypervisor. All of the instances in the environment could communicate with each other; moreover, all of the defined network services run as expected. In addition, all instances, other than

Table 3. Average processing times of the evaluation environment

Section	Disk image size [MB]	Min [s]	Quartile point [s]	Median [s]	Quartile point [s]	Max [s]
HV	10240	546.5	569.0	577.6	587.7	618.2
gr	1334	92.9	94.1	95.4	97.4	103.0
gw	1387	71.4	75.9	80.6	84.5	99.4
dm	3303	122.6	132.9	145.5	154.8	182.6
fs	4989	147.7	162.5	173.1	195.8	222.8
db	4699	133.8	152.9	161.2	181.3	213.8
win7	9987	273.0	306.1	332.5	373.8	479.4
TEAM	-	1572.6	1603.8	1624.2	1639.1	1675.1
TOTAL	-	6507.6	6565.1	6754.3	6789.4	7020.1

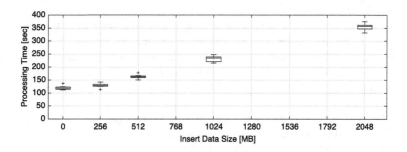

Fig. 6. Processing time for each size of inserted data content

Table 4. Support coverage of Alfons and orchestrator tools

	Facility management	Network parameter configuration	Content installation	Virtual/Physical node support
Alfons	◯	◯(Local)	◯(Local)	Physical/Virtual
SpringOS	◯	◯(Agent)	◯(Agent)	Physical
Cloud controller	×	◯	×	Virtual
Vagrant	◯	◯	×	Virtual

Global Router, do not have any management network interfaces. The user can control the Windows client instance with a VNC on the hypervisor. Thus, this evaluation environment is isolated from other testbed facilities. Alfons can configure the ownership and permission of inserted files without a special account in the instance; therefore, there is no trace of the work in the instances.

6 Conclusion

In this paper, we described the requirements for the dynamic analysis of malware and a cyber range environment construction system; moreover, we proposed the building block system "Alfons" for seamless environment construction. Alfons supports both virtual and physical nodes, and it can manage integrated with bare metal and virtual bridge management. Alfons also can configure the applications without trace in the instance; moreover, it also can insert the content files into instance without trace.

In addition, we evaluated a conceptual implementation of Alfons that utilized a sample environment assumed to be a cyber range. We constructed this environment consisting of 21 instances on five Nodebox servers in about 6754 s. The instances in the environment have no trace of processing such as a specific account and log; moreover, the instances have no management network connection, i.e., its cyber range environment was isolated. These results indicate that our proposed system is effective.

However, since this case is still insufficient, it is necessary to obtain feedback from the findings with future utilization. In addition, methods for increasing the speed of Alfons will be considered, such as simultaneous deployment to multiple Nodeboxes, because the current version of Alfons runs all processes sequentially. We are going to continue research and development for further optimization.

Acknowledgment. The authors thank S. Miwa, Ph.D. from the National Institute of Information and Communications Technology and T. Inoue, Ph.D. from the Japan Advanced Institute of Science and Technology for their insightful comments and suggestions. The authors thank H. Nakai and K. Akashi for their generous support. The authors thank the Hardening Project for giving us the opportunity to practice with the system.

References

1. SecCap: Education network for practical information technologies-security-(only available in japanese) (2015). https://www.seccap.jp
2. Hardening 10 APAC: A security competition like no other (2014). http://wasforum.jp/hardening-project/hardening-10-apac-en/
3. Miyachi, T., Nakagawa, T., Chinen, K.i., Miwa, S., Shinoda, Y.: StarBED and SpringOS architectures and their performance. In: TRIDENTCOM, vol. 90, pp. 43–58 (2011)
4. Yasuda, S., Miura, R., Ota, S., Takano, Y., Miyachi, T.: Building block type construction system for mimetic environment (only available in japanese). In: Proceedings of Internet Conference 2015 JSSST, vol. 77, pp. 69–78, October 2015
5. Cuckoo Sandbox (2015). http://www.cuckoosandbox.org/
6. Kruegel, C., Emulation, F.S.: Achieving successful automated dynamic analysis of evasive malware. In: Black Hat (2014)

7. Miwa, S., Miyachi, T., Eto, M., Yoshizumi, M., Shinoda, Y.: Design and implementation of an isolated sandbox with mimetic internet used to analyze malwares. In: Benzel, T.V., Kesidis, G. (eds.) DETER Community Workshop on Cyber Security Experimentation and Test 2007, Boston, Ma, USA, 6–7 August 2007. USENIX Association (2007)
8. OpenStack (2015). https://www.openstack.org/
9. VMWare vSphere (2015). http://www.vmware.com/products/vi/
10. Vagrant (2015). https://www.vagrantup.com
11. Ansible (2015). http://www.ansible.com/home
12. chef (2015). https://www.chef.io
13. ENCS: European network for cyber security (2015). https://www.encs.eu
14. ICS-CERT: The industrial control systems cyber emergency response team (2015). https://ics-cert.us-cert.gov
15. CRIAB. http://www.boeing.com/defense/cybersecurity-information-management/
16. Lindorfer, M., Kolbitsch, C., Milani Comparetti, P.: Detecting Environment-Sensitive Malware. In: Sommer, R., Balzarotti, D., Maier, G. (eds.) RAID 2011. LNCS, vol. 6961, pp. 338–357. Springer, Heidelberg (2011). doi:10.1007/978-3-642-23644-0_18
17. Detecting Malware and Sandbox Evasion Techniques (2015). https://www.sans.org/reading-room/whitepapers/forensics/detecting-malware-sandbox-evasion-techniques-36667

Building Low-Cost Gateways and Devices for Open LoRa IoT Test-Beds

Congduc Pham[✉]

LIUPPA, University of Pau, Pau, France
Congduc.Pham@univ-pau.fr

Abstract. While benefits of IoT are clearly stated the deployment of such devices in a large scale is still held back by technical challenges such as short communication distances. Recent long-range radio technologies such as Semtech's LoRa are promising to deploy Low Power WAN at a very low-cost for a large variety of applications. The paper describes our proposed low-cost and open IoT gateway & devices for both robust and simple deployment. Quick appropriation & customization by third parties for test-bed deployment is of utmost importance and the whole proposed architecture addresses this issue from the very beginning of the design process.

Keywords: Internet of Thing test-bed · LoRa · Low-cost test-beds

1 Introduction

While benefits of IoT are clearly stated for increased process efficiency through automation & optimization, the deployment of such devices in a large scale is still held back by technical challenges such as short communication distances. Using the telco mobile communication infrastructure is still very expensive (e.g. GSM/GPRS, 3G/4G/LTE) and not energy efficient for autonomous devices that must run on battery for months. During the last decade, low-power but short-range radio such as IEEE 802.15.4 radio have been considered by the WSN community with multi-hop routing to overcome the limited transmission range. While such short-range communications can eventually be realized on smart cities infrastructures where high node density with powering facility can be achieved, it can hardly be generalized for the large majority of surveillance applications that need to be deployed in isolated or rural environments. Recent modulation techniques where the long transmission distance (several kilometers even in NLOS conditions) can be achieved without relay nodes greatly reduces the complexity of deployment and data collection. The long-range solution has the following advantages over traditional short-range technologies:

1. Avoids relying on operator-based communications; no subscription fees;
2. Removes the complexity and cost of deploying/maintaining a multi-hop infrastructure;
3. Can offer out-of-the-box connectivity facilities.

© ICST Institute for Computer Sciences, Social Informatics and Telecommunications Engineering 2017
S. Guo et al. (Eds.): TridentCom 2016, LNICST 177, pp. 70–80, 2017.
DOI: 10.1007/978-3-319-49580-4_7

Figure 1 shows a typical extreme long-range 1-hop connectivity scenario to a gateway which is the single interface to Internet servers. Most of long-range technologies can achieve 20 km or higher range in LOS condition and about 2 km in NLOS, urban area where the RF signal has to travel through several buildings.

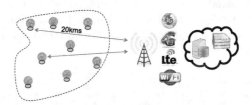

Fig. 1. Extreme long-range application

Some low-power long-range technologies such as Sigfox^{TM} are still operator-based and therefore cannot be deployed in an ad-hoc manner. However, other technologies such as LoRa^{TM} proposed by Semtech radio manufacturer can be privately used. Such technology can be deployed following the recently proposed LoRaWAN^{TM} specifications [1] for large-scale interoperability or using completely ad-hoc solutions where customization towards specific application's profile can be realized. The work presented in this paper mainly focuses on this last approach. We present here our low-cost LoRa platform & software for deploying ad-hoc LoRa IoT test-beds with a high degree of customization and flexibility.

The rest of the article is organized as follows. Section 2 details the long-range technology with focus on the LoRa technology by Semtech and explanations on low-power, long-range network architecture. In Sect. 3 we will present our low-cost architecture, hardware and software designed for test-bed deployment. Section 4 then describes how a test-bed can be rapidly set-up. We conclude in Sect. 5.

2   Review of Long-Range Transmission and LPWAN

2.1   Semtech's LoRa Technology

Semtech's long-range technology (called LoRa [2,3]) belongs to the spread spectrum approaches where data can be "spreaded" in both frequencies and time to increase robustness and range by increasing the receiver's sensitivity, which can be as low as -137 dBm in 868 MHz band or -148 dBm in the 433 MHz band. Throughput and range depend on the 3 main LoRa parameters: BW, CR and SF. BW is the physical bandwidth for RF modulation (e.g. 125 kHz). Larger signal bandwidth allows for higher effective data rate, thus reducing transmission time at the expense of reduced sensitivity. CR, the coding rate for forward error detection and correction. Such coding incurs a transmission overhead and the lower the coding rate, the higher the coding rate overhead ratio, e.g. with

$coding\_rate = 4/(4+CR)$ the overhead ratio is 1.25 for $CR = 1$ which is the minimum value. Finally SF, the spreading factor, which can be set from 6 to 12. The lower the SF, the higher the data rate transmission but the lower the immunity to interference thus the smaller is the range. Figure 2 shows for various combinations of BW, CR and SF the time-on-air of a LoRa transmission depending on the number of transmitted bytes. The maximum throughput is shown in the last column with a 255B payload. Modes 4 to 6 provide quite interesting trade-offs for longer range, higher data rate and immunity to interferences.

LoRa mode	BW	CR	SF	\multicolumn{6}{c}{time on air in second for payload size of}						max thr. for 255B in bps
				5 bytes	55 bytes	105 bytes	155 Bytes	205 Bytes	255 Bytes	
1	125	4/5	12	0.95846	2.59686	4.23526	5.87366	7.51206	9.15046	223
2	250	4/5	12	0.47923	1.21651	1.87187	2.52723	3.26451	3.91987	520
3	125	4/5	10	0.28058	0.69018	1.09978	1.50938	1.91898	2.32858	876
4	500	4/5	12	0.23962	0.60826	0.93594	1.26362	1.63226	1.95994	1041
5	250	4/5	10	0.14029	0.34509	0.54989	0.75469	0.95949	1.16429	1752
6	500	4/5	11	0.11981	0.30413	0.50893	0.69325	0.87757	1.06189	1921
7	250	4/5	9	0.07014	0.18278	0.29542	0.40806	0.5207	0.63334	3221
8	500	4/5	9	0.03507	0.09139	0.14771	0.20403	0.26035	0.31667	6442
9	500	4/5	8	0.01754	0.05082	0.08154	0.11482	0.14554	0.17882	11408
10	500	4/5	7	0.00877	0.02797	0.04589	0.06381	0.08301	0.10093	20212

Fig. 2. Time on air for various LoRa modes as payload size is varied

Electromagnetic transmissions in the sub-GHz band of Semtech's LoRa technology falls into the Short Range Devices (SRD) category. For instance, in Europe, electromagnetic transmissions in the EU 863-870 MHz ISM Band used by Semtech's LoRa technology falls into the Short Range Devices (SRD) category. The ETSI EN300-220-1 document [4] specifies various requirements for SRD devices, especially those on radio activity. Basically, transmitters are constrained to 1% duty-cycle (i.e. 36 s/h) in the general case. This duty cycle limit applies to the total transmission time, even if the transmitter can change to another channel. In most cases, however, the 36 s duty-cycle is largely enough to satisfy communication needs of deployed applications.

2.2   LoRa LPWAN Network Deployment and Architecture

As shown previously in Fig. 1, the deployment of a LoRa network is centered around a gateway that usually has Internet connectivity. Although direct communications between devices are possible, most of applications using sensors for surveillance follow the gateway-centric approach with mainly uplink traffic patterns. Data captured by end-devices are sent to the gateway which will push data to network servers. Then application servers managed by end-users could retrieve data from the network servers. If encryption is used for confidentiality, the application server can be the place where data could be decrypted and presented to end-users. Following this architecture, the LoRa Alliance proposes a LoRaWAN [1] specification for deploying large-scale, multi-gateways networks and full network/application servers.

The full network/application servers and LoRaWAN architecture can be greatly simplified for small, ad-hoc deployment scenarios where a privately owned gateway can (*i*) locally store collected data and use short range wireless radio (WiFi or Bluetooth) for direct web connection or/and, (*ii*) push data to some end-user managed servers or IoT-specific cloud platforms if properly configured. This is the approach we take in this paper to promote application-specific LoRa test-beds deployments.

3   Low-Cost LoRa Gateway and Devices

The implementation of the full LoRaWAN specification requires gateways to be able to listen on several channels and LoRa settings simultaneously. Commercial gateways therefore use advanced concentrators chips capable of scanning up to 8 different channels: the SX1301 concentrator is typically used instead of the SX127x chip series which is designed for end-devices. They cost several hundredth euros with the cost of the SX1301-capable board alone to be more than a hundred euro. In many scenarios (e.g. small farms, developing countries, test-beds, . . .) it is more important to keep both the cost of the gateway and the system's complexity low, and to target small to medium size deployments for specific use cases instead of the large-scale, multi-purpose deployment scenarios defined by LoRaWAN. Note that our approach can deploy more than 1 gateway to serve several channel settings if needed. This solution presents the advantage of being more optimal in terms to cost as incremental deployment can be realized and also offer a higher level of redundancy. We believe this statement remains true even for recent LoRa community-based deployment initiatives such as the one conducted by TheThingNetwork™ [5] where the deployment mainly targets large-scale, public and multi-purpose networks.

3.1   Single-Connection Low-Cost LoRa Gateway

Our LoRa gateway [6] could be qualified as "single connection" as it is built around an SX1272/76, much like an end-device would be. The cost argument, along with the statement that too integrated components are difficult to repair and/or replace in the context of ad-hoc deployments or developing countries, also made the "off-the-shelves" design orientation an obvious choice. Our low-cost gateway is therefore based on a Raspberry PI (version 1 or 2) which is both a low-cost (less than 30 euro) and a highly reliable embedded Linux platform, see Fig. 3. There are many SX1272/76 radio modules available and we have fully tested 3: the Libelium SX1272 LoRa, the HopeRF RFM92W/95W and the Modtronix inAir9/9B. Normally, any SX1272/76-based radio module using native SPI interface should work. The total cost of the gateway is as low as 45 euro with the HopeRF or Modtronix LoRa modules.

Together with the "off-the-shelves" component approach, the software stack is completely open-source: (a) the Raspberry runs a regular Raspian distribution, (b) ArduPi and the original SX1272 library provided by Libelium are very simple

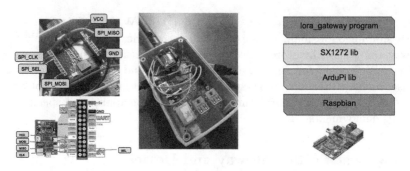

Fig. 3. Low cost gateway from off-the-shelves components

to install/understand/modify and (c) the `lora_gateway` program (which receives and forwards radio packets) is kept as simple as possible.

We improved the original SX1272 library in various ways to provide support for both SX1272 and SX1276 chip, enhanced radio channel access (CSMA-like with SIFS/DIFS) and radio activity time sharing. One of the main objectives of our architecture and software stack is to provide both robust and simple solution for either "out-of-the-box" utilization or quick appropriation & customization by third parties when deploying test-beds for specific applications.

After compiling the `lora_gateway` program, the most simple way to start the gateway is in standalone mode as shown is Fig. 4(left). By default, the LoRa mode is 4 (BW = 500 kHz, CR = 4/5 and SF = 12) and the frequency channel is 865.2 MHz. All packets received by the gateway is sent to the standard Unix-stdout stream. The gateway can also be started on a given LoRa mode, see Fig. 2, with the `--mode` option. For full customization, `--bw`, `--cr`, `--sf` and `--freq` options can indicate a bandwidth, coding rate, spreading factor and frequency channel combination. For instance, testing one of the LoRaWAN mandatory channel in the EU 863-868 MHz ISM band can be done as follows `--bw 125 --cr 5 --sf 12 --freq 868.1`.

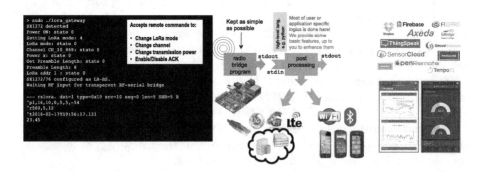

Fig. 4. Gateway architecture for radio data reception and post-processing stages

For each data packet received, `lora_gateway` provides various information that can be used by the post-processing stage. These informations are related to the packet (destination–normally the gateway–, packet type, source addr, sequence number, data length, SNR and packet's RSSI), the radio (bandwidth, coding rate and spreading factor) and the time of reception.

3.2 Post-processing and Link with IoT Cloud Platforms

Advanced data post-processing tasks are performed after the radio stage by using Unix redirection of `lora_gateway`'s outputs as shown by the orange "post-processing" block in Fig. 4(middle). We promote the usage of high-level language such as `Python` to implement all the data post-processing tasks such as access to IoT cloud platforms and even AES decryption features. Our gateway is distributed with a `Python` template that explains and shows how to upload data on various IoT cloud platforms. Examples include Dropbox™, Firebase™, ThingSpeak™, freeboard™, SensorCloud™, GrooveStream™ & FiWare™ as illustrated in Fig. 4(right).

This architecture clearly decouples the low-level gateway functionalities from the high-level post-processing features. By using high-level languages for post-processing, running and customizing data management tasks can be done in a few minutes. "Out-of-the-box" data upload to IoT cloud can be realized as most of these platforms propose free accounts that can satisfy a large number of foreseen IoT applications. For instance, a small farm can deploy in minutes the sensors and the gateway using a free account with `ThingSpeak` platform to visualize captured data in real-time.

3.3 Gateway Running Without Internet Access

One additional important issue that needs to be taken into account when deploying test-beds is the intermittent or no access to the Internet for the gateway. In all cases, received data are locally stored on the gateway in a NoSql database (e.g. `MongoDB`) and the gateway can interact with the end-users' smartphone through WiFi or Bluetooth as depicted in Fig. 4(middle). WiFi or Bluetooth dongles for Raspberry can be found at really low-cost and the smartphone can be used to display captured data (a web server is run by the gateway using `JQuery` for forms and graphs) or notify users of important events a without the need of Internet access as this situation can clearly happen in very remote areas.

3.4 Low-Cost LoRa End-Devices

Our communication library (the same library is used for the gateway) is mainly tested on Arduino boards. Figure 5 shows all the Arduino boards that have successfully been tested, from the Uno to the Nano platform. We use the MEGA as a prototyping platform. For better integration purposes, we use the Arduino Pro Mini or Nano which can be bulk purchased for about 2 euro per piece. They can be used to provide a generic platform for sensing and long-range transmission.

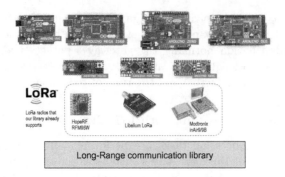

Fig. 5. Low-cost LoRa end-device for customization

We provide templates for quick and easy new behaviour customization while integrating all the necessary code for advanced channel access and data encryption if needed. By default, they run "out-of-the-box" with the gateway.

4   Deploying a Test-Bed

We describe in this section how a test-bed can be deployed and set-up with the previously described components. We will use a `ThingSpeak` channel for storing received data to the cloud.

4.1   Post-processing Data

The post-processing `Python` template `post_processing.py` contains a section to look for predefined data prefix for IoT clouds. The prefix `\!` is used to indicate the usage of a `ThingSpeak` channel. It is followed by an optional write key, an optional field index and the value to report. For instance `\!SGSH52UGPVAUYG3S#1#21.6` will be processed to upload `21.6` to the `ThingSpeak` channel which write key is `SGSH52UGPVAUYG3S` on field index 1. Using default write key and field index can be done with `\!##21.6`.

The post-processing stage can also enforce the presence of a valid application key. This application key is coded on 4 bytes and is inserted before the prefixed data. A list of valid application key is defined in the `Python` post-processing script. For the test, we use an application key list consisting in `['\x05\x06\x07\x08']`.

4.2   Deploying Gateways

The gateway can simply be started by launching `lora_gateway` with redirection of the output to the post processing stage as follows: `sudo ./lora_gateway |` `python ./post_processing.py`. Note that several gateways can be deployed to improve coverage or reliability. They can also work on the same LoRa parameters or on different settings for test purposes. All gateway's outputs can be further logged in a log file. We use the `Dropbox` file sharing service for log files therefore all the logs can be made available on various number of platforms.

4.3 Simple End-Device for Telemetry

The generic sensing template is used to drive a temperature sensor. The end-device will simple send `\!##21.6` if the sensed temperature is `21.6`. The application key `uint8_t my_appKey[4]={5, 6, 7, 8}` is inserted before. Figure 6(right) illustrates the Arduino Nano with a HopeRF RFM95W module running a temperature code based on the generic sensing template. By default, it takes a measure every 10 min and stay in sleep mode between 2 measures.

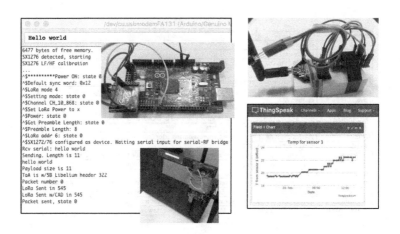

Fig. 6. Left: Interactive LoRa end-device; Right: temperature LoRa device

At this point, the basic test-bed is set-up as the gateway will receive and upload on the `ThingSpeak` channel the measured temperature. The `ThingSpeak` channel can also be used to store and plot the SNR of received packets. If the log files use `Dropbox` sharing, then one can also check the log files for link quality (SNR and missing packets).

4.4 Interactive End-Device for Deployment Tests

We also provide an interactive end-device template that can be used to interactively send ASCII strings to the gateway. Such device can be plugged and fixed to a laptop for field tests as illustrated in Fig. 6(left) which features an Arduino MEGA2560 with a Modtronix inAir9B radio. The serial monitor of the Arduino IDE is used for both input and output. Input strings beginning with `/@` are interpreted as command strings for the host program. Figure 7 shows the list of currently available commands.

Commands for configuring the LoRa parameters, for sending periodic messages and for requesting an acknowlegment (ACK) from the gateway are those that are useful in test situation. For instance, a range test can be easily realized by sending a message and requesting an ACK from the gateway: /@ACK#hello. As the gateway can also accept remote commands in ASCII format for configuring various LoRa parameters, the interactive end-device can be used to remotely configure the gateway for various test purposes. For instance the following command sequence /@ACK#/@M2#, /@M2#, /@ACK#hello switches both the gateway and the end-device to loRa mode 2 and check whether connectivity is still maintained. When an ACK is requested, the SNR value of the received message is sent back to the device in the ACK by the gateway. At the end-device, the SNR of both the message and the ACK is displayed so that both uplink and downlink quality can be monitored.

Command	Action
/@M1#	set LoRa mode 1
/@C12#	use channel 12
/@PL/H/M/x/X#	set power to Low, High, Max, extreme (PA_BOOST), eXtreme (+20dBm)
/@A9#	set node addr to 9
/@ACK#hello w/ack	sends "hello w/ack" and request an ACK
/@ACKON#	enables ACK (for all messages)
/@ACKOFF#	disables ACK
/@CAD#	performs an SIFS CAD, i.e. 3 or 6 CAD depending on the LoRa mode
/@CADON3#	uses 3 CAD when sending data (normally SIFS is 3 or 6 CAD, DIFS=3SIFS)
/@CADOFF#	disables CAD (IFS) when sending data
/@RSSI#	toggles checking of RSSI before transmission and after CAD
/@EIFS#	toggles for extended IFS wait
/@T5000#	send a message at regular time interval of 5000ms. Use /@T0# to disable periodic sending
/@TR5000#	send a message at random time interval between [2000, 5000]ms.
/@Z200#	sets the packet payload size to 200 for periodic sending
/@S50#	sends a 50B user payload packet filled with '#'. The real size is 55B with the protocol header
/@D56#	set the destination node to be 56, this is permanent, until the next D command
/@D56#hello	send "hello" to node 56, destination addr is only for this message
/@D1#/@M1#	send the command string "/@M1#" to node 1 (i.e. gateway)

Fig. 7. LoRa end-device command list

4.5   Adding Advanced Features

Improved channel access. The framework we provide is interesting especially for adding and testing new features. For instance, a CSMA-like mechanism with SIFS/DIFS has been implemented using the Channel Activity Detection (CAD) functionality of the LoRa chip and can further be customized. It can be activated with command /@CADON3# where 3 is the number of CAD for an SIFS. A DIFS is defined as 3 SIFS. Prior to packet transmission a DIFS period free of activity should be observed, see Fig. 8(left). If "extended IFS" is activated with command /@EIFS# then an additional number of CAD followed by a DIFS is required. If RSSI checking is activated with command /@RSSI90# then the RSSI should be below -90dB for the packet to be transmitted. By running a background periodic source of LoRa packets, we observed that the improved channel access succeeds in reducing packet collisions. The current framework is used to study the impact of channel access methods in a medium-size LoRa deployment.

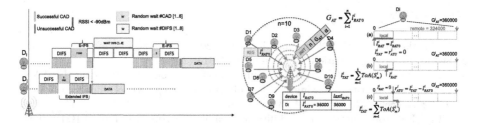

Fig. 8. Left: CSMA-like mechanism for increased robustness; Right: activity time sharing

Activity time sharing. We also implemented an exploratory activity time sharing mechanism for a pool of devices managed by a single organization. We propose to overcome the tight 36 s/h radio activity of a device by considering all the sensor's individual activity time in a shared/global manner. The approach we propose in this paper will allow a device that "exceptionally" needs to go beyond the activity time limitation to borrow some from other devices. A global view of the global activity time, G_{AT}, allowed per 1 h cycle will be maintained at the gateway so that each device knows the potential activity time that it can use in a 1-hour cycle. Figure 8(left) shows how the deployed long-range devices D_i sharing their activity time initially register (REG packet) with the gateway by indicating their local Remaining Activity Time l^i_{RAT0}, i.e. 36 s. The gateway stores all l^i_{RAT0} in a table, computes G_{AT} and broadcasts (INIT packet) both n (the number of devices) and G_{AT}. This feature is currently tested for providing better surveillance service guarantees.

5   Conclusions

Targeted for small to medium size deployment of test-beds, our low-cost, open long-range IoT framework allows for quick appropriation & customization by third parties. Developed within the EU H2020 WAZIUP project which addresses the challenges of low-cost IoT deployment in developing, low-income sub-saharan Africa countries, the platform is tested by WAZIUP's partners with a large-scale test-bed to be set-up in Senegal. The platform is also currently used by several organizations and companies for deploying LoRa test-beds and conducting field tests for various surveillance applications [6]: agriculture, oceanographic observation, pest traps monitoring....

Acknowledgments. This work is support by the WAZIUP project with funding from the EU's H2020 research and innovation program under grant agreement No 687607.

References

1. LoRaAlliance: LoRaWAN specification, v1.0 (2015)
2. Semtech: LoRa modulation basics. rev.2-05/2015 (2015)
3. McKeown, S.J.: LoRa^{TM}- a communications solution for emerging LPWAN, LPHAN and industrial sensing & IoT applications. http://cwbackoffice.co.uk/docs/jeff~20mckeown.pdf. Accessed 13 Jan 2016
4. ETSI: Electromagnetic compatibility and radio spectrum matters (ERM); short range devices (SRD); radio equipment to be used in the 25 MHz to 1000 MHz frequency range with power levels ranging up to 500 mw; part 1 (2012)
5. TheThingNetwork. http://thethingsnetwork.org/. Accessed 13 Jan 2016
6. Pham, C.: A DIY low-cost LoRa gateway. http://cpham.perso.univ-pau.fr/lora/rpigateway.html. Accessed 13 Jan 2016

Building a Prototype VANET Testbed to Explore Communication Dynamics in Highly Mobile Environments

Vishnu Vardhan Paranthaman[(✉)], Arindam Ghosh, Glenford Mapp,
Victor Iniovosa, Purav Shah, Huan X. Nguyen, Orhan Gemikonakli,
and Shahedur Rahman

Middlesex University, Hendon, London NW4 4BT, UK
v.paranthaman@mdx.ac.uk
http://www.vanet.mdx.ac.uk

Abstract. Applications for VANETs will require seamless communication between vehicle-to-infrastructure and vehicle-to-vehicle. However, this is challenging because it is being done in the context of a highly mobile environment. Therefore, traditional handover techniques are inadequate due to the high velocity of the vehicle and the small coverage radius of Road-side Units. Hence in order to have seamless communication for these applications, a proactive approach needs to be carefully investigated. This requires measurements from a real testbed in order to enhance our understanding of the communication dynamics. This paper is about building and evaluating a prototype VANET network on the Middlesex University Hendon Campus, London to explore these issues. The testbed is being used to investigate better propagation models, road-critical safety applications as well as algorithms for traffic management. In addition, the Network Dwell Time of vehicles travelling in the coverage of the RSUs is measured to explore proactive handover and resource allocation mechanisms.

Keywords: Vehicular Ad Hoc Network · Intelligent Transport System · Propagation model · Proactive handover

1 Introduction

Intelligent Transportation Systems (ITS) are a key requirement in the development of Smart Cities which will play an important part in the development of sustainable living. Significant research efforts from both the automotive industry and academia have been underway to accelerate the deployment of a wireless network based on dedicated short-range communications (DSRC) among moving vehicles (Vehicle-to-Vehicle, V2V) and road-side infrastructure (Vehicle-to-Infrastructure, V2I). This network is called a Vehicular Ad Hoc Network (VANET) and is characterized by high node speed, rapidly changing topologies, and short connection lifetime. VANETs allow several new applications to

© ICST Institute for Computer Sciences, Social Informatics and Telecommunications Engineering 2017
S. Guo et al. (Eds.): TridentCom 2016, LNICST 177, pp. 81–90, 2017.
DOI: 10.1007/978-3-319-49580-4_8

be available for road-safety, traffic efficiency, and infotainments (i.e., informa-tion and entertainment applications). VANETs are realised by the deployment of Road-side Units (RSUs) located along the transport infrastructure and On-board Units (OBUs) in the vehicles or worn by pedestrians or cyclists [1].

In order to provide new applications which can make use of the VANET environment, it is necessary to provide seamless handover as the mobile node (MN) moves between the RSUs. In VANETs, beacons are used to signal the pres-ence of both OBUs and RSUs. Since, beacons are broadcast, handover between RSUs simply involves the hearing of beacons for different networks as the MN moves from one RSU to another [2,3]. Traditional handover policies have been based on a reactive approach in which the MN reacts to signalling indicating changes in network connectivity as the MN moves around. However, in highly mobile environments with small cell coverage, such an approach can quickly lead to degradation of connections due to the small time there is to effect a handover [4].

Proactive handover in which the MN actively attempts to decide when and where to hand over can help to develop an efficient and reliable handover pol-icy mechanism. By using proactive handover, it is possible to minimize packet loss and service disruption as an impending handover can be signalled to the higher layers of the network protocol stack. Proactive handover has been widely investigated by the Y-Comm research group, this effort led to key parameters: time before vertical handover (TBVH), which is the time after which the han-dover should occur, and network dwell time (NDT), which is the time the MN spends in the coverage of the new network [5]. Therefore, in order to study seamless connectivity it is necessary to have realistic measurements of TBVH and NDT. Hence, we have designed and deployed a prototype VANET Testbed at the Hendon Campus of Middlesex University, London, funded by Department for Transport (DfT) to explore the potential of VANET Technology. In this, our first experimental study, we have analysed the coverage range of the VANET Testbed comprising four RSUs deployed and analysed the NDT of the MN.

The rest of the paper is structured as follows: Sect. 2 describes the design and implementation of the MDX VANET Testbed. Section 3 presents the coverage map results. Section 4 compares the actual received signal strength values with free space pathloss (FSPL) model. Section 5 looks at the NDT of the MNs from the trials conducted. Finally, Sect. 6 highlights some of the future work, and we conclude in Sect. 7.

2   Designing and Implementation of VANET Testbed

A VANET testbed has been fully deployed with four RSUs, as shown in Fig. 1. The RSUs and OBUs were manufactured by ARADA Systems [6] with the IEEE 802.11p (Wireless Access in Vehicular Environment: WAVE) standard specifi-cations and the maximum output power used was 200 mW or +23 dBm. The challenge was to identify the best locations to mount the RSUs in order to cover most of the Hendon Campus and the surrounding roads. This involved

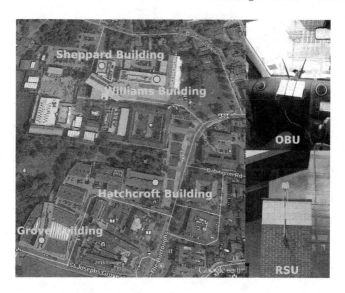

Fig. 1. RSU deployment satellite view.

making a detailed coverage map based on proposed locations of the RSUs. This was done by manually measuring the coverage of the deployment using an OBU, moving around the university roads and inside the campus. In order to determine the best location for the RSU, it was important to minimise the distance between the RSU and the router elements in the university network. This enabled us to directly backhaul data from the RSU to the central MDX VANET Server located at the basement of Sheppard library using the university network. Four RSUs have been deployed on top of the Hatchcroft building (latitude 51.5890742 and longitude −0.22848055), Williams building (latitude 51.5904948 and longitude −0.22859444), Sheppard library building (latitude 51.5908083 and longitude −0.22967222) and Grove building (latitude 51.5888797 and longitude −0.23071111) to cover the roads around the campus and to support the movement of pedestrians within the campus, hence enabling the development of vehicle-to-pedestrian (V2P) applications.

Figure 2 shows the network diagram of the MDX VANET Testbed and the applications running at the respective devices. There are different types of messages used to communicate various items of information between RSUs and OBUs such as Cooperative Awareness Messages (CAMs), Basic Safety Messages (BSMs), Road Side Alerts (RSAs), Intersection Collision Alerts (ICAs) and Probe Vehicle Data (PVD). Since we are interested in safety applications, the BSM message was used as the first message to be collected for analysis. BSMs were periodically broadcast from the OBU to the RSU and a BSM contains information regarding position, motion, time, and general status of the vehicle as shown in the Fig. 3 [7]. At the present time, we are able to only use the Message ID and 3D Position i.e., Latitude, Longitude and Elevation

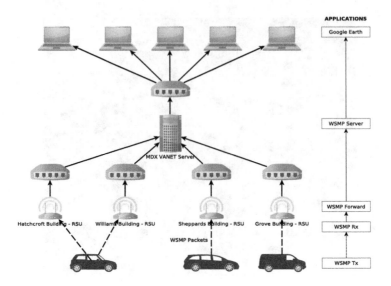

Fig. 2. Network diagram.

parameters of the BSM message. This is because all other fields such as steering wheel angle, acceleration set, brake system etc., have to be gathered from the vehicle via sensors or other mechanical devices and then added to the BSM packet and broadcast. This will be explored in the next phase of the project.

Wave Short Message Protocol (WSMP) Tx is an application used by the OBU to broadcast the BSM packets and the RSU receives these packets using WSMP Rx application. The received packets are forwarded to the server using the WSMP Forward application via an IPv6 address of the server as shown in Fig. 3. The MDX VANET Server uses a WSMP Server application to receive the packets and save the data. At this stage additional information such as a timestamp and the RSUs IP address are stored along with the message received. The received data was saved in three different files: trace.kml, live.kml and Database.csv, trace.kml contains the whole trace of the GPS coordinates contained in the received packet, live.kml contains the live or current positions of each OBU through the packets received from those OBU and this file is saved in the Apache Web Server space for remote access. Using Google Earth and by adding a network link to the live.kml file, the live tracking of the OBUs was achieved. The third file Database.csv contains the most of the available information in the packets such as the OBUs MAC address, the received signal strength indicator (RSSI) value of the received packet, GPS coordinates along with the time stamp of the packet and IP address of the RSU by which the packet has been forwarded. Every day the Database.csv file was backed up for analysis through MySQL.

The proposed network was intended to encompass the Hendon Campus of the University and surrounding roads including the Watford Way (A41). With the successful deployment of the Testbed, the Network was then used to do a

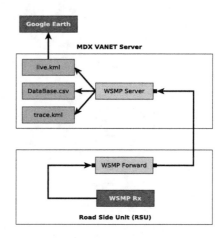

Fig. 3. BSM packet format and packet forwarding from RSU to Server.

extensive trial in which OBUs were placed in volunteered vehicles and the drivers asked to drive around the area. The trial lasted for two weeks i.e., from Jan 4th to 15th Jan 2016. Around ten people with their car volunteered for the trial.

3 Coverage Map Result

Figure 4 shows the unique GPS coordinates from the packets received by the MDX VANET Server, sent by the OBUs which were placed in the cars of the volunteers. Figure 4 displays the trial data for a 24-hour period which was collected on 8th January 2016 and a total of 390653 packets (around 17.14 MB) was received during that period. The coverage map shows the individual coverage achieved by the RSU located on each building with different colour dots. We can observe that the more coverage is achieved for the RSUs deployed at higher heights and also which have clear Line-of-Sight (LoS) in relation to the intended roads [8]. The coverage was better than anticipated but this was mainly because of the height of the RSU deployment. There are some blind spots that can be observed; these were purely due to effects of surrounding buildings. From these observations it is clear that we need more RSUs alongside the road to be deployed in an urban area. However, from our results, the deployment of RSU on high buildings and cellular masts should also be explored. The dense lines indicate very reliable communication and single spots indicate only few packets were received and hence there is no continuous communication in these regions. For example, the coverage map of RSU deployed at Grove building has almost no coverage on the A504 due to the blockade of signal propagation because of the nearby buildings.

The farthest point from where the packets were sent by the vehicles and successfully received by the RSU was approximately 1.15 Km from the Williams

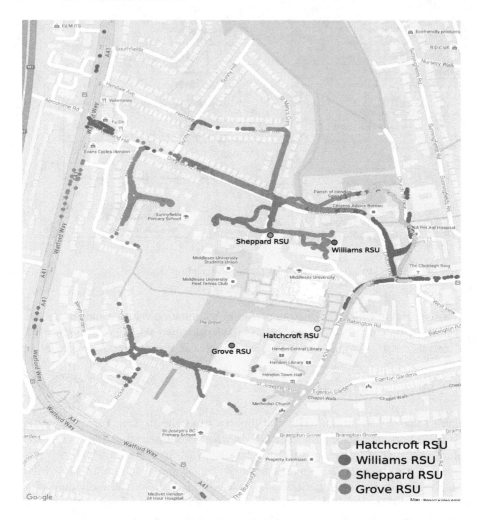

Fig. 4. Coverage map.

Building RSU to a point on the East side of Watford way close to where the A41 and A1 divide. This was achieved purely due to the very high elevation of the RSU on the Williams Building hence allowing LoS communication over a great distance.

4   Pathloss Model Analysis

These readings are omnidirectional with respect to the RSU, so only the radius of the RSU was considered, so that better readings were due to the LoS and multi-path. For Fig. 5 the detailed analysis as follows.

Figure 5a Hatchcroft Building (yellow on the coverage map):- The readings showed that in front of the Hatchcroft Building, very good coverage was received

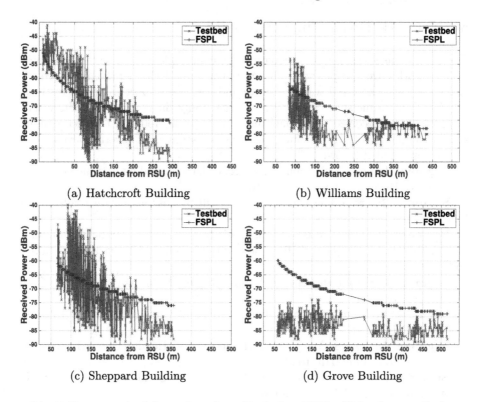

(a) Hatchcroft Building

(b) Williams Building

(c) Sheppard Building

(d) Grove Building

Fig. 5. Power received for each packet - Testbed vs FSPL. (Color figure online)

up to 120 m. However, after this the road starts to turn left towards the Church End Road resulting in less effective coverage, but as we go down the Greyhound Hill more readings are obtained.

Figure 5b Williams Building (red on the coverage map):- Here, we again see that the there is a good coverage close to the RSU, however there is a large drop due to the steep decline in the height of the road going down the Greyhound Hill. In comparison, more readings are obtained at the traffic lights further down the Greyhound Hill and along the Watford Way (A41).

Figure 5c Sheppard Library (blue on the coverage map):- This was the most consistent readings relative to the FSPL model. Therefore, signals closer to the RSU generally gave very strong readings. But there is a sharp drop due to LoS issues, further away from the RSU.

Figure 5d Grove Building (green on the coverage map):- The RSU did not really cover the surrounding roads as its position relative to the extended roads was blocked by surrounding buildings. Hence, most of the readings for the extended coverage were lower than the FSPL calculations. However, the RSU allowed most of the readings to be covered in an east-to-west direction.

5   Network Dwell Time Analysis

The aim of this section is to understand the communication time of the vehicle in a network coverage provided on the roads around the deployed testbed. A single car with the OBU was driven around the roads covered by the testbed. To identify the time spent in a coverage range, only the continuous spots where the packets are received with consistency were considered and the inconsistent spots was removed. Each RSU provides different segment of coverage around the testbed as detailed below:

Segment 1: From St Josephs Grove road, Grove building entrance till Citizens Advice Bureau in Church End Road.

Segment 2: From The Burroughs road till St Josephs Grove road, Grove building entrance gate.

Segment 3: From The Burroughs road starting at the Hatchcroft building and ending at the Greyhound Hill road (Opp. University Car park) via Church end road.

Segment 4: From the end of Sunny Hill road through St Mary's Cres Roading turing right.

Segment 5: From Citizens Advice Bureau in Church End road towards Greyhound Hill road.

Segment 6: From St Mary's Cres (Road Opp. to Hendon car park) towards north ending on Sunny Hill road.

Segment 7: From St Mary's Cres (Road Opp. to Hendon car park) towards north ending on Hendale Avenue road.

Segment 8: From St Josephs Grove near Grove building till Handowe close beyond the round about.

Segment 9: From St Mary's Cres (Road Opp. to Hendon car park) towards north.

Table 1 shows the NDT, the distance travelled for that period of NDT and the average velocity of the vehicle for the identified segments. The accuracy of the results depended on two factors; the accuracy of GPS and the timestamp which was generated at the RSU and not at the OBU. Both these factors affect the results in a minimal way because most of the relevant area was elevated and hence the GPS readings are fairly accurate as they generally were not affected by the local environment. Secondly, the network was lightly loaded and hence the timestamp given by the RSU would be close to the actual transmission time of the beacon. The RSUs were deployed at very high height thus we can observe good performance; if deployed along the road side on the lamp posts, then the coverage distance will be significantly reduced in an urban area. Hence, studying and obtaining a deep understanding of propagation models is required to estimate NDT for increasing the efficient utilization of resources and thereby achieving a seamless communication [9,10].

Table 1. Network Dwell Time for the coverage segments of RSU

Segment	NDT (s)	Distance (m)	Average velocity (m/s)	Average velocity (km/h)
Hatchcroft RSU				
1	79	536.10	6.79	24.43
2	69	308.77	4.50	16.11
Williams RSU				
3	69	533.34	7.73	27.83
4	19	129.81	6.83	24.60
Sheppard RSU				
5	31	282.93	9.13	32.86
6	48	300.14	6.25	22.51
7	40	168.64	4.22	15.20
Grove RSU				
8	42	269.40	6.41	23.10
9	61	285.53	4.70	16.80

6   Future Work

In future, the testbed will be used to explore the BSM message with all its parameters acquired from a car. This will involve interfacing the OBU to the Car Area Network (CAN) as well as the Electronic Control Unit (ECU) in the car, leading to a huge accumulation of data which will be stored in the MDX Cloud System and will be analysed using Big Data techniques. The testbed will be expanded to include sections of the A41 located behind the Hendon Campus of the Middlesex University. This will enable us to explore the interactions between different traffic types such as motorway and urban traffic. Further more, we are also building a Mobile RSU which will allow us to test the RSU setup in different environments. The next step will be to use the VANET data to form an Intelligent Information Platform for Smart Cities to develop algorithms for improved safety and traffic management.

7   Conclusion

This paper has clearly shown the potential of VANET technology and the key issues for wide scale deployment has been explored. Pathloss models and the effects on Network Dwell Time were investigated. Hence, the evolution of this technology and its potential to transform Smart Cities need to be fully understood.

Acknowledgement. This work is funded in part by Depart of Transport (DfT) through Transport Technology Research Innovation Grant (T-TRIG). We would also like to thank our technical support team at Middlesex University: Barry Harte, Jairam Reddy, Jamie Smith, Louis Slabbert and Simon Hinks.

References

1. Paier, A., Tresch, R., Alonso, A., Smely, D., Meckel, P., Zhou, Y., Czink, N.: Average downstream performance of measured IEEE 802.11p infrastructure-to-vehicle links. In: 2010 IEEE International Conference on Communications Workshops (ICC), pp. 1–5 (2010). doi:10.1109/ICCW.2010.5503934
2. Vinel, A., Staehle, D., Turlikov, A.: Study of beaconing for car-to-car communication in vehicular ad-hoc networks. In: IEEE International Conference on Communications Workshops, ICC Workshops 2009, pp. 1–5 (2009). doi:10.1109/ICCW.2009.5208066
3. Shafiee, K., Leung, V.C.M.: Connectivity-aware minimum-delay geographic routing with vehicle tracking in {VANETs}. Ad Hoc Netw. **9**(2), 131–141 (2011). Advances in Ad Hoc Networks (I)
4. Ghosh, A., Paranthaman, V., Mapp, G., Gemikonakli, O.: Exploring efficient seamless handover in vanet systems using network dwell time. EURASIP J. Wirel. Commun. Networking **2014**(1), 227 (2014)
5. Mapp, G.E., Shaikh, F., Cottingham, D., Crowcroft, J., Baliosian, J.: Y-comm: a global architecture for heterogeneous networking. In: Proceedings of the 3rd International Conference on Wireless Internet, WICON 2007, pp. 22–1225. ICST (Institute for Computer Sciences, Social-Informatics and Telecommunications Engineering), ICST, Brussels (2007)
6. ARADA Systems. http://www.aradasystems.com
7. SAE International: DSRC Implementation Guide - A Guide to Users of SAE J2735 Message Sets over DSRC. http://www.sae.org/standardsdev/dsrc/DSRCImplementationGuide.pdf
8. Gozalvez, J., Sepulcre, M., Bauza, R.: IEEE 802.11p vehicle to infrastructure communications in urban environments. IEEE Commun. Mag. **50**(5), 176–183 (2012). doi:10.1109/MCOM.2012.6194400
9. Ghosh, A., Paranthaman, V.V., Mapp, G., Gemikonakli, O., Loo, J.: Enabling seamless V2I communications: toward developing cooperative automotive applications in VANET systems. IEEE Commun. Mag. **53**(12), 80–86 (2015)
10. Paranthaman, V.V., Mapp, G., Shah, P., Nguyen, H.X., Ghosh, A.: Exploring markov models for the allocation of resources for proactive handover in a mobile environment. In: 2015 IEEE 40th Local Computer Networks Conference Workshops (LCN Workshops), pp. 855–861 (2015)

Testbed for Network Applications

The ASCETiC Testbed - An Energy Efficient Cloud Computing Environment

Marc Körner$^{(\boxtimes)}$, Alexander Stanik, Odej Kao, Marcel Wallschläger,
and Sören Becker

Department of Telecommunication Systems, Complex and Distributed IT Systems,
Technische Universität Berlin, Einsteinufer 17, 10587 Berlin, Germany
marc.koerner@tu-berlin.de

Abstract. Nowadays, the energy consumption of data centers is one of the biggest challenges in order to reduce operational expenditure (OPEX) and the carbon dioxide footprint. Most efforts are investigating the modernization of air conditions and server hardware, but also the optimization of resource allocations. Moreover, virtual server are migrated from one physical host to another in order to be able to shutdown unused physical computer nodes or even an entire rack. The Adapting Service lifeCycle towards EfficienT Clouds (ASCETiC) project tries to tackle this issue in another way. This project develops a toolbox that provides libraries and components which can be used to develop energy efficient cloud software on all three layers of the usual could stack. Thus, power consumption can be reduced by deploying energy efficient software in the cloud. This paper presents the innovative ASCETiC testbed located at the Technical University in Berlin (TUB), which is the deveopment and evaluation eviroment for the afore metioned software.

Keywords: Testbed · Cloud computing · Energy-aware · Software-defined networking

1 Introduction

In the recent years the information technology (IT) related power consumption world wide is growing rapidly. One of the biggest impact factors are data centers. They provide several IT services to customers and end-users. With the upcoming of cloud computing many companies strive to outsource their services into the cloud. However, there is an acceleration of adoption of cloud applications and services by enterprises [9]. Consequently, experts warn of a dramatic increase in energy consumption for cloud computing. Although cloud computing offers the potential for energy saving through the centralization of computing and storage technologies in large data centers, a few mechanisms to reduce energy consumption have been already exploited so far.

The ASCETiC project [5] is focused on providing novel Cloud Computing (CC) methods and tools in order to support software developers optimizing

© ICST Institute for Computer Sciences, Social Informatics and Telecommunications Engineering 2017
S. Guo et al. (Eds.): TridentCom 2016, LNICST 177, pp. 93–102, 2017.
DOI: 10.1007/978-3-319-49580-4_9

energy efficiency within their applications. This minimizes the carbon dioxide footprint resulting from designing, developing, deploying and running software in Clouds, while maintaining other quality aspects of software to adequate and agreed levels. In particular, the main objectives of the ASCETiC project are:

(i) to develop models for green and efficient software design, supporting sustainability and high quality of service levels at all stages of software development and execution
(ii) to develop and to evaluate a framework with identified energy efficiency parameters and metrics for cloud services
(iii) to develop methods for measuring, analyzing, and evaluating energy use in software development and execution, complementing quality measures
(iv) to integrate energy efficiency at the same level as other quality aspects during service requirement, design, construction, deployment, and operation leading to an Energy Efficiency Embedded Service Lifecycle

Therefore, ASCETiC is delivering a framework composed out of tools and methods covering each phase of development lifecycle for implementing energy efficient cloud services at all layers of the cloud stack [2]. Thus, the applicability of ASCETIC to achieve 20 % of energy savings will be demonstrated on two industry use cases. In order to reach this goal, ASCETiC initiative measures how software systems actually use cloud resources, in order to optimize consumption the resource consumption. Moreover, the awareness of the amount of energy needed by software will help in learning how to target software optimization where it provides the greatest energy returns. Therefore, all three layers of the cloud computing stack: Software-as-a-Service (SaaS), Platform-as-a-Service (PaaS) and Infrastructure-as-a-Service (IaaS) have to implement a MAPE (Monitor, Analyze, Plan and Execute) loop. Each layer monitors relevant energy efficiency status information locally and shares this with the other layers, assesses its current energy status and forecasts future energy consumption as needed.

This paper basically presents the testbed which is used in the ASCETiC project. This testbed provides an advanced OpenStack based cloud with additional energy monitoring capabilities. In particular, it presents the MAPE (Monitoring, Analysis, Planning, Execution) on the IaaS layer.

The remaining paper is structured as follows. Section 2 provides a brief background analysis which is followed by an introduction of the ASCETiC software stack, in Sect. 3. Afterwards the testbed architecture is introduced followed by the conclusion and futuer work, in Sect. 5. Finally a disclaimer and acknowledgment is given.

2   Background

The CC paradigm itself was generally evolving the scalability of resource allocation by virtualization. Moreover, CC is an opportunity to massively reduce OPEX costs and save energy. Overall, cloud computing provides the opportunity to save 70–90% direct energy for servers and cooling while increasing the network energy consumption by only 2–3% [7]. This demonstrates that a total energy saving of 68–87% is feasible by just switching to CC. Beside energy savings due to the CC paradigm another contemporary research challenge [1] is to use this model an integrate energy saving mechanism within and amongst the cloud layers [6]. This has the potential to increase the entire impact of this particular paradigm. To support this kind of research specific testbeds are needed. They need to provide particular hardware informations to the different components working within the cloud stack. Furthermore, an API and specific hardware functions are required to support the cloud stack based energy adaptation mechanisms.

The current State of the Art (SotA) process regarding compute and networking hardware is highly connected to Moore's Law [8]. New hardware becomes more and more energy efficient form year to year. The criteria with the almost biggest impact on the awareness of these new energy efficient demands is the hardware integration density. This process is amongst others driven by mobile devices and the approach to improve their runtime. However, this effects also regular compute hardware driven by the increasing amount of data centers and the cost-value ratio.

The ASCETiC project consortium has identified some weak points concerning the used cluster during the first project year evaluation. Unfortunately the deployed hardware was not contemporary and unable to supporting new energy saving modes. Moreover, recent hardware is also supporting specific virtualization need and provide a better scalability in this area. To overcome this issue, the first year's testbed is migrated and redeployed on SotA cluster as described in the following sections. Lessens learned during the first deployment cycles were taken into account in combination with the new identified project requirements [3] in order to design the new testbed. In particular, the aim is to support a self-adaptable optimization approach for clouds. This includs trade-offs on energy consumption, maintainability, and supportability, which builds the umbrella for the improved design.

3   The ASCETiC Toolbox

The ASCETiC Toolbox is the core component developed within the project. It is utilizing the ASCETiC testbed in order to Provide an energy efficient CC stack by using the innovative cloud testbed capabilities. It delivers the necessary mechanisms for developers and engineers to develop energy efficient applications and modules on all layers of the cloud stack. Furthermore, the testbed itself is hosting the ASCETiC toolbox, depict in Fig. 1. This is a collection of modules which are using the innovative testbed capabilities to implement the SaaS, PaaS, and IaaS stack. This includes energy awareness and self-adaptation mechanisms on all of the afore mentioned layers. The ASCETiC toolbox and its source code is available on the project website [5] and on github.

Section 4 will further introduce the ASCETiC testbed as part of this toolbox. In particular, the infrastructure manager (IM) and the distributed file system

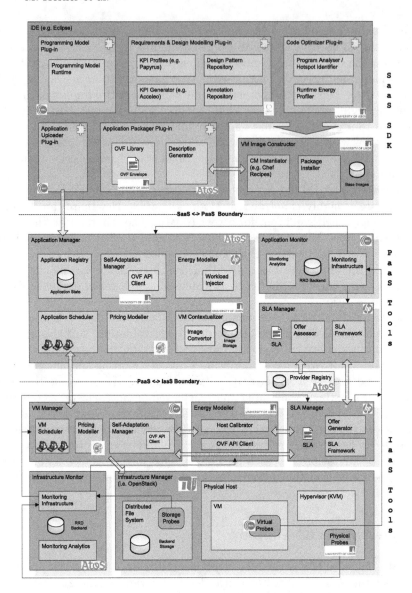

Fig. 1. ASCETiC software toolbox

(DFS). Moreover, some specific components which to obtain physical and virtual energy probes on the IaaS layer will be introduced. Thus, the next section will present the hardware and software architecture used for the ASCETiC testbed deployment at TUB.

4   Testbed Architecture

The main objective for the testbed architecture is to revise the physical infrastructure used in the first year and taking into account lessons learned during the first operational phase [4]. Moreover, the planned testbed improvements were designed to deliver an appropriate support for the ASCETiC business use-cases and further improve the sustainability of the Infrastructure Manager (IM) and the underlying cluster. In addition, the revised cluster architecture is also supposed to support full and fine-grained control over the networking resources, which further offers the opportunity to evaluate energy influences in this area. Therefore the entire cluster deployment is revised, improved and extended with:

(i)   more contemporary compute hardware - from the old 16 node based Asok (10 years old cluster) to the 200 nodes Wally cluster, which will be further introduced in this section

(ii)   increase the total amount of nodes used in the IM and the resulting experimental scalability

(iii)   integrate Software Defined Networking (SDN) resources for a comprehensive cluster network approach

(iv)   a second IM instance in order to have two environments (a small testing and large stable)

The IM is generally responsible for the entire cluster management. It is used to provide an API for the ASCETiC toolbox virtual machine manager (VMM) to allocate, parameterize and place virtual machines (VM) within the cluster infrastructure. The novelty beyond the state of the art (StoA) is a comprehensive consideration of all its cloud managed resources (compute, storage, and network) in combination with dynamic energy consumption measurements and runtime probes in order to provide a foundation for determining an energy aware cloud model. The IaaS provides power consumption probes for VMs, physical nodes, and host groups. This approach requires access to a fine-grained resource control in order compute these informations and save energy. In other words, the IM controls all resources provided by the revised and enhanced cluster testbed. It is the central management entity for all within the cluster available resources. It also manages all VM operations, from the deployment over the migration up to un-deployment. It's API is used as a communication interface for the VMM, which delegates the management interaction and uses the IM execution unit.

The utilized wally cluster is composed out of 200 heterogeneous nodes and one master node. The nodes are numbered from wally001 till wally200 and have a FQDN according to their number: <NodeName>.cit.tu-berlin.de. They are interconnected on the first Ethernet interface by one large HP5400 switch, which also provides Internet connectivity. 50 nodes on this cluster are permanently allocated in order to create the ASCETiC energy efficient cloud testbed and support the project with and appropriated test and evaluation environment.

The testbed installation is separated into two different groups or more precisely two OpenStack instances, as depict in Fig. 2. The first "unstable" instance

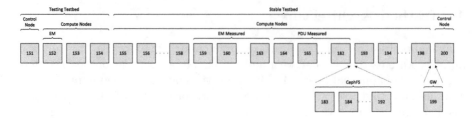

Fig. 2. Testbed environment

is for software tests with regards to the ASCETiC toolbox, while the second stable one is used to collected reference values with the three ASCETiC business use cases. One of the use cases is even deploying a large number of VMs in order to process thousands of jobs on the testbed. This is actually one of the important parameters indicating if the ASCETiC toolbox's adaption mechanisms are working. However, both OpenStack instances are using the same distribute file system also located within the allocated cluster partition. The physical deployment is composed out of the hardware listed in Table 1. In order to cover the SotA requirements, the wally cluster part belonging to the ASCETiC testbed was additionally equipped with SDN enabled network devices, as listed in Table 2.

Table 1. Wally cluster node hardware

Component	Model
CPU	Quadcore Intel Xeon CPU E3-1230 V2 3.30 GHz
Memory	16 GB RAM
Hard disk	3×1 TB
Network	2×1 GBit Ethernet NIC

Table 2. Wally cluster network hardware

Component	Model	Comment
TUB Mgmt network	HP 5400 legacy switch	public IP space with TUB addresses for the host node communication
VM Data network	2x NEC IP8800	SDN based OpenStack VM network using private IP addresses, for the VM to VM communication

The network related software deployment is composed out of the OpenStack Ice House distribution including Neutron and the OpenDaylight controller. This extends the previous approach and deliver the foundation for an additional energy aware network resource management. The VMs can be externally accessed via Network Address Translation (NAT) based user defined floating IPs. The physical hosts again can be accessed for administrative purposes over the regular TUB internal network on eth0 or the SDN data network using a private class C network addresses on eth1.

In the following subsections all testbed components will be introduced:

Testbed gateway and control node. The wally199 node is used as testbed access point. It provides all services which are not directly related to OpenStack. It hosts a layer three OpenVPN server. This VPN server is used by the clients to create their tunnel connection. It presents the central entry point for all external connections. Moreover, all traffic of the three different networks is basically routed there. TUB is also running a Chef server on this node which allows to deploy operating system (OS) images on the physical hosts on demand. This is required to e.g. roll out updates or testbed related modifications. Moreover, the on this machine installed Zabbix server is monitoring all testbed parameters including power probes from the physical and virtual machines. These values are further stored in a MySQL data-base and can be queried by modules inside the IaaS ASCETiC Toolbox layer.

Stable testbed. The stable testbed is used to deploy the use cases and explore the energy saving mechanisms implemented within the ASCETiC toolbox. The wally200 node is the cloud controller for the stable testbed. It hosts all management related OpenStack components like Neutron, Glance, and Keystone. This controller is managing a total amount of 32 compute nodes (Table 3).

Table 3. Stable testbed node distribution

Node	Comment
wally200	control node
wally193 - wally198	currently unmeasured compute nodes
wally157 - wally163	energy-meter measured compute nodes
wally164 - wally182	PDU measured compute nodes (in work)

All energy probes or more precisely power measurements are directly collected with customized scripts and pushed to zabbix, where they are available for the ASCETiC IaaS components like e.g. the VMM based VM scheduling and placement.

Testing testbed. The testing testbed serves as playground for the ASCETiC toolbox developers. It is an distinguish development environment where new implemented features can be tested without influencing the execution of the use cases running on the stable testbed. It is composed out of one master and three compute modes, as listed in Table 4.

CephFS. As distribute file system (DFS) and basic enabler for VM live migrations the testbed uses the latest from source build CephFS. The deployed CephFS installation on the testbed is composed out of ten nodes (wally183 - wally192). It uses five monitor daemons and and two one Terra-byte disks participating in

Table 4. Testing testbed node distribution

Node	Comment
wally155	control node
wally152	energy-meter measured compute node
wally153, wally154	currently unmeasured compute nodes

the DFS per node with round about 14 Terra-byte total DFS volume. In addition, every DFS node is further equipped with an 512 MB SSD, which is used as CephFS journals to increase the IOPS performance.

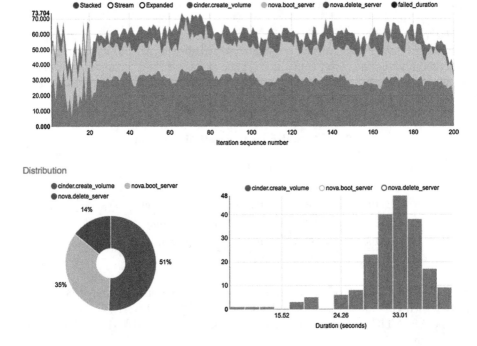

Fig. 3. Rally evaluation with 200 iterations using CephFS

A brief evaluation of the stable testbed instance with Rally [10] indicates that the deployment at TUB is working flawless. Spawning VMs with a typical Ubuntu 14.04 LTS image demonstrates that the usage of CephFS is a reasonable approach for IaaS providers to increase performance. The installation was benchmarked with a VM boot and delete process with 200 iterations running 20 concurrent deployments. As shown in Fig. 3, the testbed needs around 33 s to boot the VM. In contrast, booting from the local hard disk takes around 200 s, as depict in Fig. 4.

Atomic Action Durations

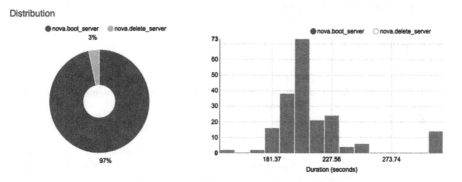

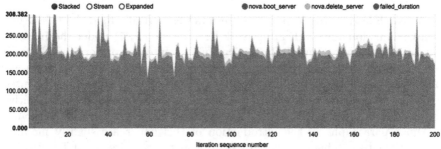

Distribution

Fig. 4. Rally evaluation with 200 iterations using the nodes local hard disk

5   Conclusion and Future Work

The currently deployed testbed presents an innovative environment for researchers to evaluate energy efficient cloud computing on all cloud layers. The ASCETiC project is currently in its third and last project year. The testbed meanwhile supports a lot of energy saving features provided by the second year ASCETiC toolbox. Nevertheless, some ambitions testbed related improvements and support opportunities are currently in progress. In particular, the TUB team is currently working on an IPMI driver to control hosts automatically. This driver will basically provide the opportunity to dynamically turn physical hosts on and off on demand. This will improve the overall energy consumption. Moreover, the TUB cluster is using smart power distribution units (PDUs) which provide a similar opportunity. Thus, with a PDU driver it would be possible to compare host and host group energy values. Furthermore, the integration of an OpenFlow capable network monitoring tool enables the opportunity to consider network streams and VM distances for the VMM related scheduling, deployment, and migration process.

6   Disclaimer and Acknowledgments

The research leading to the presented results was partially funded by the European Commission's Seventh Framework Programme (FP7) under the Information and Communications Technologies (ICT) - Internet of Services, Software and Virtualisation under the grant agreement number 610874. The views and conclusions contained herein are those of the authors and should not be interpreted as necessarily representing the official policies or endorsements, either expressed or implied, of the ASCETiC project or the European Commission.

Minor paragraphs in the introduction of this paper are slightly modified citations from [3]. Thus, we would like to thank the entire ASCETiC Project Consortium for the original paperwork.

References

1. Buyya, R., Beloglazov, A., Abawajy, J.H.: Energy-efficient management of data center resources for cloud computing: A vision, architectural elements, and open challenges. CoRR, abs/1006.0308 (2010)
2. ASCETiC Project Consortium. Ascetic whitepaper, September 2014. https://www.cetic.be/IMG/pdf/whitepaper_2014_v0.9.9.pdf
3. ASCETiC Project Consortium. D2.2.2 architecture specification - version 2, December 2014. http://www.ascetic-project.eu/sites/default/ascetic/files/content-files/articles/D2.2.2ASCETiCArchitectureSpecification.pdf
4. ASCETiC Project Consortium. D6.1.1 testbed status report - version 1, October 2014. http://www.ascetic-project.eu/sites/default/ascetic/files/content-files/articles/ASCETiCD6.1.1Testbedstatusreportv1.0.pdf
5. ASCETiC Project Consortium. Ascetic, August 2015. http://ascetic.eu
6. Djemame, K., Armstrong, D., Kavanagh, R.E., Ferrer, A.J., Perez, D.G., Antona, D.R., Deprez, J.-C., Christophe Ponsard, D., Ortiz, M.M., Guitart, J., Lordan, F., Ejarque, J., Sirvent, R., Badia, R.M., Kammer, M., Kao, O., Agiatzidou, E., Dimakis, A., Courcoubetis, C., Blasi, L.: Energy efficiency embedded service lifecycle: towards an energy efficient cloud computing architecture. In: Joint Workshop Proceedings of the 2nd International Conference on ICT for Sustainability 2014, Stockholm, Sweden, 24–27 August 2014, pp. 1–6 (2014)
7. Google. Google apps: Energy efficiency in the cloud, September 2015. http://www.google.com/green/pdf/google-apps.pdf
8. Keyes, R.W.: The impact of Moore's Law. Solid-state Circ. Soc. Newsl. 11(5), 25–27 (2006)
9. Pettey, C., van der Meulen, R.: Gartner says public cloud services are simultaneously cannibalizing and stimulating demand for external it services spending. Gartner Inc., Stamford, Press release, November 2012
10. Rally Project Core Team.: Rally, January 2016. https://wiki.openstack.org/wiki/Rally

Towards an Interoperability Certification Method for Semantic Federated Experimental IoT Testbeds

Mengxuan Zhao[1(✉)], Nikos Kefalakis[2], Paul Grace[3], John Soldatos[2],
Franck Le-Gall[1], and Philippe Cousin[1]

[1] Easy Global Market, Sophia Antipolis, Nice, France
{mengxuan.zhao,franck.le-gall,
philippe.cousin}@eglobalmark.com
[2] Athens Information Technology, Athens, Greece
{nkef,jsol}@ait.gr
[3] IT Innovation Centre, University of Southampton, Southampton, UK
pjg@it-innovation.soton.ac.uk

Abstract. IoT deployments and then related experiments tend to be highly heterogeneous leading to fragmented and non-interoperable silo solutions. Yet there is a growing need to interconnect such experiments to create rich infrastructures that will underpin the next generation of cross sector IoT applications in particular as using massive number of data. While research have been carried out for IoT test beds and interoperability for some infrastructures less has been done on the data. In this paper, we present the first step of the FIESTA certification method for federated semantic IoT test bed, which provides stakeholders with the means of assessing the interoperability of a given IoT testbed and how it can be federated with other ones to create large facility for experimenter. Focus is given on data and semantic context of the test beds and how they can interoperate together for larger experiments with data.

Keywords: Semantic interoperability · Federation · Certification · Testbeds · IoT

1 Introduction

The advent of the Internet-of-Things (IoT) paradigm has led to the emergence of a large number of context-aware human-centric applications that leverage data and services from sensors and other internet-connected objects. These applications are in several cases supported by IoT platforms, which facilitate the integration, and processing of IoT data streams, as well as their orchestration of IoT services in-line with the business requirements driving the IoT deployments [1]. Nevertheless, the vast majority of the platforms do not provide the means for building interoperable applications [2]. Hence, IoT deployments and also experiments tend to be fragmented and non-interoperable. This results in disaggregated and fragmented silo solutions, which can hardly be integrated into added-value applications [3].

© ICST Institute for Computer Sciences, Social Informatics and Telecommunications Engineering 2017
S. Guo et al. (Eds.): TridentCom 2016, LNICST 177, pp. 103–113, 2017.
DOI: 10.1007/978-3-319-49580-4_10

One major aspect of the boom of IoT deployments is the growing and massive number of data which themselves can become non interoperable as data cannot be understood by different silos. It is therefore very important to provide environment such as test beds which can help to experiment the use of large data sets and get some tools to ensure data (semantic) interoperability [4]. Before providing techniques to ensure such data interoperability it is very important to provide large test facilities and this is often provided by federation of testbeds. While federation of testbeds are promoted through regional program (i.e. GENI (https://www.geni.net) in US, FIRE and fed4-FIRE [6] in EU), there is no specific federation techniques focusing on data and semantic interoperability.

To address this limitation the FIESTA project (http://www.fiesta-iot.eu) is developing a certification method for IoT interoperability, which provides testbed owners with the means to assess the interoperability features and capabilities of a given IoT testbed, while at the same time providing concrete guidelines to facilitate data interoperability. Such a certification method is motivated by the need to interconnect diverse IoT testbeds, to create richer experimental facilities.

The purpose of this paper is to introduce the FIESTA interoperability certification framework which is a set of tools and methodology. It is structured as follows: Sect. 2, following the present introduction provides more details about the framwork. Section 3 elaborates the methodology used to derive the suite, which included consultation with owners of IoT infrastructures and IoT software developers. Section 4 is devoted to the presentation of the suite, in the form of a scorecard, along with concrete examples of its use. Section 5 is the concluding section of the paper, which also highlights future work.

2   A Semantic Interoperability Certification Framework

The purpose of testbed is to provide an environment that allows experimentations and testing to be performed which can require the participation of selected end-users [5]. FIESTA is an experimental facility that is a federation of heterogeneous IoT testbeds. Experimenters can utilize tools and services to run IoT experiments across different testbeds (covering different heterogeneous technology domains) [6]. Interoperability is clearly at the heart of this federation. In order for testbeds and tools to participate in the federation—they must interoperate. Hence, the objective of the *certification framework* is to ensure that an individual testbed which applies to be a part of the federation conforms to the certification specifications in order to guarantee the service level of the federation. Such a framework ensures that the key stakeholders can behave as shown in Fig. 1:

- **IoT Infrastructure Providers and Testbed Owners** provide the test environment, including resources and services (e.g. resource discovery, data access). The certification framework ensures that their testbed will gain wider visibility and will be used more extensively by applications and users.
- For **Experiments Developer and Integrators.** These are the people or organizations who develop and perform experimentations, which are in the form of new applications or services designed to get specific results, using the testing environment together with all available tools from the testbed. They are most interested in

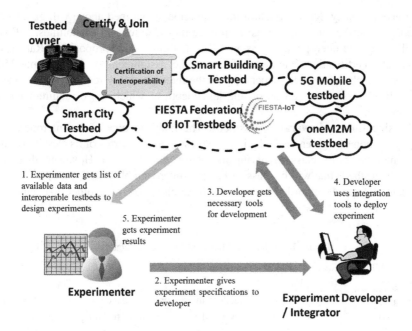

Fig. 1. Interactions between stakeholders in the certification framework

features such as the ease of use of the testbeds, the performance of services and tools provided by the testbeds for development and deployment, and the effectiveness of collecting experimentation results.

- For **Experimenters/Researchers.** They are the people who use the experiments running on the test federation to obtain the results they want. They need the certification framework to get ensured about what testbeds are interoperable to be used together, and what are the data accessible from the federation, in order to design their experiments and give the requirements to the experiments developer.

A certified testbed will help the other two stakeholders to have the confidence to concentrate on their core business without taking care of the details on the testing infrastructure. Conversely, once the two other stakeholders have confidence in the federation of certified testbeds, they will use more this testing infrastructure for their experiments. The **federator** (the FIESTA facility) is also a beneficiary of the certification framework that will provide guarantees that a given testbed complies and interoperates within the federation, thus being able to maintain the service level of the whole platform.

The structure of the certification framework comprises three elements:

- **Interoperability Aspects and Requirements:** The interoperability capabilities of each IoT platform or testbed will be defined in terms of a set of interoperability requirements (or capabilities) that it will have to fulfil. These requirements are discussed in the next paragraph.

- **Interoperability Scores:** Each of the requirements outlined above will give rise to scoring a testbed in terms of its interoperability features and capabilities. FIESTA will not define interoperability as an "all-or-nothing" value proposition. Rather, the project's certification framework foresees the assignment of an interoperability score to each IoT testbed, depending on the interoperability requirements/concerns that it addresses, as well as on the level/depth at which those requirements are addressed.
- **Classification and overall assessment:** The final outcome of the interoperability specification of a given testbed will be expressed also in terms of its classification to an interoperability class signifying its interoperability level. However, there will also be testbeds that will be classified as non-interoperable ("fail" class) i.e. lacking essential features in order to be used in conjunction with other IoT platforms (Table 1).

Table 1. Indicative interoperability classification.

Interoperability class	Score (0–100) (example)	Explanation
"Platinum" (A)	$S \geq 90$	Excellent interoperability, exceeding the set of criteria
"Gold" (B)	$90 > S \geq 80$	Very good interoperability, fulfilling all the set of criteria
"Silver" (C)	$80 > S \geq 70$	Good interoperability, implementing most of the set interoperability criteria
"Bronze" (D)	$70 > S \geq 60$	Acceptable interoperability, providing support for a set of important requirements that enable interoperability
Fail (E)	$60 > S$	The testbed has serious interoperability weaknesses and fails to meet essential interoperability requirements

3 Certifying IoT Testbeds: Aspects and Requirements

The production of the certification scorecard was developed by studying the interoperability requirements collected from our analysis of four testbeds aiming to integrate into the FIESTA federation (the requirements are documented [7]). These testbeds are not necessarily compliant with the FIESTA certified testbed definition from the beginning, because they may have different approaches or conflict of interest as they are independent. However, they should be the first to adapt the criteria of FIESTA testbed as soon as the definition of "FIESTA-compliant testbed", which is a mutual-agreement between them, is available, in order to establish the federation and enable first experiments running on the federation. This analysis of the requirements produced the following key themes where interoperability must be certified:

- **Data models.** Achieving interoperability by establishing and using a semantic model for the data in the federation.
- **Interfaces and services.** Certification of the services and interfaces which should be provided by the federation and each testbed.

- **Security.** Ensuring that testbeds maintain the end-to-end security properties of the federation.
- **Quality Auditing Aspects.** Ensuring that testbeds maintain the end-to-end Quality of Service Aspects of the federation.

3.1   Data Models

A key interoperability characteristic of an IoT experimental infrastructure is its ability to represent and exchange data in standards-based models and formats. The rationale behind supporting such format is two-fold:

- **Syntactic Interoperability:** To facilitate developers in accessing and processing data, on the basis of popular, mainstream and widely use standards such as REST and JSON. This is a major step towards syntactic interoperability across IoT applications that use/leverage data from multiple testbeds.
- **Semantic Interoperability:** To ensure that IoT applications leveraging data from multiple testbeds have compatible semantics, thanks to their compliance to a common (standards-based) data model or ontology. The interoperability score of a testbed will be defined on the basis of the number and type of supported data models and ontologies

3.2   Interfaces and Services

Another interoperability feature of a testbed relates to the interfaces that it supports for accessing its IoT services and resources. The support of a standards-based interface can facilitate third-parties (i.e. integrators of IoT experiments) to develop interoperable applications, on the basis of the principle: "Build once and interface across multiple testbeds".

Interfaces. Apart from the provision of support for access interface, a testbed's interoperability is affected by the type of IoT services that it supports, such as for example services for discovery of resources (e.g., services, sensors) and data processing functionalities (e.g., CEP). To facilitate the FIESTA platform access across multiple testbeds some of the most known IoT and/or proprietary interfaces are going to be utilized:

- **SPARQL interface:** SPARQL Protocol and RDF Query Language interface is a web service for conveying SPARQL queries to an SPARQL query processing service and returning the query results to the entity that requested them
- **NGSI:** Next Generation Services Interface is a RESTful API via HTTP. Its purpose is to exchange context information.
- **OCCI:** Open Cloud Computing Interface is a Protocol and API for Management tasks. It can serve models in addition to IaaS, including e.g. PaaS and SaaS.
- **IoT-A Virtual Entity end point:** virtual entities representing physical entities can be discovered

- **Relational DB end point**.
- **Document DB end point**.

IoT Services. Some of the testbeds could provide additional services that will enable the experimenter and the FIESTA platform of having more advanced interaction with it. These services include:

- **Resource Discovery:** this service will enable FIESTA platform to discover available resources of the testbed and list them to the experimenter.
- **Direct access to sensors through services:** this service will enable the experimenter, based on an agreed access policy, to access the data feed of the sensor directly for retrieving real time data.
- **Actuation true offered services:** will enable the experimenter, based on an agreed access policy, to control a sensor/actuator by exposing its control interface.

3.3   Security

Security must be considered in an end-to-end manner across the federation. Interoperability covers both functional and non-functional properties. Each testbed that joins and participates in the FIESTA federation must comply with the security technologies, protocols and practices in order that it interoperates with the same secure characteristics. A fully interoperable testbed (syntactically and semantically) at both the data and interface/service levels still cannot operate within the FIESTA federation without considering conformance with the security architecture and requirements (and indeed other non-functional properties). For a testbed to be considered maintaining security compliance it must achieve the following elements:

- **Secure encrypted communication channel** between all testbed interfaces and FIESTA. The testbed must implement fully secure interface endpoints. That is all communication between the testbed and systems in the federation are encrypted.
- **Authentication.** The testbed must trust the FIESTA federation to identify and authenticate experimenters on its behalf. A request received by a testbed in the federation is deemed to be authentic.
- **Identity Management** (optional). A testbed may wish to determine who is using what features of the testbed, e.g. for accounting purposes.
- **Authorization.** The testbed may trust FIESTA to authorize users on its behalf. The testbed must then provide FIESTA a set of access policies for its resources.
- **Testbed-based Access Control** (optional). A testbed can choose to perform local access control decisions and enforcement.

By conforming to these security features the key requirements of the federation are maintained: (i) single-sign of experimenters to use all testbeds and services in the federations; (ii) authorized access to resources; and (iii) secure and protected communication in the federation.

3.4 Quality Auditing Aspects

Quality expectations depend on the evaluated subject which is testbed in the current case clarified earlier. Testbeds aim to provide better services to attract experimenters. In a given testbed, the most important impacts on the quality of service are the technological and service enablers that experimenters and developers use directly to implement the experiments.

Quality of Service (QoS) aims at evaluating the end to end service delivery quality and correlating it with the users' quality of experience. From [7], we identify the QoS-related indicators for the certification framework which are:

- **Response time.** The maximum delay to give a response to a received request.
- **Processing time.** The maximum delay that the testbed must finish the processing even in the most complex case.
- **Computational assets.** Resource assignment for computing should be optimized.
- **Service prioritization.** If a testbed provide several services, as resources are limited, it should be able to prioritize some services.
- **Reliability.** The testbed should be enough reliable to not interrupt experiments too often.

Good quality of a testbed is also related to how easy and clear that an experimenter can develop and deploy their experiments on it. **Best practice** such a support which is a guide for platform/framework users to design and run services/applications conform to the specifications in an efficient way. It helps to improve the reusability of the testbed for conducting various experiments on it. This guide will also help other testbeds in the federation to understand and cooperate with the current testbed. This is a part of the whole documentation. In a similar way, we identify the best practice-related indications from the requirement document of Fiesta.

- **Documentation.** The most essential part of the best practice about a platform.
- **High level interface description.** This will guide the users to use provided services.
- **Tools.** Available tools will help development, deployment and management of experiments.

4   Testbed Interoperability ScoreCard

Based on the items presented in the previous sections we have generated a scorecard, based on the criteria presented in Table 2, which was implemented in an Excel file and when completed during the certification process will provide a score to the testbed owner based on the features that is capable to provide.

Application of scorecard to certify a testbed. Figure 2 is shows an example of a filled up scorecard with the relevant mock-up result/advice guide. This example is from the input and feedbacks from the Santander Smart City testbed. In the generated Excel file, the testbed owner is able to choose the level of support for the listed items above by ticking the appropriate box on the right and as soon as it finishes it can get an overall score (72.7/100 on upper right) of the testbed/FIESTA Interoperability. In the current

Table 2. The interoperability scorecard content

Testbed/FIESTA Interoperability	
Items	Description
Data Models	
SSN Ontology	Does the testbed supports the SSN ontology
FIESTA Ontology	Does the testbed supports the FIESTA ontology
SensorML	Does the testbed supports SensorML language to represent the sensor data
SWE	Does the testbed supports Sensor Web Enablement (SWE) language to represent the sensor data
Proprietary Format	Does the testbed supports a proprietary language to represent the sensor data
Data Extraction	Does the testbed provides the ability to extract data in a document format (i.e. CSV, Excel, XML, RDF, JSON, etc.)
Graph Database	Does the testbed store its data in a Graph Database
Document Database	Does the testbed store its data in a Document Database
Relational Database	Does the testbed store its data in a Relational Database
Interfaces and Services	
SPARQL End Point	Does the Testbed offer a SPARQL (Graph DB) endpoint
NGSI Interface	Does the Testbed offer NGSI
OCCI Interface	Does the Testbed offer OCCI
Virtual Entity Endpoint	Does the Testbed offer an Virtual Entity end point
Relational Database End Point	Does the Testbed offer a Relational DB endpoint
Document DB Endpoint	Does the Testbed offer a document DB endpoint
IoT Services End Point	Resource Discovery, Direct access to sensors thru services, Actuation true offered services
Security	
Data Encryption	Offer secure encrypted communication channel between all testbed interfaces and FIESTA
Authentication	Can trust FIESTA to identify and authenticate experimenters on its behalf
Identity Management	Determine who is using what features of the testbed
Authorization	Is the testbed able to specify access rights to specific resources?
Testbed-based Access Control	Can the testbed choose to perform local access control decisions and enforcement?
Quality Auditing Aspects	
Response time	Do you control or set a threshold before which your testbed must give a response to the received request?
Processing time	Do you control or set a threshold before which your testbed must finish processing the request in the most complex case?
Computational assets	Does your testbed implement any resource optimizing mechanism?

(continued)

Table 2. (*continued*)

Testbed/FIESTA Interoperability	
Items	Description
Service prioritization	Does the testbed support the execution of services with different priorities?
Reliability	Do you define a ratio of failure time/working time that the testbed must respect?
Generic	
Documentation	Does the Testbed provide Documentation
Tools	Does the testbed provide development, deployment and management tools
Adaptors	Can the Testbed offer the ability to run third party software (i.e. FIESTA adaptors)
Additional DB	Can the testbed replicate/annotate its current data to the FIESTA format in a local Database

#	Check Items (double click topics to expand / collapse)	Descriptions	Yes (double click to	Partially (double click to	No (double click to
1	**Data Models**		■	■	■
1.1	SSN Ontology	Does the testbed supports the SSN ontology	☐	☑	☐
1.2	FIESTA Ontology	Does the testbed supports the FIESTA ontology	☐	☐	☑
1.3	SensorML	Does the testbed supports SensorML language to represent the sensor data	☐	☐	☑
1.4	SWE	Does the testbed supports Sensor Web Enablement (SWE) language to represent the sensor data	☐	☐	☑
1.5	Proprietery Format	Does the testbed supports a proprietary language to represent the sensor data	☑	☐	☐
1.6	Data Extraction	Does the testbed provides the ability to extractr data in a document format (i.e. CSV, Excel, XML, RDF, JSON, etch)	☐	☑	☐
1.7	Graph Database	Does the testbed store its data in a Graph Database	☐	☐	☑
1.8	Document Database	Does the testbed store its data in a Document Database	☑	☐	☐
1.9	Relational Database	Does the testbed store its data in a Relational Database	☑	☐	☐
2	**Interfaces and Services**		■	☐	■
2.1	SPARQL End Point	Does the Testbed offer a SPARQL (Graph DB) endpoint	☐	☐	☑
2.2	NGSI Interface	Does the Testbed offer an OMA Next Generation Services Interface	☑	☐	☐
2.3	OCCI Interface	Does the Testbed offer an Open Cloud Computing Interface	☐	☐	☑
2.4	Virtual Entity Endpoint	Does the Testbed offer an Virtual Entity end point	☐	☐	☑
2.5	Relational Database End Point	Does the Testbed offer a Relational DB endpoint	☐	☐	☑
2.6	Document DB Endpoint	Does the Testbed offer a document DB endpoint	☐	☐	☑
2.7	IoT Services End Point	Resource Discovery	☑	☐	☐
		Direct access to sensors thru services	☑	☐	☐
		Actuation thru offered services	☑	☐	☐
3	**Security**		■	■	☐
3.1	Data Encryption	Offer secure encrypted communication channel between all testbed interfaces and FIESTA	☑	☐	☐
3.2	Authentication	Can trust FIESTA to identify and authenticate experimenters on its behalf	☑	☐	☐
3.3	Identity Management	determine who is using what features of the testbed	☐	☑	☐
3.4	Authorization	Is the testbed able to specify access rights to specific resources	☑	☐	☐
3.5	Testbed-based Access Control	Can the testbed choose to perform local access control decisions and enforcement.	☑	☐	☐
4	**Quality Auditing Aspects**		■	■	■
4.1	Response time	Do you control or set a threshold before which your testbed must give a response to the received request?	☐	☑	☐
4.2	Processing time	Do you control or set a threshold before which your testbed must finish	☑	☐	☐
4.3	Computational assets	Does your testbed implement any resource optimizing mechanism?	☐	☐	☑
4.4	Service prioritization	Does the Testbed support the execution of services with different priorities?	☐	☐	☑
4.5	Reliability	Do you define a ratio of failure time/working time that the testbed must respect?	☑	☐	☐
5	**Generic**		■	■	■
5.1	Documentation	Does the Testbed provide Documentation	☑	☐	☐
5.2	Tools	Does the testbed provide development, deployment and management tools	☑	☐	☐
5.3	Adaptors	Can the Testbed offer the abbility to run third party software (i.e. FIESTA	☐	☐	☑
5.4	Addittional DB	Can the testbed replicate/anotate it's current data to the FIESTA format in a	☐	☑	☐

Testbed/FIESTA Interoperability   Overall Score: 72,7%

Fig. 2. An interoperability scorecard mock-up sample

case, a "Yes" give a score of 1.35, a "Partially" gives 0.75 and a "No" gives 0. It should be noted here that for the reason of ease of use for the scorecard users, some criteria in Table 2 are split into several finer items. We also investigate to generate automatically a report with a results/advice guide on what a testbed could easily support further or what needs to be done to make it interoperable with the FIESTA platform. according to specific items (i.e. "The testbed could adapt FIESTA ontology with some effort" (in data models category in Table 2)) is an advice given based on the "NO" answer of "Does the testbed supports the FIESTA ontology?"), or according to a score calculated within a category (i.e. "The testbed provides satisfactory quality of service" is given based on the scored calculated from the answers to items in the category "Quality Auditing Aspects"). It is mapped to the interoperability class "Sliver (C)" to give the testbed owner an intuitive information about how much effort to investigate in the future to make the testbed interoperable regarding to FIESTA (Table 3).

Table 3. An interoperability scorecard mock-up result/advice guide sample

Data Models
The testbed could adapt FIESTA ontology with some effort
Interfaces and Services
The testbed could adapt FIESTA architecture by implementing SPARQL endpoint
The testbed could utilize the FIESTA adaptors thru NGSI interface
The testbed can provide direct access to sensors and actuators thru its own interfaces
Security
The testbed provides satisfactory level of security
The testbed can only provide complete access to one user type which will be controlled by FIESTA
One Fiesta User will require to be created to access the Data offered by the testbed
Quality Auditing Aspects
The testbed provides satisfactory quality of service
Generic
The testbed could offer FIESTA compliant database without the need of additional software

5   Conclusions and Outlook

As part of this paper we have highlighted the importance of federating IoT test beds to ensure data interoperability experiments, along with the need of a framework for auditing IoT applications against their interoperability characteristics. The framework addresses a wide range of aspects that underpin interoperability, including supported interfaces, data models, security mechanisms and more. Special emphasis is given in the provision of support for standards, which is an aspect that can greatly facilitate interoperability. The certification framework is currently provided in the form of a scorecard, which has been subject to small scale validation on the basis of the involvement of few testbed owners and IoT developers. As part of on-going work we are transforming the scorecard to an interactive on-line tool, which will facilitate its use by stakeholders, while at the same time enabling the reception of feedback for fine-tuning the implementation. Furthermore, a larger scale validation targeting owners and administrators of commercial IoT infrastructures (rather than experimental testbeds only) is also planned. This future work is expected to increase the number and scope of the potential beneficiaries of the certification framework, which will be provided as an on-line service. Furthermore the framework currently addressing test beds will be extended to the whole data IoT interoperability world where there are a lot of expectations in particular within Standards organizations such as ETSI or oneM2M, just to mention few ones.

Acknowledgments. Part of this work has been carried out in the scope of the FIESTA-IoT project (H2020-643943) (http://www.fiesta-iot.eu/). The authors acknowledge help and contributions from all partners of the project.

References

1. Soldatos, J., Serrano, M., Hauswirth, M.: Convergence of utility computing with the internet-of-things. In: 2012 Sixth International Conference on Innovative Mobile and Internet Services in Ubiquitous Computing (IMIS), 4–6 July 2012, Palermo, Italy. IEEE (2012)
2. Soldatos, J., Kefalakis, N., Hauswirth, M., Serrano, M., Calbimonte, J.-P., Riahi, M., Aberer, K., Jayaraman, P.P., Zaslavsky, A., Žarko, I.P., Skorin-Kapov, L., Herzog, R.: OpenIoT: open source internet-of-things in the cloud. In: Podnar Žarko, I., Pripužić, K., Serrano, M. (eds.) FP7 OpenIoT Project Workshop 2014. LNCS, vol. 9001, pp. 13–25. Springer, Heidelberg (2015). doi:10.1007/978-3-319-16546-2_3
3. Manyika, J., Chui, M., Bisson, P., Woetzel, J., Dobbs, R. Bughin, J., Aharon, D.: Unlocking the Potential of the Internet of Things. McKinsey Global Institute, June 2015
4. Serrano, M., Quoc, H.N.M., Le Phuoc, D., Hauswirth, M., Soldatos, J., Kefalakis, N., Jayaraman, P.P., Zaslavsky, A.: Defining the stack for service delivery models and interoperability in the internet of things: a practical case with OpenIoTVDK. IEEE J. Sel. Areas Commun. 33(4), 676–689 (2015)
5. MyFire project (http://www.my-fire.eu) deliverable D1.2-taxonomy on common interpretation of testing, testing approaches and test bed models
6. Fed4Fire project (http://www.fed4fire.eu) deliverable D2.3 First sustainability plan
7. Fiesta project deliverable D2.1, Stakeholders Requirements

Design and Architecture of an Industrial IT Security Lab

Steffen Pfrang$^{(\boxtimes)}$, Jörg Kippe, David Meier, and Christian Haas

Fraunhofer IOSB, Fraunhoferstr. 1, 76131 Karlsruhe, Germany
{steffen.pfrang,joerg.kippe,david.meier,
christian.haas}@iosb.fraunhofer.de

Abstract. IT security for Industrial control systems or the Industrial Internet of Things is an emerging topic in research and development as well as for operators of real production facilities. In this paper, we will present the Fraunhofer IOSB IT Security Laboratory for industrial control systems, that enables security research, development and testing of products and training of IT security personnel. Due to its architecture based on both real hardware components and a flexible virtual environment, the IT Security Lab offers a realistic setup of today's production facilities and at the same time a high flexibility with regard to future networking technologies and protocols.

Keywords: IT security · Industrial Internet of Things · Industrie 4.0 · Testbed

1 Introduction and Motivation

Future industrial production facilities will be highly networked. Controllers and embedded systems such as programmable logic controllers (PLC) and sensors or actors communicate with each other, cloud-based systems plan tasks and machine utilization, plant operators monitor and control the system remotely, maintenance staff can access and change the plant's configuration remotely from anywhere on the planet. With more networking and connectivity, IT security mechanisms become an urgent and integral topic well beyond factory or production sites. Attackers could potentially infiltrate critical production networks and therefore harm or destroy production lines or even cause severe injuries.

To protect against damage and production stoppages, suitable measures to prevent security incidents are urgently needed. Yet, the research and development of countermeasures or attack research and vulnerability scanning are often not possible in real production networks due to availability issues or the risk of malfunctions. On the other hand, nearly no test data, e.g. packet capture (PCAP) files of network traffic in industrial sites is available, as this data is often related to intellectual property protection and kept secret. Nevertheless, IT security research and development requires an IT infrastructure that is isolated from productive networks and yet replicates the target environment as

S. Guo et al. (Eds.): TridentCom 2016, LNICST 177, pp. 114–123, 2017.
DOI: 10.1007/978-3-319-49580-4_11

accurately as possible. In this paper we will present the Fraunhofer IOSB IT Security Laboratory for Industrial control systems that enables us to perform security research, development and testing of products and education or training of security personnel in an isolated environment that contains most of today's industrial networks and components in real hardware and software as well.

1.1 Requirements

There are several requirements that the IT Security Laboratory has to fulfill. At first and most important, there is the necessity to perform attack research including Vulnerability scanning and Intrusion detection in a testbed that consists of real automation components connected with real industrial protocols without endangering any real production process.

In order to gain flexibility and reduce costs, there should both real hardware components (e.g. PLCs, industrial switches etc.) and virtualized components. Using a virtualization environment for the production site allows for constructing larger, more realistic production processes and workflows as well as for attacking devices without the danger of destroying components irrecoverably. On the other hand, attacks have to target real components to transfer research results to real production sites.

The laboratory has to be built up to integrate arbitrary automation equipment. Additionally, there has to be the flexibility for reconfiguring the whole laboratory setup by exchanging components through standardized interfaces: Mechanically, electrically as well as the networking infrastructure.

For attack and detection purposes, there has to be a powerful virtualized computing infrastructure which can be used from different locations (e.g. offices) with the ease of virtual machines. And last but not least, the whole laboratory has to be protected from attacks coming from the Internet as well as the Internet, that has to be protected from attacks performed by malicious software that is run within the laboratory.

2 Design

The IT Security Laboratory is a test- and demonstration environment dedicated to the security of industrial IT systems and providing a high degree of flexibility to perform IT security research. From the top-level point of view, the lab consists of two parts:

Virtualization environment (also called the cloud infrastructure): This environment shown on the left side of Fig. 1 is implemented using the Open source software platform Proxmox VE [4] and runs on a three node hardware cluster. In this environment different networks have been set up using virtual switches (Open vSwitch [15]) as well as virtual firewalls (pfsense [10]). Virtual machines connected to these networks provide components of automation systems (e.g. PLC programming stations, SCADA servers), management tools and – to support security research – different attack and detection tools.

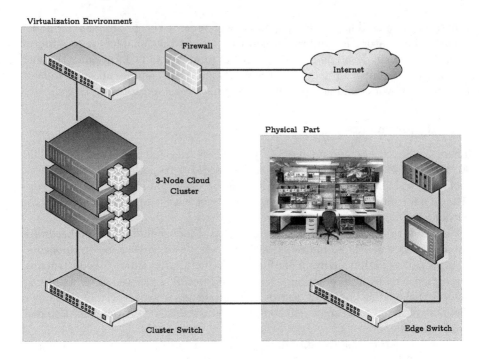

Fig. 1. The virtualization environment and related physical part

The hardware cluster is connected to the Internet and protected by a hardware firewall (Cisco ASA) controlling incoming traffic as in any other Internet connected enterprise network, but additional protection has been implemented to control outgoing traffic and to prevent malicious software from passing from the laboratory networks into the outside world. A cluster switch connects the nodes and provides on a trunk port several virtual LANs set up within the cloud infrastructure building the network infrastructure for the experiments to be run in the laboratory.

Physical part: The physical part shown on the right side of Fig. 1 consists of a mechanical framework construction into which different experiments can be mounted. Experiments consist of slabs, which on turn carry real physical components known from industrial automation systems (like PLCs, industrial switches, HMIs, etc.). The framework construction provides electrical power (different voltages as needed by typical automation equipment) and connection to the networks in the virtualization environment via an edge switch that is connected to the cluster switch.

Both the virtual and the physical part together provide the test- and demonstration environment which allows to run attacks against real automation equipment (which hardly can be simulated using virtual machines) in a flexible way. The slabs carrying the experiments are designed in a modular way and can be changed easily (Fig. 2).

Fig. 2. Picture of the IOSB Industrial IT security laboratory

Figure 3 shows an example network structure with three subnets: The Field network comprising PLCs, sensors and actors, is connected via a firewall with the SCADA network homing a SCADA system. Another firewall connects this network with the Office network. The management, attack and detection tools reside in a separate network which is linked to all of the other networks.

2.1 Monitoring Infrastructure

With respect to network traffic analysis one has to consider the fact that sub-networks/VLANs are spread over different switches in the virtual as well as in the real part of the lab environment. To get a complete view of the network traffic the traffic passing through the different switches has to be monitored and those mirror streams have to be merged. That has been achieved by setting up the mirroring within the Open vSwitch infrastructure and sending the collected mirror streams through Generic Routing Encapsulation (GRE) tunnels to a concentrator which provides a merged mirror stream to the analyzer machine. A visualization of this mirroring infrastructure is shown in Fig. 4.

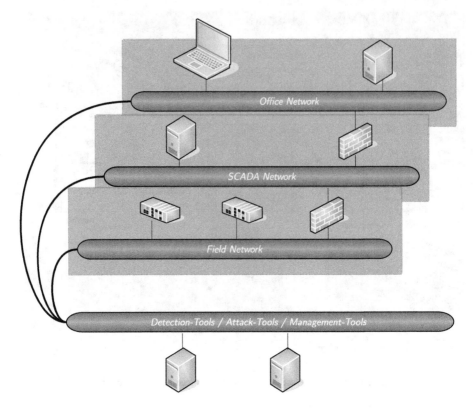

Fig. 3. Example network view with different typically used networks

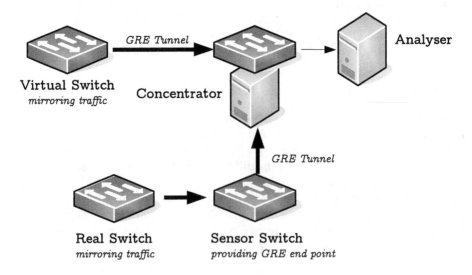

Fig. 4. A mirror infrastructure example comprising one real and one virtual switch

2.2   Detection Tools

The placement and usage of any detection tools depends on the experiments to be conducted. For network based detection tools e.g. a sensor component performing packet capture would be connected to the mirror stream provided by the monitoring infrastructure as described above. For the analysis/testing of host based detections tools, collectors and correlators would be installed in the management network receiving alerts directly from the components under test. In the same way any GUI applications would be located within this network. A dual-homed installation typically would be used for vulnerability assessment scanners, which have one interface in the management network and another where the components to be scanned are residing.

3   Attack Case Study

To demonstrate the capabilities of the Industrial IT Security Lab, an attack case study is presented. This example attack will involve multiple parts of the lab to illustrate security weaknesses and their impact on Industrial IT components.

3.1   Scenario

This scenario is built upon a simulated production process involving multiple simulated machines. The simulated production process is based on a real factory installation from Festo Didactic and simulated using CIROS 6.0 software, also by Festo [3]. The simulated machines are controlled by individual programmable logic controllers (PLC) by wiring their signal in- and outputs to the simulation. This has the advantage that the PLCs can be operated with the same firmware and configuration used in a completely real environment. One part of the production process contains a rotary disk where workpieces are tooled with a molding cutter and a drill. This part of the process is controlled by a single PLC that reacts on sensor input when a new workpiece is ready to get processed. It is then brought into position by the rotary disk and cutter and drill are positioned accordingly. The actual cutting and drilling is also controlled by the signal outputs from the PLC. The real-world installation of this production process part is shown in Fig. 5.

The PLCs are communicating with each other and have industrial Ethernet connections to a OPC-UA server [9], where production data gets aggregated. No security hardening procedures or methods were used on the automation devices. While this would not be common practice in modern IT environments, this is still often found in the industrial IT domain, because of a false perception of security [11]. This also means that access to the PLC is not restricted, for example by using default passwords or no passwords at all.

In this scenario, we assume an attacker has gained access to the plant communication network with typical attack vectors [7] comprising of, for example, infected control stations or manipulated mobile maintenance equipment.

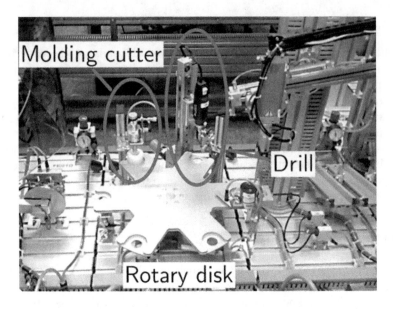

Fig. 5. Picture of process part used for the attack scenario

The attacker has access to the SCADA parts of the network in particular (refer to Fig. 3) and is able to inject arbitrary data into the network. He is therefore also able to intercept data by using ARP spoofing, for example. This also enables the attacker to start communication with devices of his choice.

3.2 Attack Description

The attacker is first starting to scan the network silently to avoid affecting automation devices yet, which often react with errors when confronted with simple network scans. This enables the attacker to learn the devices present in the network. By analyzing MAC addresses, a target PLC can be identified. The attacker can now start communicating with the targeted PLC by using an applicable SCADA protocol. As the PLC in this scenario is a *SIEMENS S7-300*, the *S7 protocol* is the protocol of choice. The protocol enables the attacker not only to read data from the PLC, the attacker can also send commands to the PLC. By issuing a *force order* command, arbitrary values can be set on the in- and outputs. This is a debugging feature to enable quick reaction options, for example in the case of hardware failures. The attacker can now provide the executed PLC program with manipulated inputs or set the outputs of the PLC directly. By setting almost all output signals, the attacker can provoke a constant rotation of the dish while molding cutter and drill are still active and in position. This would, of course, immediately cause damage to the current workpieces and the hardware itself and ultimately lead to the destruction of crucial elements of this process part.

During the attack, the internal computation cycle of the PLC is not altered in any way. As soon as the *force order* is deactivated by the attacker, the current cycle outputs are set and the PLC continues regular operation. This also means that neither the firmware nor the current configuration of the PLC are altered by the attack.

3.3 Detection and Alert Processing

Our simple showcase detection workflow starts with the network-based Intrusion Detection System (IDS) SNORT [12]. Initially, SNORT gets configured with a whitelist containing the information of allowed connections to the PLC.

Once SNORT detects a network packet addressing the PLC whose sender doesn't match the whitelist, it fires an alert. This alert gets forwarded to the correlation engine OSSEC [1] which simply converts the alert into the standardized Intrusion Detection Message Exchange Format (IDMEF) [2]. The alert might be processed by an Incident Management System (IMS). In our case, for demonstration purposes, it triggers a traffic light which is mounted on the mechanical part of the lab and sets it to red.

3.4 Case Study Conclusion

We are able to demonstrate a simple, yet effective attack to a production process. The attack arises because an attacker has got direct access to the SCADA components with the PLCs. This scenario is not only fictitious, it is even ordinary in many production sites based on our experiences with talks to employees and responsable persons: Network separation isn't performed in production sites as it is common in the Office IT.

Additionally, as a second point, Intrusion detection is being performed in the virtualization infrastructure and an alarm gets raised once malicious activities are being discovered. That allows for alerting cyber security personnel that can react properly.

4 Related Work

Testbeds for the Industrial Internet of Things is a hot topic all over the world. For example, there are several testbeds in the Industrial Internet Consortium (IIC) for different emerging topics in the industrial internet, e.g. for condition monitoring an asset efficiency testbed [5]. Another set of testbeds can be found in the German *Plattform Industrie 4.0* consortium, where several testbeds are hosted in the so-called *Labs Network Industrie 4.0*. These testbeds address several hot topics for Industrie 4.0, e.g. Smart Factories, PLUG and WORK or Smart Data Innovation [8]. Neverless, very few testbeds are designed and used for research and development on IT security for the industrial internet. For some educational purposes, some smaller training and test scenarios can be found from commercial cyber training vendors, e.g. [13,14] or [6]. These smaller test environments usually are used to showcase some specific attacks or detection technique for industrial control systems, yet they often lack the flexibility to use both real hardware and virtual components. Also, often times no real production processes are simulated or run.

5   Discussion and Future Work

With the attack case study presented in Sect. 3, we were able to prove that the testbed fulfills the requirements for an Industrial IT security laboratory enumerated in Subsect. 1.1: A cyber attack disturbing a physical but simulated process gets detected by an IDS component which triggers an alarm.

The architecture is chosen rather flexible allowing for the inclusion of arbitrary physical as well as virtualized components. Using a powerful cloud infrastructure, even heavy-weight attack tools can be run. With the monitoring infrastructure in place, different types of detection tools can be launched and used for both research and educational purposes. Furthermore, it allows for the recording of process automation communication as well as cyber attack traffic resulting in PCAP files which can be used for analysis outside of the laboratory.

Nevertheless, there are some minor limitations of our approach to be mentioned. Even with the flexibility of the lab, it is not possible to reproduce the whole complexity of some real-world automation scenarios because there are nearly no industrial components which can be virtualized with full industrial real-time protocol support.

A limitation might also be the fact that the lab doesn't involve any human operators or workflows which are an essential part of a complete automation scenario. But many infections of production networks arise via the Office network through infected email attachments, malicious code on websites, phishing attacks or infected USB drives because human personnel is vulnerable for social engineering attacks. An inadequate separation of the networks then allows for the spreading of the attack.

5.1   Future Work

Within this paper, we have presented a basic attack and detection scenario. We are planning to elaborate more enhanced attacks on the Field layer as well as on the SCADA layer including attack research on ProfiNet, S7 and OPC UA. In order to detect these security breaches, we are experimenting with more enhanced Intrusion detection and correlation techniques. A goal is also to include the gathered information about security alerts into a security overview of the situation. As a future step, we plan to use our IT security lab in education, using it as an easy way to create awareness for security risks in industrial control systems as well as a good tool to demonstrate how to secure these systems.

Using the flexibility of the laboratory infrastructure, we are also planning to include remote production sites into the lab in order to perform advanced security monitoring.

References

1. Bray, R., Cid, D., Hay, A.: OSSEC Host-Based Intrusion Detection Guide. Syngress (2008)
2. Debar, H., Curry, D., Feinstein, B.: The Intrusion Detection Message Exchange Format (IDMEF). RFC 4765 (Experimental). Internet Engineering Task Force, March 2007. http://www.ietf.org/rfc/rfc4765.txt
3. Festo AG & Co. KG. Festo Didactic (2016). http://www.festo-didactic.com/. Accessed 01 February 2016
4. Proxmox Server Solutions GmbH. Open Source Virtualization (2016). https://www.proxmox.com/en/. Accessed 01 February 2016
5. Industrial Inernet Consortium (IIC). Industrial Inernet Consortium Testbeds (2016). http://www.iiconsortium.org/test-beds.htm. Accessed 01 February 2016
6. International Society of Automation. International Society of Automation Hands-on Training (2016). https://www.isa.org/training-certifications/isa-training/about-isa-training/hands-on-laboratories/. Accessed 01 February 2016
7. Johnson, R.E.: Survey of SCADA security challenges and potential attack vectors. In: 2010 International Conference for Internet Technology and Secured Transactions (ICITST), pp. 1–5 (2010)
8. Labs Network Industrie 4.0. Labs Network Industrie 4.0 Testbeds (2016). http://lni40.de/. Accessed 01 February 2016
9. OPC Foundation. OPC Unified Architecture (2016). https://opcfoundation.org/. Accessed 01 February 2016
10. pfSense. Open Source Security (2016). https://www.pfsense.org/. Accessed 01 February 2016
11. Piètre-Cambacédès, L., Tritschler, M., Ericsson, G.N.: Cybersecurity Myths on Power Control Systems: 21 Misconceptions and False Beliefs. IEEE Trans. Power Delivery **26**(1), 161–172 (2011). doi:10.1109/TPWRD.2010.2061872. ISSN: 0885-8977
12. Roesch, M., et al.: Snort: lightweight intrusion detection for networks. In: LISA, vol. 99(1), pp. 229–238 (1999)
13. SANS. Assessing and Exploiting Control Systems (2016). http://www.sans.org/course/pentesting-smartgrid-scada. Accessed 01 February 2016
14. SANS. Critical Infrastructure and Control System Cybersecurity (2016). http://www.sans.org/course/critical-infrastructure-csc. Accessed 01 February 2016
15. Proxmox Server Solutions. Open vSwitch (2016). http://openvswitch.org/. Accessed 01 February 2016

Test Bench to Test Protocols and Algorithms for Multimedia Delivery

Jose M. Jimenez[1], Jaime Lloret[1(✉)], Juan R. Diaz[1],
and Raquel Lacuesta[2]

[1] Instituto de Investigación para la Gestión Integrada de Zonas Costeras,
Universidad Politécnica de Valencia, Camino Vera s/n, 46022 Valencia, Spain
{jojiher,jlloret}@dcom.upv.es,
juanramon.diazsantos@gmail.com
[2] Escuela Politécnica Superior de Teruel, Universidad de Zaragoza,
C/ Ciudad Escolar s/n, 44003 Teruel, Spain
lacuesta@unizar.es

Abstract. Nowadays, the study of Quality of Service (QoS) in multimedia streaming is generally carried out by simulators. However, the results of these tests are not quite real. This forces researchers to work with approximations. In this paper, we implement a test bench to test the performance and assess the protocols and algorithms for multimedia delivery. This test bench let us evaluate the network parameters performance, by manipulating the devices under controlled conditions, and allow us to identify different application cases. We can confirm that the designed test bench gives us more real measures than a simulators, which allows us to do many types of tests with low cost.

Keywords: Multimedia · Test bench · QoS · Protocols and algorithms

1 Introduction

The evolution of multimedia delivery has been possible thanks to the development of control mechanisms to promote Quality of Service (QoS) and Quality of Experience (QoE) in IP networks: traffic prioritization, streaming protocols, etc. [1, 2]. They have brought benefits to both service operators and users in many aspects such as: obtaining an efficient communication, optimizing resources and reducing costs in both, the part of the service providers and in consequence to the users, optimizing network administration, delivery of new services, and efficient and secure network infrastructure developing. New technologies such as adaptive streaming [3] and Software Defined Networks [4] are providing research advances in this topic.

A QoS categorized model of user-centric let us know the performance quality goals of audio, data and video. These goals are detailed in the Recommendation UIT T G.1010 [5] and Recommendation UIT R M.1079-2 [6]. So, we primarily must take into account parameters such as latency, jitter, and bandwidth and packet loss in both wired and wireless networks [7, 8]. Others parameters we are interested in are shown in Cisco VNI report [9]. Some of them are internet user demand, network connections

© ICST Institute for Computer Sciences, Social Informatics and Telecommunications Engineering 2017
S. Guo et al. (Eds.): TridentCom 2016, LNICST 177, pp. 124–134, 2017.
DOI: 10.1007/978-3-319-49580-4_12

growth, as well as the generation of internet video minutes per month in a global scale and especially the number of video users in Internet.

In this work, we study the effect of stressing the network. In order to achieve this goal, we study the most well-known network parameters such as latency, jitter and number of lost packets, which provide relevant information to the network operators. We test different cases and analyze the received video quality. It is performed for both wireless and wired networks. First, we get a baseline that is later used to compare different study cases. These cases are designed taking into account the impact of multimedia delivery when there are few network resources.

The paper is organized as follows. In next section, we show several related works that include testbeds to show the performance of the network when there is multimedia delivery. In Sect. 3, we describe the test bench implemented to test the case studies and the experiments. Section 4 explains the case studies as well as the experimentation process. In Sect. 5 we analyze the results. Finally, in Sect. 6, we show the conclusions we have reached and our future work.

2   Related Work

This section shows the most relevant related works.

In [10], Lu et al. show the potential benefits of a "quality-based" adaptation approach for video applications. They discuss the joint impact of packet loss and encoding rate on video quality, based on which a simple quality feedback-control system has been built. Adaptation is carried out by measuring the quality of the received video and comparing it to a baseline reference. Their preliminary experimental results show both the viability and the benefits of using video quality as the basis of adaptation. Lee et al. [11] introduced an IP Multimedia Subsystem (IMS) based testbed which provides a platform for the study of real-time services integration and orchestration. This open-source based testbed is built on the principle of Service Oriented Architecture (SOA), with an emphasis for real-time network services. They developed service-oriented system functionalities such as optical network connection and bandwidth management, mobile client authentication protocols, and video streaming services. They are packaged as interoperable service components, so that they can be integrated and orchestrated through their respective standard interfaces. Finally, they elaborated a proof-of-concept environment via a use-case scenario of having various client-server interactions over a heterogeneous network environment. The work presented by Mu et al. in [12] introduces a system where digital video can be corrupted according to established loss patterns and the effect is measured automatically. The corrupted video is then used as input for user tests. Their results are analyzed and compared with the automatically generated. Within this paper they present the complete testing system that makes use of existing software as well as introducing new modules and extensions. The system can test packet loss in H.264 coded video streams and produce a statistical analysis detailing the results. The user tests can also be used to test the effectiveness of the objective video quality assessment models. Thus, the testbed is designed to provide a common testing platform on which objective and subjective evaluations can be performed with different testing scenarios (such as codec, transmission pattern) with the least human intervention (in terms of set-up and analysis). In [13], Kuwadekar et al. present the performance results obtained on a IP Multimedia Subsystem (IMS) based Next Generation Network test-setup connected to a live operator network. These results are based on the Quality of Experience (QoE) that end user perceive. They can help service operators to deliver content rich applications to the end users as per their expectations. The aim of this work was to understand, with a series of experiment, the behavior of video streaming across various devices and changing network conditions. Through passive measurements, they characterized the behavior of video streaming and evaluated the users QoE.

3 Description of the Test Bench Design

In order to perform the test bench design, we have taken into account the current technologies used by service providers and the usual features of the networks focused on video streaming. The equipment include a Cisco 2811 Router, a Cisco Catalyst 3560 Switch WS-C3560-24PS-E, a Cisco AIR-AP 1231G-E-K9 Access Point, 3 PC's with Intel Core Processor i5-2400, CPU @3.10 GHz, 4 GB Memory RAM, Wireless adapter LINKSYS WUSB600N and Ethernet Intel 82579V gigabit network connection and Win7 Operative System, and 1 PC with Intel Core Processor i5-2400 CPU @3.10 GHz, 4 GB Memory RAM, Wireless adapter Cisco AIR-PI21AG-E-K9, 802.11 a/b/g, Ethernet Intel 82579V gigabit network connection; and Windows XP Professional Service Pack 3 Operative System. The video used to perform the test was the Big Buck Bunny, Sunflower version, which is accessible at [14]. We use FFmpeg program [15] to encode the video with the following features: video time 35 s, encoded in H.264 [16], with a resolution of 1024 × 768 at 30 fps (frames per second) and a bitrate of 1338 Kbps. We use VLC media player, version 2.1.3, for both server and client. To capture and analyze network parameters, under the Real Time Protocol (RTP), we use Wireshark, version 1.10.5. The main analyzed parameters are the delay (interval between two consecutive packets), jitter (deviation of each packet with respect to the latency), packet loss and BW (bandwidth).

3.1 Physical Topology

The proposed topology consists of different LANs connected by serial interfaces. The LANs use IEEE 802.3 and IEEE 802.11 technology, while the serial connections use ISO 3309 and ISO 4335 (HDLC) technology. We used Routers Cisco 2811 to connect the LANs. In the LANs we used switches Cisco Catalyst 3560-24PS, which support IEEE 802.1q protocol and Cisco PVST + (Plus per vlan spanning tree). We configured the switch interfaces in different VLANs for each end user. The proposed physical topology can be observed in Fig. 1.

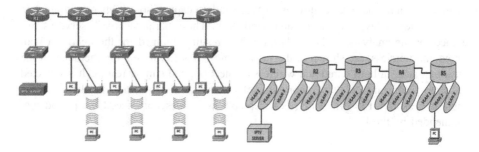

Fig. 1. Proposed physical topology   **Fig. 2.** Proposed logical topology

3.2 Logical Topology

The logical topology used VLANs, which allow building networks even when they are not sharing the same physical medium. The proposed logical topology can be observed in Fig. 2.

4 Cases of Study and Experimentation

In this section we develop a testbed for media streaming, which allow us to perform a series of actions based on network parameters, both internal and external, in order to evaluate the influence on the quality of the received video. The study is divided as follows: first we extract the base line on video streams both wired and wireless, then, we study the effect on the external and external parameters in such streaming.

4.1 Base Line Study in Wired/Wireless Video Delivery

For the study of the base line we used an IPTV server located at five hops between the VLC Clients (one in the wireless and another in the wired LAN), as shown in Fig. 3. This study allows evaluating the quality of video in the reception when there is no internal or external factor affecting the transmission delivery. At the reception, we use Wireshark to capture and evaluate the network parameters.

Fig. 3. Transmission from an IPTV server to a VLC Client (wireless or wired).

We conduct a series of experiments using this network design to gather measurements of network parameters. They will be the basis for analyzing and comparing them with respect to other study case. For the extraction of these measures we have delivered video through the network and we used Wireshark to capture some network parameters such as jitter, delay, packet loss and bandwidth. These parameters will serve as reference for the analysis of the study case. The results obtained for the delay, in both wired and wireless, are shown in the Figs. 4 and 5. As can it be seen, the delay at the customer side, in both wired and wireless connection, had similar results. It is detected an almost constant delay of approximately 18 ms along the time. Furthermore the highest peak has 130 ms, which is acceptable as it does not exceed the period recommended by the ITU.

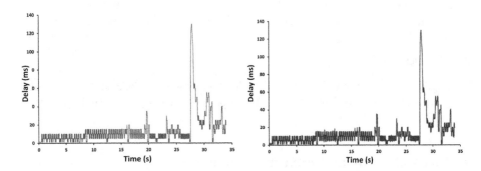

Fig. 4. Delay of the wired baseline.   **Fig. 5.** Delay of the wireless baseline.

Figures 6 and 7 show the jitter at VLC clients side. The results show a peak of 5.5 ms at the beginning of the reception of the video until it stabilizes. Then, the graph follows an almost constant pattern that reaches a value of approximately of 2.5 ms.

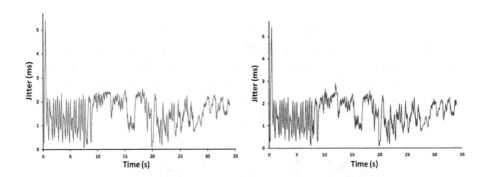

Fig. 6. Jitter of the wired base line.   **Fig. 7.** Jitter of the wireless base line.

To estimate the bandwidth over the time, we calculated at each instant the average bandwidth consumed by the last 50 packets received. Considering that the average size of the transmitted packet is 1370 bytes, the bandwidth BW_t at time T_t in which is received the 'i' packet is calculated by the Eq. (1).

$$BW_i = \frac{N^\circ \, bits}{Time \; interval} = \frac{1370 * 50 * 100000}{(T_i - T_{i-50}) * 1000} \tag{1}$$

Where, T_{i-50} indicates the time instant reception of packet number 'i−50'. Factors 100000 and 1000 have been included to normalize the time, which originally are given in tens of microseconds, and bits units respectively, so that the result is displayed in Kbps. Figures 8 and 9 show the estimated bandwidth timely manner at each instant of time. It is possible to observe that in both cases, the mean values consumed at the reception, for both wired and wireless network, range approximately 2 Mbps. It also exists values that can exceed 9 Mbps. Finally, remark with respect to the loss of packets, that all transmitted packets (5092 packets), have been successfully received. This data will also be included in the baseline. Since neither losses of packages nor mistakes exist in the transmission, we obtained an optimal quality of video reception.

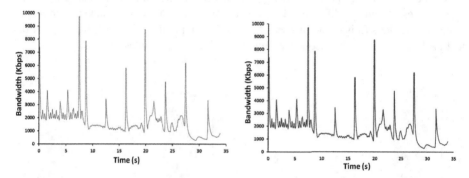

Fig. 8. Bandwidth wired base line.   **Fig. 9.** Bandwidth wireless base line.

4.2 Study of the Internal Network Parameters and the Transmission Effects

In this section we study the effect on the multimedia traffic. Concretely, we study, the video quality perceived when we modify internal parameters of the network configuration and protocols such as the transmission rate of WAN links, and when we decrease the available bandwidth by increasing other traffic type.

(1) *Effects of Speed Transmission in WAN Links - Point to Point*

In this first case study we measure the video reception, in both wired and wireless environments, by varying the transmission speed of the WAN links. The values of the bandwidth selected for the study are 2 Mbps, 4 Mbps and 5.3 Mbps. The design proposed for the studio is observed in Fig. 10.

After the analysis of the network parameters captured during video delivery through the WAN links at different speeds, we obtained the following results. Regarding the delay, we observe that at a transmission speed of 2 Mbps in the WAN links, the average value obtained is 6.2 ms. However, for 4 Mbps and 5.3 Mbps the

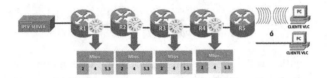

Fig. 10. Transmission from the IPTV server to the VLC Client using different WAN links.

average was 7.36 ms, in both wired and wireless (it is shown in Fig. 11). Concerning the jitter, we obtain different values for wired than wireless. For a transmission rate of 2 Mbps in WAN links, the obtained average results are superior when the links are 5.3 Mbps and 4 Mbps, as it can be observed in Fig. 12.

To determine the average percentage of lost packets, we performed the following calculations. First, we subtracted the sequence of packets between the last and the first visible package. Then, the number of packets is obtained, which in this case is 5092. Later, we estimated the difference between the sequence number of packets minus the number of packets (this is the number of lost packets). Finally, we divide the number of lost packets by the packet sequence, thus obtaining the percentage of lost packets.

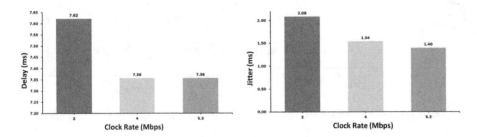

Fig. 11. Average delay at different transmission speeds in the WAN links.

Fig. 12. Average jitter at different transmission speeds in the WAN links.

We can see in Fig. 13 that with a transmission rate of 2 Mbps at WAN links, the average percentage of lost packets is 3.44% for wired environments, and 3.48% for wireless. For a transmission speed of 4 Mbps and 5.3 Mbps in WAN links, we obtained an overall average of 0%. This means that there are no packet losses for both cases in the reception. Given that there is a percentage of loss in estimating the transmission speed of 2 Mbps WAN link, we evaluate in this particular case which is the number of packets lost during the delivery and thus make a proper balance.

In Fig. 14, it is shown the average bandwidth of the video streams obtained when we vary the transmission speed in WAN links at 2 Mbps, 4 Mbps and 5.3 Mbps. For a WAN link with 2 Mbps, there was an average value of 2181 Kbps. For 4 Mbps and 5.3 Mbps we observed an average value of 2456 Kbps.

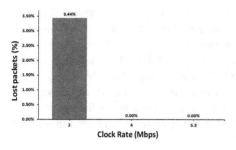

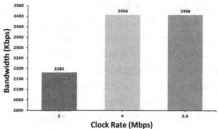

Fig. 13. Average lost packets for different transmission speeds of the WAN links.

Fig. 14. Average bandwidth for different transmission speeds of the WAN links.

5   Result Analysis

In this section, we analyze the results we have obtained in the previous section. We carry out an analysis of the statistical variance to compare the effect of the studied parameters in relation to the base line in order to test the null hypothesis H0 defined in each case. The null hypothesis H0 is defined as follows. H0 is met when there is no statistically significant difference among the parameters: average latency, jitter, packet loss or bandwidth of each measure compared to those in the baseline. A value of $\alpha = 0.01$ is established to carry out the calculation. We focus our study only on the analysis of the internal parameters in multimedia transmissions, because the results of the effect of external ones have not been conclusive. We compare the results obtained in these cases with the baseline.

In this case, we change the transmission speed of the WAN links in the wired LAN and study the QoS parameters. The statistical calculations summary of the delay is shown in Table 1. If we establish the transmission speed of the WAN links to 2Mbps the average delay value is 7.62 ms. Statistically, it shows a significant difference, but from the point of view of QoS, it may be considered negligible or insignificant. Likewise, we cannot exclude the results with the other experimental conditions: 4 Mbps and 5.3 Mbps. Therefore, it indicates that with those values an increment of the link bandwidth does not affect the latency behavior respect to the one obtained in the baseline. In Table 2, we show the summary of the statistical calculations for the jitter. The average jitter value is 2.08 ms. when we establish the transmission speed of the WAN link to 2 Mbps and 1.54 ms when we establish it to 4 Mbps. The jitter obtained for 2 Mbps and 4 Mbps is out of the confidence interval range established in the baseline measure. Therefore, we found in this experiment, with a 99.9% of guarantee, that when the transmission rate of the WAN links is 2 Mbps or 4 Mbps, there is a significant increase of the jitter. Likewise, the jitter when there is a transmission speed of 5.3 Mbps in the WAN links is 1.40 ms. There is a significant difference from the statistical point of view. However, we consider it negligible from the viewpoint of the QoS. The summary of the statistical calculations for packet loss in shown in Table 3. The average value of packet loss is 3.46% when the transmission speed of the WAN links is established to 2 Mbps. That value is out of the confidence interval range established in the baseline measure. Therefore, we found in this experimental condition, with a 99.9% of guarantee, that when the transmission speed of the WAN links is 2 Mbps, there is a significant increase in the number of packet loss. We cannot exclude the difference of the other experiments: 4 Mbps and 5.3 Mbps. They indicate that an increment of the bandwidth in the WAN link, respect to those initially shown in the baseline, does not affect to the packet loss. To sum up, in this first case, we can see that the transmission is affected when the transmission speed of the WAN links is reduced to 2 Mbps. The most affected parameter is the packet loss. Jitter is affected in a lesser grade. Delay is not affected.

Table 1. Study of the delay when comparing the baseline with different transmission speeds of the WAN Links.

Transmission speed of WAN links (Mbps.)	Network parameters		Statistical parameters		
	Number of packets (bytes)	Delay (ms)	Standard deviation (ms)	Subhead	
				Min. (ms)	Max. (ms)
Base Line	5092	7.36	7.10	7.10	7.61
2	4917	7.62	5.76	7.41	7.83
4	5092	7.36	6.86	7.11	7.60
5.3	5092	7.36	7.03	7.10	7.61

Table 2. Study of the jitter when comparing the baseline with different transmission speeds of the WAN Links.

Transmission speed of WAN links (Mbps.)	Network parameters		Statistical parameters		
	Number of packets (bytes)	Jitter (ms)	Standard deviation (ms)	Subhead	
				Min. (ms)	Max. (ms)
Base Line	5092	1.37	0.70	1.34	1.39
2	4917	2.08	1.55	2.03	2.14
4	5092	1.54	0.83	1.51	1.57
5.3	5092	1.40	0.75	1.37	1.42

Table 3. Study of the packet loss when comparing the baseline with different transmission speeds of the WAN Links.

Transmission speed of WAN links (Mbps.)	Network parameters		Statistical parameters		
	Number of packets (bytes)	Packet loss (ms)	Standard deviation (ms)	Subhead	
				Min. (ms)	Max. (ms)
Base Line	5092	0.00	0.00	0.00	0.00
2	4917	3.46	18.27	2.79	4.13
4	5092	0.00	0.00	0.00	0.00
5.3	5092	0.00	0.00	0.00	0.00

6   Conclusion

We have implemented a test bench to observe both the network traffic QoS parameters variations of the received video and the impact in the image quality due to the network parameters variations. We have designed, assembled and configured a WAN network for multimedia traffic transmission. To carry out the test we have used routers, switches, PCs and an access point. We have obtained measurements from the test bench and we have analyzed the significant differences in order to evaluate the QoS parameters basing it on a variance statistical analysis of the different study cases.

We have noticed a significant packet loss when the WAN point-to-point links transmission speed values decrease to near the video transmission average bandwidth (2 Mbps). Some significant changes (but less) are also noticed in the jitter. Delay parameter is not significantly affected.

The study results show that service operators should have both video and QoS tests, in order to have a data transmission statistical database (video, voice, etc.). As far as multimedia communication services demand tends to grow every day, it is necessary to deliver reliability and confidence to customers in order to offer them a good QoS. Therefore, that testbech should be able to reproduce the conditions in both wired and wireless environments.

In future works we intend to use the testbench defined to test the received video quality using different types of queues, video streaming applications quality, and different video codecs performance and quality after the transmission. Moreover, due to the proliferation of the video streaming applications for Content Delivery Networks (CDNs), Peer-to-Peer (P2P) networks, Multimedia Cloud Computing, etc., we will use the implemented testbench in new streaming applications. In addition, it will allow us to test on any device (laptops, phones, etc.) the performance and quality of different video and audio codecs after transmission [17].

References

1. Lloret, J., Garcia, M., Atenas, M., Canovas, A.: A QoE management system to improve the IPTV network. Int. J. Commun Syst **24**(1), 118–138 (2011)
2. Garcia, M., Canovas, A., Edo, M., Lloret, J.: A QoE management system for ubiquitous IPTV devices. In: The Third International Conference on Mobile Ubiquitous Computing, Systems, Services and Technologies, UBICOMM 2009, Sliema, Malta, 11–16 October 2009
3. Álvarez, A., Pozueco, L., Cabrero, S., García Pañeda, X., García, R., Melendi, D., Díaz Orueta, G.: Adaptive streaming: a subjective catalog to assess the performance of objective QoE metrics. Netw. Protoc. Algorithms **6**(2), 123–136 (2014)
4. Jimenez, J.M., Romero, O., Rego, A., Dilendra, A., Lloret, J.: Study of multimedia delivery over software defined networks. Netw. Protoc. Algorithms **7**(4), 37–62 (2015)
5. Recomendation UIT/T G.1010: End-user multimedia QoS categories (2001). https://www.itu.int/rec/T-REC-G.1010-200111-I/en
6. Recomendation UIT R M.1079-2: Performance and quality of service requirements for International Mobile Telecommunications-2000 (IMT-2000) access networks. https://www.itu.int/dms_pubrec/itu-r/rec/m/R-REC-M.1079-2-200306-I!!PDF-E.pdf

7. Garcia, M., Lloret, J., Edo, M., Lacuesta, R.: IPTV distribution network access system using WiMAX and WLAN technologies. In: Proceedings of the 4th Edition of the UPGRADE-CN Workshop on Use of P2P GRID and Agents for the Development of Content Networks, Munich, Germany, 11–13 June 2009

8. Atenas, M., Sendra, S., Garcia, M., Lloret, J.: IPTV performance in IEEE 802.11 n WLANs. In: IEEE GLOBECOM Workshops 2010, Miami, USA, pp. 929–933, December 2010

9. Cisco Systems Inc. Cisco's Visual Networking Index Forecast Projects Nearly Half the World's Population Will Be Connected to the Internet by 2017. http://newsroom.cisco.com/press-release-content?articleId=1197391

10. Lu, X., Tao, S., El Zarki, M., Guérin, R.: Quality based Adaptive Video Over the Internet. Department of ESE, University of Pennsylvania, Philadelphia, PA 19104 (2003)

11. Lee, T.K., Chai, T.Y., Ngoh, L.H., Shao, X., Teo, J.C.M., Zhou, L.: An IMS-based testbed for real-time services integration and orchestration. In: IEEE Asia-Pacific Services Computing Conference (APSCC 2009), Singapore, 7–11 December 2009

12. Mu, M., Mauthe, A., Casson, J., Tyson, G., Garcia, F.: LA1 TestBed: evaluation testbed to assess the impact of network impairments on video quality. In: 5th International Conference on Testbeds and Research Infrastructures for the Development of Networks & Communities and Workshops (TridentCom 2009), Washington, DC, 6–8 April 2009

13. Kuwadekar, A., Al-Begain, K.: User centric quality of experience testing for video on demand over IMS. In: First International Conference on Computational Intelligence, Communication Systems and Networks (CICSYN 2009), Indore, India, 23–25 July 2009

14. Downline Guide, Big Buck Bunny, Sunflower version. http://bbb3d.renderfarming.net/download.html

15. FFmpeg. http://www.ffmpeg.org/about.html

16. Sullivan, G.J., Wiegand, T.: Video compression - from concepts to the H.264/AVC standard. Proc. IEEE 93(1), 18–31 (2005)

17. Estepa, A.J., Estepa, R., Vozmediano, J., Carrillo, P.: Dynamic VoIP codec selection on smartphones. Netw. Protoc. Algorithms 6(2), 22–37 (2014)

QoS and QoE on Networks

Direct Feature Point Correspondence Discovery for Multiview Images: An Alternative Solution When SIFT-Based Matching Fails

Jinwei Xu[1]([⊠]) and Jiankun Hu[2]

[1] Marketing Analytics and Insight, Data2Decisions, Sydney, NSW 2000, Australia
link.xu.job@gmail.com
[2] School of Engineering and Information Technology,
The University of New South Wales, Canberra, ACT 2600, Australia
j.hu@adfa.edu.au

Abstract. 3D fingerprint identification is an emerging biometric authentication method, which is powerful against spoofing attacks. For actualizing 3D fingerprint identification, this paper develops a 3D fingerprint minutiae cloud reconstruction technique based on 2D multiview touchless fingerprint images. This technique provides a practical solution for 2D minutiae matching for multiview fingerprint images, when traditional feature correspondence finding based on 2D SIFT (Scale Invariant Feature Transformation) feature points fails. In this case, developing a new 2D feature point correspondence establishment algorithm is necessary to cover the deficiency of the SIFT-based technique. In this paper, minutiae, a type of detailed ridge-valley features in fingerprint images, are utilized for the correspondence discovery. Furthermore, differential evolution, an efficient evolutionary computing framework is employed to directly infer the possible correspondence of minutiae sets from the different posed fingerprint images. Our experiments demonstrate that the proposed direct 2D feature point correspondence discovery strategy is able to handle the cases when the SIFT-based matching fails. To further illustrate the advantages of the proposed algorithm, 3D fingerprint minutiae cloud construction is conducted based on the feature correspondence discovered by the proposed algorithm. The experiments on 2D different posed fingerprint image matching and 3D fingerprint minutiae cloud construction show that the proposed algorithm can be used as an alternation when SIFT-based matching fails.

Keywords: 3D fingerprint reconstruction · Feature matching · Minutiae cloud · Differential evolution

1 Introduction

3D fingerprint identification system is an emerging biometric authentication method, which is powerful for anti-spoofing attacks. Beyond 2D image domain, finger object built on point cloud and curved surface can be displayed within 3D

© ICST Institute for Computer Sciences, Social Informatics and Telecommunications Engineering 2017
S. Guo et al. (Eds.): TridentCom 2016, LNICST 177, pp. 137–147, 2017.
DOI: 10.1007/978-3-319-49580-4_13

space, which provides more stereo sense [5]. Being different from traditional 2D fingerprint identification systems, 3D fingerprint identification systems hold the following advantages.

– **Contactless Fingerprint Image Acquisition:** Traditional 2D fingerprint images have to be captured by placing, pressing or rolling fingers against optical scanning devices or finger trace cards. Such operations usually result in distorted, incomplete and low resolution fingerprint images. Instead, 3D fingerprint imaging systems provide contactless scanning setting, which directly prevent finger from touching imaging devices. The resultant fingerprint images are non-distorted, complete, multi-posed and resolution guaranteed. The 2D multi-posed fingerprint images captured by 3D fingerprint imaging system are shown in Fig. 1.

– **Man-made Finger Model Prevention:** Traditional 2D fingerprint identification systems are being challenged by man-made finger models in recent years. That is, the imposter finger models, which are made by printing finger ridge-valley patterns onto rubber, plastic, and other soft materials, are intended to fool the 2D fingerprint identification systems. Consequently, the 2D fingerprint identification systems are unable to distinguish whether the fingers under investigation are genuine human fingers. On the contrary, 3D fingerprint identification systems can easily validate whether the investigated fingers are artificially made ones.

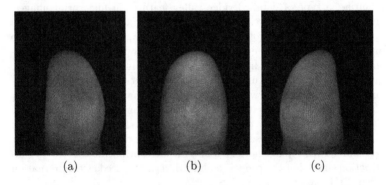

    (a)   (b)   (c)

Fig. 1. 2D Multi-posed fingerprint images (left thumb): (a) left lateral view; (b) frontal view; and (c) right lateral view.

3D fingerprint construction process plays an essential role for 3D fingerprint identification system. Within 3D fingerprint identification system, the target finger can be captured by multiple built-in cameras. Since these built-in cameras are differently posed, the resultant pictures are differently posed. To generate 3D finger model, 3D construction process works on the obtained multi-posed 2D images [2,4]. To be explicit, as an initial step, correspondence between different posed images should be discovered. In most cases, the correspondence discovery depends on feature points obtained by specific feature point detection method such as SIFT. Afterward, based on the discovered correspondence in 2D domain, the spatial coordinates for the detected feature points in 3D space are calculated by 3D triangle reconstruction. Furthermore, other points' 2D correspondence can be inferred based on the prior correspondence establishment. Then their 3D coordinates are also calculated via 3D triangle reconstruction. At the end, the point cloud can be generated and it is further used to form the curved surface of the 3D finger model [1,3].

For discovering feature level correspondence between two differently posed images, SIFT is one of the most popular methods. After SIFT point detection process, the image points, whose multi-scale Gaussian filtering response are salient, are labeled as feature points. For each individual feature point, it holds a high-dimension feature vector. Such feature vector is a summary of local gradient information in terms of gradient magnitude and direction. Furthermore, two points whose feature vectors have higher similarity are matched between different images, while two points with lower feature vector similarity are not matched. The correspondence between different images is discovered via the matched feature points [5]. For fingerprint images, however, the feature vectors are generally similar, as the local regions centered at every feature points have very similar ridge-valley structures (the local summarized gradient information are also very similar). Such local structure similarity significantly reduces the discrimination of the feature vector-based matching. Therefore, massive mismatches happen between the different posed fingerprint images. In this case, the SIFT-based feature point matching approach is unable to work. Figure 2 shows an example when SIFT-based feature matching method is applied to the left and frontal images in Fig. 1.

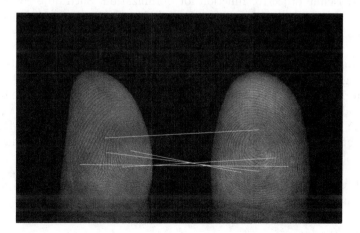

Fig. 2. An example: SIFT-based feature matching method fails to find the correspondence between the left and frontal views in Fig. 1.

For covering the SIFT deficiency, we propose a direct feature point correspondence discovery algorithm based on evolutionary computing in this paper. As an initial step, the minutiae in fingerprint images are utilized instead of using the SIFT feature points. Furthermore, the proposed technique treats the feature point matching problem as the optimization problem. To maximize the number of the matched feature points between two images, differential evolution, a fast searching evolutionary computing algorithm is adopted. The rest of this paper is organized as follows: in Sect. 2, the differential evolution-based minutiae matching method is introduced; in Sect. 3, the experiments for 2D different posed minutiae set matching and 3D minutiae point cloud construction are conducted; in Sect. 4, the conclusion and future research directions are given.

2 Proposed Method

The minutiae matching process can be regarded as the process to search for more and more mated minutiae points from differently posed fingerprint images. To actualize this process, we utilize differential evolution algorithm [6,7]. A summary for the proposed differential evolution-based minutiae matching program is provided as follows.

- **Step 1:** Input two differently imposed 2D fingerprint images.
- **Step 2:** Employ Verifinger SDK to extract minutiae points for input images. The outputs obtained from Verifinger SDK are minutiae points' coordinates in 2D image domain.
- **Step 3:** Generate fundamental matrix and initially set up its elements. These elements belonging to the fundamental matrix are treated as the parameters which need to be optimized by the differential evolution algorithm. Also, the generated fundamental matrix must be a rank-two matrix.
- **Step 4:** Define objective function for optimization. Such objective function is required to represent the underlying relationship between the fundamental matrix's elements and the number of the matched minutiae points for both images.
- **Step 5:** Define epipolar constraint and spatial constraint for point-to-point matching.
- **Step 6:** Iteratively run the differential evolution algorithm until the termination conditions are satisfied.
- **Step 7:** Export the optimized fundamental matrix's parameters. Based on these optimized parameters, the minutiae point correspondence relationship can be obtained.

To be explicit, the technical details involved in each individual step are described as follows.

2.1 Minutiae Extraction

Minutiae extraction is the first step for the subsequent procedures. To ensure the reliability of the extracted minutiae points, Verifinger SDK, a widely used

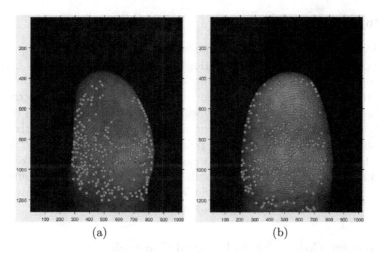

(a)   (b)

Fig. 3. The extracted minutiae by Verifinger SDK for the left and frontal views in Fig. 1: (a) left view's minutiae points; and (b) frontal view's minutiae points.

commercial software development kit for biometric applications, is employed in this paper. We believe that VeriFinger SDK is the most reliable minutiae extractor in public domain as far as we know. For the multi-posed fingerprint images captured by the 3D imaging system, we cannot find any other softwares or computer programs for fingerprint minutiae detection and extraction, which can be competitive or even better than VeriFinger SDK. Figure 3 shows the extracted minutiae for the left and frontal views in Fig. 1 respectively.

2.2 Fundamental Matrix

Fundamental matrix is a core concept in computer vision system, which explains projective geometric relationship for associated 2D objects. Also, the fundamental matrix is a low-rank matrix whose dimension is 3×3 and rank should be equal to two. This strict equality imposed on the matrix rank to regulate the epipolar lines in one view can be converged into a point (such point is called epipole). To guarantee the fundamental matrix's rank equals to two, the following matrix decomposition strategy is applied.

$$F = A \cdot B = \begin{bmatrix} A_1 & A_2 \\ A_3 & A_4 \\ A_5 & A_6 \end{bmatrix} \cdot \begin{bmatrix} B_1 & B_2 & B_3 \\ B_4 & B_5 & B_6 \end{bmatrix} \tag{1}$$

where the elements in matrixes A (dimension 3×2) and B (dimension 2×3) can be assigned by arbitrary numeric values (all zeros are exceptional) and $rank(F) = 2$. Due to the multiplication between A and B, the number of the parameters which need to be optimized for F is twelve.

2.3   Objective Function

The objective function pushes the differential evolution algorithm approaching to the optimal parameters and solutions. By evaluating individual fitness in whole population, the algorithm is not only to preserve the individuals with higher fitness but also to weed out the ones with lower fitness. To better drives the differential evolution algorithm to work towards the optimum, an objective function which can map the twelve parameters for fundamental matrix F onto the number of the matched minutiae points is created. In this sense, the increment of the matched minutiae points can positively feedback the evolution of the parameter's values. When the maximal number of the matched minutiae is achieved, it means the differential evolution algorithm has already converged to the optimal solutions for the target parameters.

2.4   Epipolar Constraint and Spatial Constraint

Both epipolar and spatial constraints are required to be considered simultaneously to avoid invalid solutions for target parameters during differential evolution searching process. Figure 4 illustrates how the epipolar constraint works.

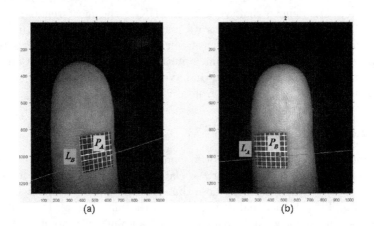

Fig. 4. An example to show how the epipolar constraint works.

In Fig. 4, the images are captured from left and frontal views respectively. A point, located at the same position of the chessboard, appears in the two different views. We denote it as P_A in left view image and P_B in frontal view image. Under the projective transformation of the fundamental matrix, P_A is projected into an epipolar line L_A in the frontal view image and P_B is mapped to an epipolar line L_B in the left view image. In the left view image, the epipolar line L_B passes through P_A. Also, in the frontal view image, the epipolar line L_A passes through P_B. This observation evidences a very important characteristic for the fundamental matrix. It demonstrates that P_A can be matched against

P_B when P_A's epipolar line passing through P_B. This important characteristic directs the differential evolution algorithm to seek for the points, whose epipolar lines should pass through another view's points. Mathematically, a valid point-to-point match should be counted when the following condition is satisfied.

$$[P_B, 1] \cdot F \cdot [P_A, 1]^T = [P_B, 1] \cdot L_A = 0 \qquad (2)$$

where $P_A = \left[P_A^{(x)}, P_A^{(y)} \right]$ and $P_B = \left[P_B^{(x)}, P_B^{(y)} \right]$ (dimension 1×2).

Being different from the epipolar constraint, spatial constraint only focuses on the minutiae points' relative locations in both horizontal and vertical directions. Figure 5 shows how the horizontal spatial constraint works. For the horizontal-axis constraint, the matched minutiae points' relative shifts along horizontal-axis should be the same. The point relative shift is calculated according to the following formula. In Fig. 5, the yellow and pink reference lines are determined according to the fingertip.

$$\tilde{x}_{point} = \frac{x_{point} - x_{yellow}}{x_{pink} - x_{yellow}} \qquad (3)$$

where $\tilde{x}_{point}$ is the horizontal relative shift of the minutiae point. x_{point}, x_{yellow} and x_{pink} stand for the x coordinates for the minutiae point, the yellow reference line and the pink reference line respectively.

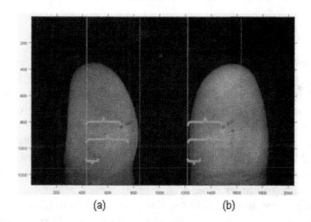

(a)   (b)

Fig. 5. An example to show how the horizontal spatial constraint works. (Color figure online)

Besides, Fig. 6 exhibits how the vertical spatial constraint works. For the vertical-axis constraint, the matched minutiae points' y coordinates should be the same. That is, the matched minutiae points' heights are at the same level in image domain.

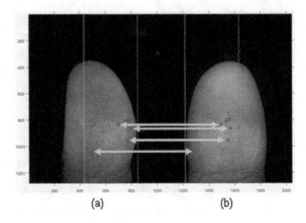

Fig. 6. An example to show how the vertical spatial constraint works.

3   Experiments

To validate the feasibility and effectiveness of the proposed direct minutiae matching algorithm, we conduct the following two experiments: (i) the minutiae point level's correspondence discovery between two differently posed 2D fingerprint images; and (ii) minutiae point cloud construction within 3D space.

3.1   Minutiae Point Correspondence Discovery

The data set used for this study is collected from the internal volunteers from the University of New South Wales. This data set consists of 150 volunteers' 3D fingerprint imaging records. Each volunteer case includes 10 fingers from left palm to right palm. For each single finger, we capture its left, frontal and right view images by 3 built-in cameras in 3D fingerprint imaging system. For ensuring robustness and reliability, we scan every single finger twice. In total, we collect $60 = 10 \times 3 \times 2$ 2D fingerprint images for each volunteer. Afterwards, we extract the minutiae points by using VeriFinger SDK. Therefore, we obtain 60 minutiae point files for each volunteer case.

As an example, we demonstrate the minutiae point matching results in Fig. 7. The result shown in Fig. 7(a) is obtained based on a single run of the proposed algorithm. To search for more matched minutiae points, Monte Carlo simulation based on multiple runs is conducted (the result is shown in Fig. 7(b)). For each independent trial, the proposed differential evolution-based algorithm starts with a group of randomly initialized solutions. The randomly initialized solutions could be different for each independent run, since the random number generator built in the differential evolution approach works on the different random number seed every time. The Monte Carlo simulation repeatedly runs the proposed algorithm to make sure the randomly initialized solutions could be uniformly distributed. After multiple runs, we aggregate the final result by selecting the

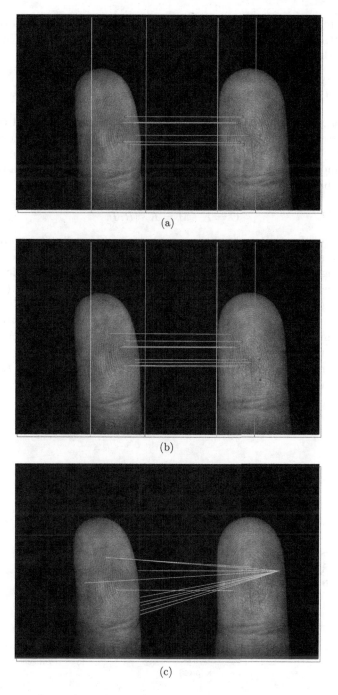

Fig. 7. An example to show the results after running the proposed direct minutiae point matching algorithm for a right index finger. Also the SIFT matching result is compared: (a) a single run result; (b) an aggregated result after multiple runs; and (c) SIFT matching result.

repeatedly matched minutiae pairs. Compared with the results achieved by the proposed algorithm, the feature point correspondence discovered by SIFT is unreliable (the result is shown in Fig. 7(c)).

3.2 Minutiae Point Cloud Construction

The minutiae point cloud construction is based on the minutiae point correspondence discovered in Sect. 3.1. To calculate minutiae points' spatial coordinates in 3D space, camera parameter matrix for the built-in camera in the 3D fingerprint imaging system is firstly necessary. Mathematically, the camera parameter matrix can be denoted as follows.

$$C = K \cdot M = K \cdot [R, T] \tag{4}$$

where C stands for the camera parameter matrix. K is a 3×3 camera internal parameter matrix, which can be obtained via camera calibration based on chessboard testing. M ia a 3×3 camera external parameter matrix, which contains two components: (i) camera pose matrix R (dimension 3×3); and (ii) camera shift vector T (dimension 3×1). The camera pose matrix R is determined by the camera's rotations $(\theta_x, \theta_y, \theta_z)$ along x, y and z axis in 3D coordinate system. The camera shift vector $T = [T_x, T_y, T_z]$ is the bias apart from the origin in 3D coordinate system. The values for $(\theta_x, \theta_y, \theta_z, T_x, T_y, T_z)$ are given by the manufacturer of the used 3D fingerprint imaging system, therefore the camera external parameter matrix M can be calculated.

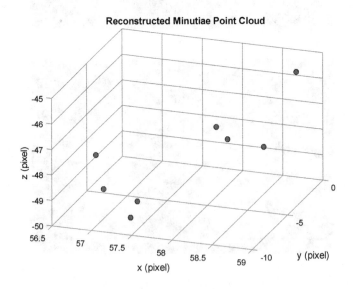

Fig. 8. An example to show the constructed 3D minutiae point cloud based on the calculated camera parameter matrixes and the discovered minutiae point correspondence in Fig. 7(b).

Furthermore, given the camera parameter matrixes and the minutiae points correspondence in Fig. 7(b), the minutiae points' 3D coordinates can be computed via triangulation reconstruction method. As an example, we demonstrate the resultant 3D minutiae point cloud in Fig. 8.

4   Conclusion and Future Work

This paper proposes a novel minutiae point correspondence discovery strategy based on differential evolution for 3D fingerprint imaging system. Such algorithm can be adopted to align the minutiae point set in one view against the point set in another one. As an alternative solution for tackling the feature point level matching, this algorithm is able to produce reliable matching result, when the SIFT-based matching approach cannot work at all. Furthermore, this algorithm can solidly support the subsequent 3D minutiae cloud construction. The effectiveness and superiority of the proposed algorithm are evidenced by the experiments.

However, the proposed algorithm still needs to be further improved in the following aspects: (i) the number of the matched minutiae pairs are still limited after taking Monte Carlo simulation; and (ii) the minutiae point matching method in 3D space is in demand.

References

1. Liu, F., Zhang, D.: 3D fingerprint reconstruction system using feature correspondences and prior estimated finger model. Pattern Recogn. **47**, 178–193 (2014)
2. Choi, H., Choi, K., Kim, J.: Mosaicing touchless and mirror-reflected fingerprint images. IEEE Trans. Inf. Forensics Secur. **5**, 52–61 (2010)
3. Liu, F., Zhang, D., Song, C., Lu, G.: Touchless multiview fingerprint acquisition and mosaicking. IEEE Trans. Instrum. Meas. **62**, 2492–2502 (2013)
4. Kumar, A., Kwong, C.: Towards contactless, low-cost and accurate 3D fingerprint identification. IEEE Trans. Pattern Anal. Mach. Intell. **37**, 681–696 (2015)
5. Hartley, R., Zisserman, A.: Multiple View Geometry in Computer Vision. Cambridge University Press, Cambridge (2004)
6. Storn, R., Price, K.: Differential evolution - a simple and efficient heuristic for global optimization over continuous spaces. J. Global Optim. **11**, 341–359 (1997)
7. Qin, A., Huang, V., Suganthan, P.: Differential evolution algorithm with strategy adaptation for global numerical optimization. IEEE Trans. Evol. Comput. **13**, 398–417 (2009)

An Optimized Probabilistic Routing Protocol Based on Scheduling Mechanism for Delay Tolerant Network

Yuxin Mao[1(✉)], Chenqian Zhou[1], and Jaime Lloret[2]

[1] School of Computer and Information Engineering,
Zhejiang Gongshang University, Hangzhou 310018, Zhejiang, China
maoyuxin@zjgsu.edu.cn
[2] Department of Communications, Universidad Politecnica de Valencia,
Valencia, Spain

Abstract. How to achieve efficient data transmission in delay tolerant network (DTN) is an important issue to many wireless or mobile systems. In this study, we propose a new routing protocol to improve delivery rate and optimize delivery delay with low overhead in DTN. We extend the classic PROPHET routing protocol by a scheduling policy to increase delivery rate and reduce delivery delay in DTN. We try to improve the performance of traditional PROPHET from both storage and transmission. Moreover, we evaluate the performance of the scheduling protocol by ONE Simulator. The simulation result illustrates that the proposed protocol is able to achieve better performance compared with the classic protocols like PROPHET and Epidemic in several key aspects.

Keywords: Scheduling mechanism · Routing · Delay Tolerant Network · ONE simulator

1 Introduction

The development of communication technologies and the wide spread of hand-held devices such as smart-phones and tablets have made unstructured wireless networks more and more common. These unstructured networks can be considered as a type of delay/disruption tolerant networks (DTN) [1, 2]. In DTN, when a node (source) intends to deliver messages to another node (destination) but there doesn't exist a fully connected path between them, messages are then forwarded to intermediate nodes. However, the intermediate nodes may not encounter other nodes during a given period of time. Due to the store-carry-forward mechanism, the uncertainty delivery paths, and the dynamic network topology, traditional routing protocols can not work well in this case. Recent years, numerous protocols were proposed to maximize delivery success, such as First Contact [3], Epidemic [4], Spray and Wait [5], PROPHET [6] etc. PROPHET (Probabilistic Routing Protocol using History of Encounters & Transitivity) is a typical routing protocol based on historical data. However, we notice that there exist some drawbacks with PROPHET [6]:

© ICST Institute for Computer Sciences, Social Informatics and Telecommunications Engineering 2017
S. Guo et al. (Eds.): TridentCom 2016, LNICST 177, pp. 148–157, 2017.
DOI: 10.1007/978-3-319-49580-4_14

1. Some delivered messages form source may be damaged by some malicious intermediate nodes.
2. As there are too many intermediate nodes and hops on connected paths, messages are more likely to be aborted.
3. A number of messages may be dropped because of TTL and buffer congestion.

In order to overcome the above drawbacks, we propose a new routing protocol called Scheduling-PROPHET, which can be directly applied to DTN. The protocol is designed to increase the delivery rate, reduce the loss of messages, and improve the efficiency of information transmission in this work. The remainder of the manuscript is organized as follows: Sect. 2 presents the related work. In Sect. 3, we illustrate a new protocol to improve PROPHET routing. Section 4 presents the experimental setting and simulation results. Finally, we conclude the manuscript in Sect. 5.

2 Related Work

There are a series of routing protocols for DTN, each with its own characteristic and optimal goal, and they are suitable for different scenarios. For example, Epidemic [4] is a classic flooding-based protocol that exchanges messages in a simple way that seems like epidemic. This protocol utilizes the movement of nodes to make more connected paths, and increases the delivery rate by replicating messages. To improve routing performance, Lindgren A. et al. considered probabilistic routing and thus proposed PROPHET [6], which is a probabilistic routing protocol computing the probability of success by historical transmission information, and selecting decent intermediate nodes which are more likely (based on past history statistics) to form a reliable path to destination nodes.

In recent years, prediction encountering opportunity and node mobility are two key factors in many new routing protocol design. Many researchers focus on the node movement environment. They consider that the area of nodes' movement and encountering opportunity are closely related to the geographic position at particular time point. For this reason, Anna S. et al. in [7] and W.Z. Li et al. in [8] show the importance of nodes' mobility and distribution in city environment, and try to improve the routing performance. Similarly, Lebrun J. in [9] and Leguay J. in [10] consider that the physical location and mobility behavior of nodes are also common parameters. In [6, 11, 12], protocols used the history of encounters to measure transmission reliability. E. Bulut et al. introduce a new metric called CIT, which computes the average inter-meeting time between two nodes to improve its performance [13]. Some protocols exploit two parameters to improve performance, such as the works in [14–16]. Moreover, some protocols make their decision of transmission by using game theory, such as [17].

3   Proposed Routing Protocol

We present an optimized routing protocol called Scheduling-PROPHET, which improves over PROPHET in buffering and transmission. In this section, we illustrate our assumptions and describe the protocol in detail.

3.1   Network Model

In order to formalize the operation of the Scheduling-PROPHET routing protocol, we first give a basic network model for illustrating the protocol as follows.

Nodes Each node is assumed to have a unique nonzero identifier i, which is bound to a public identity. We assume that each node has a finite buffer space for carrying messages originated from others, but an unlimited buffer for messages generated by itself. The core of our protocol is delivery predictability. When two nodes encounter each other within communication range, the delivery predictability will be calculated.

Transfer As nodes are not always stationary, we assume that the transfer opportunity is limited in both duration and bandwidth. When two nodes encounter, the number of messages they can transfer is confined. Under communication range, nodes are able to discover each other, and transmit messages to each other.

Storage As nodes receive messages from others, each node must manage its limited buffer space by assigning priority to messages and selecting messages to delete according to the protocol. There are only three cases that nodes will delete messages. Case 1: The messages have been transmitted to the destination, which sends ACK to all senders. Then, nodes will remove the messages from their buffer. Case 2: The messages do not have enough time to stay in buffer space. In our evaluations, the TTL of messages is set to 300 s. Case 3: The messages are with the lowest priority when the buffer space is full.

3.2   Protocol Definition

In order to reduce the impact of network failures on delivery predictability, we propose a new routing protocol called Scheduling-PROPHET. The core of Scheduling-PROPHET routing protocol is delivery predictability according to the encountering frequency among nodes.

We use the incremental average value of delivery predictabilities to make the change of delivery predictability more smooth. The calculation model for delivery predictability is given as follows. We establish a probabilistic value called delivery predictability, noted as $P(A, B) \in [0, 1]$. It refers to the probability that node A encounters node B in the network. For each node, it is required to preserve a table to store the information about delivery predictability. When node A encounters node B, they will exchange their table information to determine whether to transfer messages or not. We set an initial value called $P_{init} \in (0, 1]$, which is an initialization constant for each node.

When node A encounters node B, the delivery predictability is calculated by Eq. (1), where $\beta \in (0.5, 1)$.

$$P(A, B)_{new} = P(A, B)_{old} + [1 - P(A, B)_{old}] * \beta \tag{1}$$

After that, the delivery predictabilities of all nodes will be recalculated according to Eq. (2), and N denotes the set of all nodes.

$$P(i, j) = \frac{P(i, j)_{old}}{2}, (i, j \in N) \tag{2}$$

When node A encounters note B for the first time, the delivery predictability is calculated by Eq. (3).

$$P(A, B)_{new} = P_{init} \tag{3}$$

Therefore, P is directly related to the frequency by which they meet each other. According to Eq. (2), if two nodes can't encounter each other, the value of P will be much lower.

In the worst case, forwarding messages to intermediate nodes that rarely encounter the destination node will cause delivery failure. Therefore, we try to calculate the complete delivery predictability from current node to destination node. The complete delivery predictability is calculated by Eq. (4), where $S(i, i+1, \cdots, D)$ denotes the total predictability from current node i to destination node D.

$$S(i, i+1, \cdots, D) = \prod_{x=i}^{D-1} P(x, x+1) \tag{4}$$

From source node A to destination node B, we can get a series of values for $S(i, i+1, \cdots, D)$ by Eq. (4), and then we can choose an appropriate path with the highest value for $S(i, i+1, \cdots, D)$.

3.3   Transmitting Messages

To reduce the number of invalid messages in network and increase successful delivery rate of significant messages, we propose two scheduling mechanisms: Message Management Mechanism and Message-Transfer Mechanism.

(1) Message Management Mechanism: In order to make bandwidth more efficient and save buffer space, we set some criteria to coordinate the priority of in-transit messages. The core of the management involves dropping messages and assigning priority. All nodes in a network are notified by ACK and then remove delivered messages from their buffer. If the messages have lower delivery predictability, we assign lower priority to them in order to restrain their transmission. If the buffer space is full, messages with the lowest priority will be removed to make more room for forth-coming messages.

In this way, the routing protocol avoids generating copies for messages with low priority, and improves the utilization of network resources.

(2) Message-Transfer Mechanism: In Scheduling-PROPHET, when node I encounters node J, node I will transmit messages to node J, and the Messages-Transfer Mechanism is illustrated as follows: Firstly, transmit messages to node J which is the destination of those messages. Secondly, exchange the table which holds the delivery predictabilities of all nodes, and decide the transmission path. The determinate values are complete predictability ($S(i, i+1, \cdots, D)$), the amount of hops of path ($h(i, i+1, \cdots, D)$) and traffic load (tl_i).

The algorithm for the proposed routing protocol to explain the procedure is given below (Algorithm: Scheduling-PROPHET). When two nodes (A and B) encounter, they will exchange their tables with each other, and then Scheduling-PROPHET transmits messages by following the rules shown in the algorithm. Moreover, the notations we have mentioned in this algorithm are shown in Table 1 for convenience.

Table 1. Notations in algorithm.

Notation	Description
A	a node carrying messages(M)
B	a node encountered by A
M	the message node A intends to send
D	the destination of M
K	any other node that is not encountered by A
N	the set of all nodes
L_i	the connected path from source to destination
$S(L_i)$	the complete predictability of L_i

(1) The value of $P(A, B)$ is calculated by Eq. (1), and then all values of P are re-normalized by Eq. (2).

(2) Messages are transmitted to the encountered node based on its priority. Specifically, if node A discovers the destination (node D) of the messages (M), A will transmit M to D firstly. In addition to this, transmission is based on a ranked list of messages stored in nodes.

(3) The message receiver (node D) confirms that it has already received the correct message, and notifies acknowledgement character (ACK) to all senders.

(4) Messages that have not been transferred in the buffer space will be transmitted one by one according to the priority. Scheduling-PROPHET calculates the possible paths (L) from current sender to destination according to the historical delivery predictability. In our protocol, we denote the maximum amount of paths to compare as $\triangle\lambda$. In the meanwhile, each possible path is normalized by Eq. (4). For all paths, we rank them from high predictability to low based on the value of $S(i, i+1, \cdots, D)$. Scheduling-PROPHET selects the path with the highest predictability for transmission.

Algorithm: Scheduling-PROPHET

```
1:  for each node A :
2:    when node A encounters node B , they exchange their tables;
3:    P(A, B)_new = P(A, B)_old + [1 - P(A, B)_old] * β
4:  end for;
5:  for each node pair i and j :
```

$$6: \quad P(i, j) = \frac{P(i, j)_{old}}{2} , \ (i, j \in N)$$

```
7:  end for;
8:  for each message M of A :
9:    if( D == B ){
10:      A forwards M to B ;
11:      D notifies that M has arrived and it can be deleted from all
      node buffers;
12:    }
13:    else{
14:      A exchanges table with B and gains the set of connected paths
      (denoted as L );
15:      if( L ≠ NULL ){
16:        Arrange the paths in L from high to low according to the value
      of S ;
17:        Get the top three paths L₁, L₂, L₃ from L
18:        if( S(L₁) = S(L₂) ☐ S(L₁) = S(L₂) = S(L₃) ){
19:          A calculates the hops of L₁ , L₂ , L₃ respectively;
20:          if( h(L₁) = h(L₂) ☐ h(L₁) = h(L₂) = h(L₃) ){
21:            A compares the traffic load of next hop on L₁, L₂, L₃
      respectively;
22:            A forwards M to the next hop with the least traffic
      load;
23:          }
24:        }
25:        else {
26:          A forwards M according to L₁ ;
27:        }
28:      }
29:      else {
30:        do nothing;
31:      }
32:    }
33:  end for;
```

---

(5) We found that there will be more than one path with the highest predictability in real-life applications, but Scheduling-PROPHET forbids choosing two or more paths concurrently. Therefore, we attempt to give an additional factor, the hop count of path $(h(i, i+1, \cdots, D))$. For the paths with the same predictability, the hop count of path is calculated by Scheduling-PROPHET, and those paths are arranged in order according to their hop counts. Scheduling-PROPHET will choose the path with the fewest hop counts to transmit. In our protocol, we set the maximum amount of paths to compare to 3.

(6) Finally, in the real applications, traffic load is a significant factor for transmission efficiency. Thus, in our protocol, we take traffic load (tl_i) into account. For the

paths with the same hop count, traffic load which is kept by the nodes will be compared. Scheduling-PROPHET will chooses next node with the least traffic load to transmit.

Scheduling-PROPHET keeps choosing paths with the highest predictability of successful delivery, the fewest hop count and the least traffic load. In this way, we are able to choose the most efficient transmission path, to improve transmission efficiency and reduce the message drop rate.

4   Simulations and Results

4.1   Simulation Setting

We implemented a test-bed based on ONE (Opportunistic Network Environment) simulator [18] to simulate the proposed routing protocol and evaluate its performance through a variety of simulations. We also compare the performance of Scheduling-PROPHET routing protocol with two classic protocols, Epidemic [4] and PROPHET [6] for DTN.

We have carried out a series of simulations in order to evaluate how the Scheduling-PROPHET routing protocol performs. The experimental scenario is confined to a 4500*3400 m^2 area of Helsinki city, which is included in the ONE by default. There are six groups of nodes in total. Group1 and Group3 are pedestrians groups, and their moving speed is about 0.5 to 1.5 m/s. Pedestrians follow the movement model called ShortestPathMapBasedMovement. Group2 is an automobile group and the nodes in this group can drive only on road, their moving speed is about 2.7 to 13.9 m/s. Group4, Group5 and Group6 are tram groups, and their moving speed is about 7 to 10 m/s, and they must drive on given roads by their movement model called MapRouteMovement. In our simulations, nodes transmit messages to others by using Bluetooth in 250 k/s. When Scheduling-PROPHET compares the possible paths, we have $\triangle\lambda \leq 10$.

4.2   Nodes Distribution

In order to evaluate the adaptability of our protocol in different network scales, we ran the simulation program for several times, with the density of the nodes varying from 10 to 700. The buffer size at Group1, 2, 3 remains as a constant of 5 M, and that of Group 4, 5, 6 is 50 M. The transmission range is a circle with the radius of 10 m. In our simulation, we mainly focus on evaluating the performance with four metrics: Delivery Ratio, Delivery Delay, Overhead and Hop Count.

Figure 1 shows the performance of the three protocols with different nodes distribution. Figure 1(a) illustrates the results of message delivery rate for the three protocols with different node density. There are no significant differences in performance for these three protocols with low density. However, with the density increasing, the proposed protocol has higher delivery ratio than others. The average delivery delay of the three protocols is given in Fig. 1(b). Delivery delay refers to the time of messages be transformed from source node to destination node, and we take the average delivery delay to evaluate the performance. It is easy to see that the proposed protocol performs much better than the other protocols at high density. Moreover, we find that two classic routing protocols perform better than ours at low density. That is mainly because they use simplex and direct mechanisms to transfer messages, and such direct mechanisms may perform efficient at low density, but the drawback will be exposed at high density. To make our protocol more efficient, we propose two improved mechanisms in Sect. 3.3. The overhead for these protocols is shown in Fig. 1(c). Overhead refers to the amount of messages have been transformed by each node in time unit. Figure 1(c) shows that our protocol gets the best performance in this simulation. This is mainly because that Scheduling-PROPHET takes the hop count into consideration, and chooses the shortest path to transmit messages while keeping a high delivery predictability. The result of hop count in Fig. 1(d) has depicts the similar truth with Fig. 1(c).

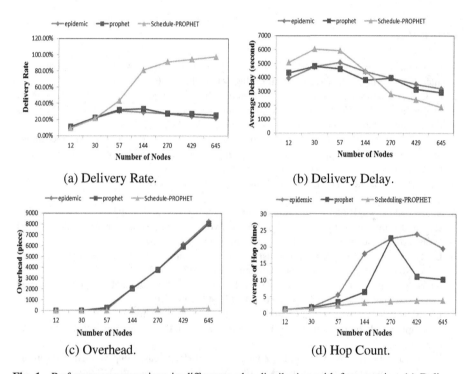

(a) Delivery Rate.

(b) Delivery Delay.

(c) Overhead.

(d) Hop Count.

Fig. 1. Performance comparison in different nodes distribution with four metrics: (a) Delivery Rate; (b) Delivery Delay; (c) Overhead; (d) Hop Counts.

5   Conclusions

In this paper, we proposed a new routing protocol called Scheduling-PROPHET for DTN. Scheduling-PROPHET is able to achieve high delivery rate and reduce delivery delay with low overhead in transmission. Moreover, the protocol can improve the management of messages in buffer. We also implement simulations to evaluate the performance of the proposed protocol and compare the protocol with classical routing protocols for DTN. There is also room for improvement, e.g. to evaluate Scheduling-PROPHET in different environments. We only simulated this protocol in one specific scenario, and therefore we can't guarantee that the protocol we used will be suitable for other situations in applications. In the future, we will focus on the performance of the proposed protocol and update it to satisfy different application environments.

Acknowledgments. This work is partially supported by Grants from the NSFC Program (NSFC61379121 and NSFC 61305148), the Science and Technology Department of Zhejiang Province Program (no. 2014C33097, 2014C33079, 2014C33099 and 2015C33062), the ZJNSF Program (no. LY14F020003).

References

1. Burleigh, S., Hooke, A., Torgerson, L., et al.: Delay-tolerant networking: an approach to interplanetary internet. IEEE Commun. Mag. **41**(6), 128–136 (2003)
2. Fall, K.: A delay-tolerant network architecture for challenged internets. In: SIGCOMM Proceedings of the Conference on Applications, Technologies, Architectures and Protocols for Computer Communications, vol. 33(4), pp. 27–34. ACM (2003)
3. Jain, S., Fall, K., Patra, R.: Routing in a delay tolerant network. In: SIGCOMM Proceedings of the Conference on Applications, Technologies, Architectures and Protocols for Computer Communications, vol. 34(4), pp. 145–158. ACM (2004)
4. Vahdat, A., Becker, D.: Epidemic Routing for Partially Connected Ad Hoc Networks. Technical report (2000)
5. Spyropoulos, T., Psounis, K., Raghavendra, C.S.: Spray and wait: an efficient routing scheme for intermittently connected mobile networks. In: Proceeding of ACM SIGCOMM Workshop on Delay-Tolerant Networking, pp. 252–259 (2005)
6. Lindgren, A., Doria, A.: Probabilistic routing in intermittently connected networks. ACM SIGMOBILE Mob. Comput. Commun. Rev. **7**(3), 19–20 (2003)
7. Anna, S., Stavros, T.: Wireless mobile DTN routing with the extended minimum estimated expected delay protocol. Ad Hoc Netw. **42**(15), 47–60 (2016)
8. Li, W.Z., Lin, F., Zhou, J.L., Wang, Y.: DTN routing with fixed stations based on the geographic grid approach in an urban environment. Wirel. Pers. Commun. **82**(4), 2033–2049 (2015)
9. Lebrun, J., Chuah, C.N., Ghosal, D., Zhang, M.: Knowledge based opportunistic forwarding in vehicular wireless ad hoc networks. IEEE Veh. Technol. Conf. **4**(4), 2289–2293 (2005)
10. Leguay, J., Friedman, T., Conan, V.: Evaluating mobility pattern space routing for DTNs. In: IEEE 25th International Conference on Computer Communications, pp. 1–10 (2006)
11. Musolesi, M., Hailes, S., Mascolo, C.: Adaptive routing for intermittently connected mobile ad hoc networks. In: Proceeding of the Sixth IEEE International Symposium on World of Wireless Mobile and Multimedia Networks, pp. 183–189. IEEE Computer Society (2005)
12. Nelson, S.C., Bakht, M., Kravets, R.: Encounter-Based Routing in DTNs. Infocom IEEE **13** (1), 846–854 (2009)
13. Bulut, E., Geyik, S.C., Szymanski, B.K.: Utilizing correlated node mobility for efficient DTN routing. Pervasive Mob. Comput. **13**(4), 150–163 (2014)

14. Satya, B.S., Nanaji, U.: Efficient implementation of conditional shortest path routing in delay tolerant networks. Int. J. Comput. Sci. Commun. Netw. **1**(3), 252–257 (2011)
15. Burns, B., Brock, O., Levine, B.N.: MV routing and capacity building in disruption tolerant networks. In: 24th Annual Joint Conference of the IEEE Computer and Communications Socierties, vol. 1(4), pp. 398–408. Infocom IEEE (2005)
16. Spyropolous, T., Psounis, K., Raghavendra, C.S.: Single-copy routing in intermittently connected mobile networks. In: First Annual IEEE Communications Society Conference on Sensor and Ad Hoc Communications and Networks, IEEE Secon 2004, pp. 235–244 (2004)
17. Lenormant, F.: GTDM: a DTN routing on noncooperative game theory in a city environment. J. Sens. **2015**, 1–9 (2015)
18. Keränen, A., Ott, J., Kärkkäinen, T.: The ONE simulator for DTN protocol evaluation. In: Proceedings of the 2nd International Conference on Simulation Tools and Techniques (2009)

Inverse Multicast Quality of Service Routing Problem with Bandwidth and Delay Under the Weighted l_1 Norm

Longcheng Liu[1(✉)], Yu'an Chen[1], Wenhao Zheng[1], and Deqing Wang[2]

[1] School of Mathematical Sciences, Xiamen University,
Xiamen 361005, People's Republic of China
`longchengliu@xmu.edu.cn`
[2] School of Information Science and Engineering, Xiamen University,
Xiamen 361005, People's Republic of China

Abstract. Quality of Service (QoS) Routing problem has been attracting considerable attention thanks to the rapid development of the high-speed communication network, image processing and computer science. In the past decades, many Quality of Service Routing algorithms were presented based on the QoS requirements and the resource constraints.

The idea of the inverse optimization problem is to modify the given or estimated parameters such that the given feasible solution became an optimal solution. The modification costs are measured by different norms, such as l_1 norm, l_2 norm, l_∞ norm, Hamming distance and so on.

In this paper, we consider the inverse multicast quality of service routing problems under the weighted l_1 norm. We present combinatorial algorithms which can be finished in strongly polynomial time.

Keywords: Communication network · Quality of service routing · Inverse problem · Strongly polynomial combinatorial algorithm

1 Introduction

The notion of Quality of Service has been proposed to capture the qualitatively or quantitatively defined performance contract between the service provider and the user applications in communication networks. The quality of service requirement of a connection is given as a set of constraints, which can be link constraints, path constraints, or tree constraints. The routing problems can be divided into two major classes: unicast routing and multicast routing.

The unicast quality of service routing problem with bandwidth and delay is defined as follows: given a graph (V, E, s, t), $V = \{1, 2, \ldots, n\}$, $E = \{e_1, e_2,$

This research is supported by the National Natural Science Foundation of China (Grant No. 11001232, 61301098), Fujian Provincial Natural Science Foundation of China (Grant No. 2012J01021) and Fundamental Research Funds for the Central Universities (Grant No. 20720160035, 20720150002).

$\ldots, e_m\}$, s is the service provider and t is the terminal user. Let each edge e_i has associated bandwidth b_i and delay d_i, and let $b = \{b_1, b_2, \ldots, b_m\}$ denote the bandwidth vector, $d = \{d_1, d_2, \ldots, d_m\}$ denote the delay vector. Then we want to find an $s - t$ path P which satisfies the quality of service requirement, i.e., $\min_{e_i \in P} b_i \geq B$ and $\sum_{e_i \in P} d_i \leq D$, where B and D are given threshold.

The multicast quality of service routing problem with bandwidth and delay is defined as follows: given a graph (V, E, s, t), $V = \{1, 2, \ldots, n\}$, $E = \{e_1, e_2, \ldots, e_m\}$, s is the service provider and $t = \{t_1, t_2, \ldots, t_k\}(k \leq m)$ is the set of terminal users. Let each edge e_i has associated bandwidth b_i and delay d_i, and let $b = \{b_1, b_2, \ldots, b_m\}$ denote the bandwidth vector, $d = \{d_1, d_2, \ldots, d_m\}$ denote the delay vector. Then we want to find a tree T covering s and all nodes in t which satisfies the quality of service requirement, i.e., $\min_{e_i \in P_j} b_i \geq B_j$, $\sum_{e_i \in P_j} d_i \leq D_j$, $j = 1, 2, \ldots, k$, where P_j is the unique path from s to t_j on the tree T, and B_j, D_j are given threshold.

Multicast routing can be viewed as a generalization of unicast routing in many cases. For more details, the readers may refer to the survey paper [4] and papers cited therein.

Conversely, an inverse quality of service routing problem is to modify the parameters as little as possible such that a given $s - t$ path P can satisfy the quality of service requirement for the unicast routing, or a given tree T which covering s and all nodes in t can satisfy the quality of service requirement for the multicast routing. The parameters considered in this paper are bandwidth and delay, and the modification cost is measured by the weighted l_1 norm. Note that a path is a special tree, i.e., inverse unicast routing problem is a special case of the inverse multicast routing problem. Hence, we only consider the inverse multicast routing problem in detail.

Inverse multicast routing problem

Let each edge e_i has associated bandwidth modification cost w_i^b and delay modification cost w_i^d, and let $w^b = \{w_1^b, w_2^b, \ldots, w_m^b\}$ denote the bandwidth modification cost vector, $w^d = \{w_1^d, w_2^d, \ldots, w_m^d\}$ denote the delay modification cost vector. Let T be a given tree which covering s and all nodes in t, but under the current b and d, the T can not satisfy the quality of service requirement, i.e., $\min_{e_i \in P_j} b_i < B_j$, $\sum_{e_i \in P_j} d_i > D_j$, $j = 1, 2, \ldots, k$. Then for the inverse multicast routing problem with bandwidth and delay under the weighted l_1 norm, we look for a new bandwidth vector b^* and a new delay vector d^* such that

(a) the given tree T satisfies the quality of service requirement, i.e., $\min_{e_i \in P_j} b_i^* \geq B_j$, $\sum_{e_i \in P_j} d_i^* \leq D_j$, $j = 1, 2, \ldots, k$;

(b) for each $e_i \in E$, $-l_i^b \leq b_i^* - b_i \leq u_i^b$, $-l_i^d \leq d_i^* - d_i \leq u_i^d$, where $l_i^b, u_i^b, l_i^d, u_i^d \geq 0$ are respectively given bounds for bandwidth and delay;

(c) the total modification cost for change bandwidth and delay of all edges, i.e., $\sum_{e_i \in E} w_i^b |b_i^* - b_i| + \sum_{e_i \in E} w_i^d |d_i^* - d_i|$, is minimized.

In general, in an inverse optimization problem, a feasible solution is given which is not optimal under the current parameter values, and it is required to modify some parameters with minimum modification cost such that the given feasible solution becomes an optimal solution. Burton and Toint [3] were the first who investigate the inverse version of the shortest path problem. Since then, different inverse optimization problems have been well studied when the modification cost is measured by (weighted) l_1 norm, l_2 norm, l_∞ norm and Hamming distance. Some examples are the inverse minimum cost flow problem [1,5,9], the inverse center location problem [2,12,14], the inverse shortest path problem [3,13,15], the inverse minimum cut problem [7,10,11] and so on. For more details, readers may refer to the survey paper [6] and papers cited therein.

The problem considered in our paper has so far not been treated in literature, but seems to have some potential applications in real world. For example, the service provider has built his own network (path for one to one service, tree for one to many service) to service his customers. At the beginning, the network is optimal for the service provider. But as the service requirement is growing, the exist network is not optimal any more, i.e., it can not satisfies the customers' requirement. Hence, the service provider need to improve the exist network to meet the customers' requirement. Which is the model considered in this paper.

The remainder of the paper is organized as follows. Section 2 considers the inverse multicast quality of service routing problem with bandwidth and delay under the weighted l_1 norm. Strongly polynomial combinatorial algorithms are presented. Some final remarks are made in Sect. 3.

2   Inverse Multicast Quality of Service Routing Problem

In this section, we are going to consider the inverse multicast quality of service routing problem with bandwidth and delay under the weighted l_1 norm, which can be formulated as follows.

$$\min \sum_{e_i \in E} w_i^b |b_i^* - b_i| + \sum_{e_i \in E} w_i^d |d_i^* - d_i|$$
$$\text{s.t.} \min_{e_i \in P_j} b_i^* \geq B_j, j = 1, 2, \ldots, k;$$
$$\sum_{e_i \in P_j} d_i^* \leq D_j, j = 1, 2, \ldots, k; \tag{1}$$
$$-l_i^b \leq b_i^* - b_i \leq u_i^b, i = 1, 2, \ldots, m;$$
$$-l_i^d \leq d_i^* - d_i \leq u_i^d, i = 1, 2, \ldots, m.$$

Note that b and d are independent when they be changed. Hence problem (1) can be divided into the following two problems:

$$\min \sum_{e_i \in E} w_i^b |b_i^* - b_i|$$
$$\text{s.t.} \min_{e_i \in P_j} b_i^* \geq B_j, j = 1, 2, \ldots, k; \tag{2}$$
$$-l_i^b \leq b_i^* - b_i \leq u_i^b, i = 1, 2, \ldots, m.$$

$$\min \sum_{e_i \in E} w_i^d |d_i^* - d_i|$$
$$\text{s.t.} \sum_{e_i \in P_j} d_i^* \leq D_j, j = 1, 2, \ldots, k; \tag{3}$$
$$-l_i^d \leq d_i^* - d_i \leq u_i^d, i = 1, 2, \ldots, m.$$

Theorem 1. *Suppose b^* is an optimal solution of problem (2) and d^* is an optimal solution of problem (3). Then the optimal solution of problem (1) is $\{b^*, d^*\}$, and the associate optimal value is $\sum\limits_{e_i \in E} w_i^b |b_i^* - b_i| + \sum\limits_{e_i \in E} w_i^d |d_i^* - d_i|$.*

Hence, we need to solve problems (2) and (3), respectively.

For problem (2), it is to modify the bandwidth under the given bound as little as possible such that the given tree T meet the bandwidth constraint. First, it is clear that the bandwidth of the edges out of the tree T need not be changed. Second, for the edges belong to the tree T, we need to increase the bandwidth for some of them to meet the bandwidth constraint. Due to the objective function and the bandwidth bound constraint of problem (2), for the edges belong to the unique path from s to t_j, if $b_i \geq B_j$, then the bandwidth need not be changed, otherwise, the bound must satisfies $b_i + u_i^b \geq B_j$ and we increasing the bandwidth to B_j. Hence, we have the following algorithm to solve problem (2).

Algorithm 1

Step 1. Let $j = 1$.

Step 2. Let P_j denote the unique path from s to t_j. If there exist an edge $e_i \in P_j$ such that $b_i + u_i^b < B_j$, then output problem (2) is infeasible and stop. Otherwise, set

$$u_i^b = \begin{cases} u_i^b, & e_i \notin T, \\ u_i^b, & e_i \in P_j \text{ and } b_i \geq B_j, \\ u_i^b - (B_j - b_i), & e_i \in P_j \text{ and } b_i < B_j, \end{cases}$$

$$b_i = \begin{cases} b_i, & e_i \notin T, \\ b_i, & e_i \in P_j \text{ and } b_i \geq B_j, \\ B_j, & e_i \in P_j \text{ and } b_i < B_j, \end{cases}$$

Step 3. If $j = k$, output the current bandwidth vector b as an optimal solution of problem (2). Otherwise, set $j = j + 1$ and go back to the Step 2.

Theorem 2. *The Algorithm 1 solves problem (2) with a time complexity $O(k) \leq O(n)$.*

Proof. First, from the above analysis, the validity of the Algorithm 1 is straight-forward.

Second, let us consider the time complexity of the algorithm. We designate computations starting from Step 2 until switching back to the next Step 2 as one iteration. In each iteration, we will modify the bandwidth of some of the edges on the path P_j to let the associate t_j meet the bandwidth constraint or find problem (2) is infeasible, which means the Algorithm 1 will terminate at most k iterations. Combining with the computation of the Step 2, the Algorithm 1 runs in $O(k) \leq O(n)$. □

For problem (3), it is to modify the delay as little as possible such that the given tree T meet the delay constraint. First, it is clear that the delay of the edges out the tree T need not be changed. Second, for the edges belong to the tree T, we need to decrease the delay for some of them to meet the delay constraint. Hence, we can rewrite problem (3) as following.

$$\min \sum_{e_i \in T} w_i^d (d_i - d_i^*)$$
$$\text{s.t.} \sum_{e_i \in P_j} d_i^* \leq D_j, j = 1, 2, \ldots, k; \tag{4}$$
$$0 \leq d_i - d_i^* \leq l_i^d, i = 1, 2, \ldots, m.$$

For simplicity, denote $\Delta d_i = d_i - d_i^*, \Delta D_j = \sum_{e_i \in P_j} d_i - D_j$. Then problem (4) is simplified to

$$\min \sum_{e_i \in T} w_i^d \Delta d_i$$
$$\text{s.t.} \sum_{e_i \in P_j} \Delta d_i \geq \Delta D_j, j = 1, 2, \ldots, k; \tag{5}$$
$$0 \leq \Delta d_i \leq l_i^d, i = 1, 2, \ldots, m.$$

To solve problem (5), we first consider a special case: $\Delta D_j = C$ for $j = 1, 2, \ldots, k$, where C is a given threshold, i.e., the following problem.

$$\min \sum_{e_i \in T} w_i^d \Delta d_i$$
$$\text{s.t.} \sum_{e_i \in P_j} \Delta d_i \geq C, j = 1, 2, \ldots, k; \tag{6}$$
$$0 \leq \Delta d_i \leq l_i^d, i = 1, 2, \ldots, m.$$

To solve problem (6), we construct a new weighted graph $\widetilde{G}$ based on the given tree T. The node set of $\widetilde{G}$ is $V(T) \cup \{r\}$, i.e., add a new node r to the tree T. The edge set of $\widetilde{G}$ is $E(T) \cup \{(t_i, r), i = 1, 2, \ldots, k\}$, i.e., besides the tree edges, add new edges connect the terminal nodes t_i and the new node r. And we set the weight of the edges as

$$w_i = \begin{cases} w_i^d, & e_i \in T, \\ +\infty, & e_i = (t_i, r). \end{cases}$$

An illustration of the weighted graph $\widetilde{G}$ is shown in Fig. 1.

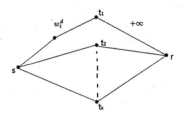

Fig. 1. An illustration of the weighted graph $\widetilde{G}$.

Theorem 3. *Suppose M is the edge set of a minimum $s-r$ cut of the weighted graph $\widetilde{G}$. Then the following $\{\Delta d_i^*\}$ form an optimal solution of problem (6) with $C \leq \min\limits_{e_i \in M} l_i^d$.*

$$\Delta d_i^* = \begin{cases} C, \ e_i \in M, \\ 0, \ e_i \in T \setminus M. \end{cases}$$

Proof. First, the $\{\Delta d_i^*\}$ given by the theorem satisfies the first constraint of problem (6) since M is the edge set of a minimum $s-r$ cut of the weighted graph $\widetilde{G}$. Second, the $\{\Delta d_i^*\}$ given by the theorem satisfies the second constraint of problem (6) since we set $C \leq \min\limits_{e_i \in M} l_i^d$ before. Hence, the $\{\Delta d_i^*\}$ given by the theorem is a feasible solution of problem (6).

Furthermore, we say the $\{\Delta d_i^*\}$ given by the theorem is an optimal solution of problem (6). Otherwise, there exist another optimal solution $\{\widetilde{\Delta d_i}\}$. Denote $M' = \{e_i \in T \mid \widetilde{\Delta d_i} \neq 0\}$. Then for $e_i \in M$, denote $e_i = (x, y)$, P_x is the unique path form s to x and T_y is the subtree whose root is y (we will use the same notation for other nodes in the following). If $\widetilde{\Delta d_i} \neq \Delta d_i^*$ for $e_i \in M$, then at least one of the following two cases will occur.

Case 1. $M' \cap T_y \neq \emptyset$. In this case, we can transfer the modification of the delay from $M' \cap T_y$ to $e_i \in M$ without increasing the modification cost since M is a minimum $s-r$ cut of the weighted graph $\widetilde{G}$.

Case 2. $M' \cap P_x \neq \emptyset$. For $\widetilde{e}_i = (\widetilde{x}, \widetilde{y}) \in M' \cap P_x$, we can transfer the modification of the delay from $\widetilde{e}_i$ to $M \cap T_y$ without increasing the modification cost since M is a minimum $s-r$ cut of the weighted graph $\widetilde{G}$. Hence, consider the edges belong to $M' \cap P_x$ one by one, we can transfer the modification of the delay from $M' \cap P_x$ to M without increasing the modification cost.

Combining the above two cases, consider the edges belong to M' one by one, we can transfer the modification of the delay from M' to M without increasing the modification cost, which means the $\{\Delta d_i^*\}$ given by the theorem is an optimal solution of problem (6). □

Theorem 4. *Suppose Δd_i is a feasible solution of problem (5), then Δd_i can be presented as $\Delta d_i = \Delta d_i^1 + \Delta d_i^2$, where Δd_i^1 is a feasible solution of problem (6) and Δd_i^2 is a feasible solution of the following problem.*

$$\min \sum_{e_i \in T} w_i^d \Delta d_i$$
$$\text{s.t.} \sum_{e_i \in P_j} \Delta d_i \geq \Delta D_j - C \geq 0, j = 1, 2, \ldots, k; \qquad (7)$$
$$0 \leq \Delta d_i \leq l_i^d, i = 1, 2, \ldots, m.$$

Proof. First, let

$$V_h = \{v \in V(T) \mid \text{ the number of the edges of the path from } s \text{ to } v \text{ is } h\}.$$

In this way, $V(T)$ is decomposed to its subsets $V_0, V_1, \ldots, V_q$, where q is the number of the edges of the longest path from s to the nodes in the tree T.

Suppose Δd_i is a feasible solution of problem (5), then it is easy to know the $\Delta d_i^1, \Delta d_i^2$ given by the following algorithm will satisfy the theorem.

Algorithm 2

Step 1. Set $h = 0$.

Step 2. Select an $e_i = (x, y)$ such that $x \in V_h, y \in V_{h+1}$. Let $\Omega = C - \sum_{e_i \in P_x} \Delta d_i^1$, where P_x is the unique path form s to x.

Step 3. If $\Delta d_i \leq \Omega$, then set $\Delta d_i^1 = \Delta d_i, \Delta d_i^2 = \Delta d_i - \Delta d_i^1$.
Otherwise, set $\Delta d_i^1 = \Omega, \Delta d_i^2 = \Delta d_i - \Delta d_i^1$.

Step 4. Set $V_{h+1} = V_{h+1} \setminus \{y\}$. If $V_{h+1} \neq \emptyset$, then go back to the step 2.

Step 5. If $h + 1 = q$, stop. Otherwise, set $h = h + 1$ and go back to the step 2. □

Theorem 5. *Suppose Δd_i^{1*} and Δd_i^{2*} are optimal solutions of problems (6) and (7), respectively. Then $\Delta d_i^* = \Delta d_i^{1*} + \Delta d_i^{2*}$ is an optimal solution of problem (5).*

Proof. First, it is easy to know that Δd_i^* is a feasible solution of problem (5) since Δd_i^{1*} and Δd_i^{2*} are optimal solutions of problems (6) and (7).

Next, we will show that Δd_i^* is an optimal solution of problem (5).

Suppose Δd_i is a feasible solution of problem (5). Then by the Theorem 4, the Δd_i can be represented as $\Delta d_i^1 + \Delta d_i^2$ such that Δd_i^1 is a feasible solution of problem (6) and Δd_i^2 is a feasible solution of problem (7). We have

$$\sum_{e_i \in T} w_i^d \Delta d_i^1 \geq \sum_{e_i \in T} w_i^d \Delta d_i^{1*},$$

$$\sum_{e_i \in T} w_i^d \Delta d_i^2 \geq \sum_{e_i \in T} w_i^d \Delta d_i^{2*},$$

since Δd_i^{1*} and Δd_i^{2*} are optimal solutions of problems (6) and (7).

Hence

$$\sum_{e_i \in T} w_i^d \Delta d_i$$

$$= \sum_{e_i \in T} w_i^d \Delta d_i^1 + \sum_{e_i \in T} w_i^d \Delta d_i^2$$

$$\geq \sum_{e_i \in T} w_i^d \Delta d_i^{1*} + \sum_{e_i \in T} w_i^d \Delta d_i^{2*}$$

$$= \sum_{e_i \in T} w_i^d \Delta d_i^*,$$

which implies Δd_i^* is an optimal solution of problem (5). □

Combining the above analysis, we can solve problem (5) by the following algorithm.

Algorithm 3

Step 1. Construct a weighted graph $\widetilde{G}$ as showed in the Fig. 1. Let $\Delta d_i = 0$ for $e_i \in T$.

Step 2. Find a minimum $s - r$ cut M for the current weighted graph. If the weight of the $s - r$ cut M is equal to $+\infty$, then output problem (5) is infeasible. Otherwise, set

$$\underline{l^d} = \min\{l_i^d \mid e_i \in M \text{ and } l_i^d > 0\},$$

$$\underline{\Delta D} = \min\{\Delta D_j \mid j = 1, 2, \ldots, k \text{ and } \Delta D_j > 0\},$$

$$C = \min\{\underline{l^d}, \underline{\Delta D}\},$$

$$\Delta d_i = \begin{cases} C, & e_i \in M, \\ \Delta d_i, & e_i \in T \setminus M. \end{cases}$$

$$l_i^d = \begin{cases} l_i^d - C, & e_i \in M, \\ l_i^d, & e_i \in T \setminus M. \end{cases}$$

$$w_i = \begin{cases} +\infty, & l_i^d = 0, \\ w_i, & l_i^d > 0. \end{cases}$$

$$\Delta D_j = \Delta D_j - C.$$

Step 3. If $\Delta D_j = 0$ for all $j = 1, 2, \ldots, k$, stop and output the current $\{\Delta d_i\}$ as an optimal solution of problem (5). Otherwise, go back to the Step 2.

Theorem 6. *The Algorithm 3 solves problem (5) with a time complexity*

$$O(n_1 m_1^2) \leq O(nm^2),$$

where n_1 is the node number of the given tree T and m_1 is the edge number of the given tree T.

Proof. First, we show the validity of the algorithm.

If the algorithm stops at the Step 2, i.e., there exists at least one $\Delta D_j > 0$ and the weight of the minimum $s-r$ cut of the current weighted graph is equal to $+\infty$, that is to say there exists at least one $s-t_j$ path P_j such that $\sum_{e_i \in P_j} d_i > D_j$ and the delay of the edges on the path P_j can not be changed anymore, which implies problem (5) is infeasible.

We next consider the case that problem (5) is feasible, i.e., the algorithm stops at the Step 3. We designate computations starting from the Step 2 until switching back to the next Step 2 as one iteration. From the Theorem 3, we find an optimal solution of an instance of problem (6) in each iteration. Furthermore, combining all iterations we find an optimal solution of problem (5) due to the Theorem 5.

Finally, we study the time complexity of the Algorithm 3. It is clear that the Step 1 takes $O(m_1)$ to construct the weighted graph $\widetilde{G}$, where m_1 is the edge number of the given tree T. In each iteration, the main computation is to find a minimum $s - r$ cut which can be done in $O(n_1 m_1)$ [8], where n_1 is the node number of the given tree T. Furthermore, in each iteration, we will set at least one of l_i^d equals 0 or at least one of ΔD_j equals 0, which means the algorithm iterates for at most $k + m_1$ times. Hence, the algorithm runs in $O(m_1 + n_1 m_1 \cdot (k + m_1)) = O(n_1 m_1^2) \leq O(nm^2)$ time in the worst case, which is a strongly polynomial time algorithm.   □

3   Concluding Remarks

In this paper, we study the inverse multicast quality of service routing problem with bandwidth and delay under the weighted l_1 norm in detail and present strongly polynomial algorithms.

There are some related inverse problems that deserve further study. First, it is interesting to study the inverse quality of service routing problem with bandwidth and delay with other norms, such as l_2, l_∞ and Hamming distance. Second, it is meaningful to consider the inverse quality of service of routing problem with other parameters. Studying computational complexity results and proposing optimal/approximation algorithms are promising.

References

1. Ahuja, R.K., Orlin, J.B.: Combinatorial algorithms for inverse network flow problems. Networks **40**, 181–187 (2002)
2. Berman, O., Ingco, D.I., Odoni, A.: Improving the location of minimax facilities through network modification. Networks **24**, 31–41 (1994)
3. Burton, D., Toint, P.L.: On an instance of the inverse shortest paths problem. Math. Program. **53**, 45–61 (1992)
4. Chen, S.G., Nahrsted, K.: An overview of quality of serice routing for next-generation high-speed networks: problems and solutions. IEEE Netw., Special Issue Transm. Distrib. Digit. Video **12**(6), 64–79 (1998)
5. Güler, C., Hamacher, H.W.: Capacity inverse minimum cost flow problem. J. Comb. Optim. **19**, 43–59 (2010)
6. Heuberger, C.: Inverse optimization: a survey on problems, methods, and results. J. Comb. Optim. **8**, 329–361 (2004)
7. Liu, L.C., Yao, E.Y.: A weighted inverse minimum cut problem under the bottleneck type Hamming distance. Asia. Pac. J. Oper. Res. **24**, 725–736 (2007)
8. Orlin, J.B.: Max flows in $O(nm)$ time, or better. In: Proceedings of STOC 2013, pp. 765–774 (2013)
9. Tayyebi, J., Aman, M.: Note on "Inverse minimum cost flow problems under the weighted Hamming distance". Eur. J. Oper. Res. **234**, 916–920 (2014)
10. Yang, C., Zhang, J.Z., Ma, Z.F.: Inverse maximum flow and minimum cut problems. Optimization **40**, 147–170 (1997)
11. Zhang, J.Z., Cai, M.C.: Inverse problem of minimum cuts. Math. Method. Oper. Res. **47**, 51–58 (1998)
12. Zhang, J.Z., Liu, Z.H., Ma, Z.F.: Some reverse location problems. Eur. J. Oper. Res. **124**, 77–88 (2000)

13. Zhang, J.Z., Ma, Z.F., Yang, C.: A column generation method for inverse shortest path problems. ZOR-Math. Method. Oper. Res. **41**, 347–358 (1995)
14. Zhang, B.W., Zhang, J.Z., He, Y.: The center location improvement problem under the Hamming distance. J. Comb. Optim. **9**, 187–198 (2005)
15. Zhang, B.W., Zhang, J.Z., Qi, L.Q.: The shortest path improvement problems under Hamming distance. J. Comb. Optim. **12**, 351–361 (2006)

Distance and Cooperation Based Broadcast in Wireless Ad Hoc Networks

Xinxin Liu, Yanping Yu$^{(\boxtimes)}$, Yuanyan Zheng, Dongsheng Ning, and Xiaoyan Wang

College of Information and Electronic Engineering,
Zhejiang Gongshang University, Hangzhou 310018, China
liumickey@126.com, yuyanping@zjgsu.edu.cn,
{470309041,95688033,806161048}@qq.com

Abstract. Broadcasting is one of common data dissemination techniques in wireless ad hoc networks. Thus, it is critical to improve the broadcast efficiency. Flooding, which is simple but has reliable coverage, results in high broadcast redundancy, channel contending and message collision when the network is densely distributed. In this paper, a new broadcast algorithm named as distance and cooperation based broadcast (DCBB) is proposed. In DCBB, four neighbor nodes at most are determined to forward broadcast packets based on the number of neighbors and the distance between neighbors. Redundancy can be reduced by limiting the number of relay nodes. And, through the time-division forwarding scheme, channel contending is reduced and the network utilization is improved effectively. Moreover, due to the limited number of relay nodes, DCBB saves energy of nodes and prolongs the network lifetime. The simulation results show that DCBB achieves higher reachability and lower retransmitted ratio compared to dynamic probabilistic broadcasting algorithms (DP). Meanwhile, the average maximum end-to-end delay is significantly decreased. Therefore, DCBB is applicable to densely distributed network environment.

Keywords: Wireless ad hoc networks · Broadcasting · Distance and corporation based broadcasting

1 Introduction

A wireless ad hoc network is a multi-hop and temporary autonomous system, which consists of mobile devices, equipped with wireless communication capacities. One of the fundamental operations in wireless ad hoc networks is broadcasting by which a source node disseminates a message to all other nodes. Broadcasting is widely used in many ad hoc network protocols. For instance, it can be used to find a route in Ad hoc On-Demand Distance Vector Routing (AODV) and Dynamic Source Routing (DSR) protocols. It can also be used to update network topology, to deliver multi-media information, to release control and warning messages, etc. [1, 2].

In wireless ad hoc networks, flooding is the simplest way to broadcast. In flooding, every node retransmits the broadcast message received first time. In general, flooding achieves high coverage. However, blind flooding causes significant redundant

S. Guo et al. (Eds.): TridentCom 2016, LNICST 177, pp. 168–178, 2017.
DOI: 10.1007/978-3-319-49580-4_16

transmissions, which results in substantial waste of network resource in densely distributed networks [3, 4]. The main problems caused by flooding are redundant transmissions, channel contentions and packet collisions, which are called as the broadcast storm problem. Redundant transmissions refer to that a node receives the same messages more than once. Upon receiving a message, a node retransmits the message to its neighbors. Those neighbors, which are adjacent to each other, receive and retransmit the messages almost in the same time, which result in the contending for the channel. With the number of neighbors increasing, the probability of contending increases. Signal collision may be caused by hidden or neighbor nodes. For example, if the distributed coordination function (DCF) of medium access control (MAC) in IEEE 802.11 is used in ad hoc networks, hidden terminal problems as well as collisions are unavoidable. Moreover, collisions lead to broadcasting unreliability [3, 5].

To achieve reliable broadcast in wireless ad hoc networks, we propose a distance and cooperation based broadcasting algorithm (DCBB), in which the broadcast storm and unreliability are resolved simultaneously. In DCBB, every node selects four neighbor nodes at most, acting as relay nodes to transmit the packet at different time point according to the distribution of nodes. Redundancy is reduced by limiting the number of relay nodes. At the same time, collisions are avoided by transmitting at different time slots for those relay nodes, which mitigate the channel contentions. Moreover, due to the limited number of relay nodes, DCBB saves the energy of nodes and prolongs the network lifetime, which are crucial for wireless ad hoc networks since nodes in the networks have limited energy and frequent retransmission consumes a large amount of energy.

The rest of the paper is organized as follows: related work is presented in Sect. 2, and the design of the DCBB algorithm is presented in Sect. 3. Its performance is examined via simulation in Sect. 4. Finally, the conclusion is given in Sect. 5.

2 Related Work

Broadcast is a fundamental communication operation in wireless ad hoc networks. However, the broadcasting storm problem, caused by flooding, severely deteriorates the performance of networks in terms of the throughput and other QoS metrics. The broadcasting unreliability, caused by collisions, also affects the performance. Therefore, it is crucial to develop efficient broadcasting algorithms to solve the above problems. Currently, researches on wireless network broadcast mainly focus on the broadcast storm mitigating technique [5–11], followed by the reliable broadcast and its acknowledgement storm [12, 13].

At present, algorithms for broadcast storm mitigation can be classified into four categories: probability based [2, 7, 8], area based [2, 14, 15], neighborhood based [6] and hybrid algorithms [16]. Although the above algorithms reduce broadcasting redundancy to some extent, they are still not satisfied in many scenarios. The probability based algorithms are simple, but their efficiency to reduce redundancy are not good enough or they have lower coverages. The neighborhood based algorithms which are sensitive to topological change and are involved in the NP problem, are complex. The area based algorithms need the support of GPS and have their limitation in applications.

Compared with the broadcast storm problem, fewer researches focus on unreliable broadcasting. Some routes are not discovered and route information is out of date due to unreliable broadcasting. In wireless ad hoc networks, upon an upstream node sending a message, a collision occurs at some receivers if all neighbors forward the message at the same time. Ultimately, the receivers are unable to receive the message correctly, i.e., the unreliable broadcasting problem. Reliable broadcast schemes can be classified into four categories: flooding based algorithms, the minimum spanning tree based algorithms, hybrid algorithms and acknowledgement based algorithms. The flooding based algorithms are simple but highly reliable. However, the broadcasting storm problem is severe. The reliable minimum spanning tree (RMST) algorithm [5] is the most popular one among the minimum spanning tree based algorithms. In wireless ad hoc networks, however, it needs a large amount of calculations to construct the minimum spanning tree and is hard to realize the distributed computation. In the acknowledgement based algorithms, the acknowledgement storm problem emerges.

Due to the importance of broadcasting in wireless ad hoc networks, many novel approaches for broadcast have been proposed recently. We are going to elaborate the most recent advancements to this issue as following.

A. Hybrid algorithms: neighborhood and probability based

Abdalla et al. [16] proposed a hybrid approach based on probability and neighbor information, named as Dynamic Probabilistic broadcasting algorithms (DP). In DP, every node periodically sends HELLO packets to acquire network topology information. Each node dynamically adjusts rebroadcasting probability P_i according to the number of neighbors. P_i varies with the density of network nodes. P_i is larger in a sparse area and is smaller in a dense area. Therefore, the transmission redundancy is reduced.

B. Neighborhood based algorithms

S. Leu proposed a distributed algorithm to construct a connected dominating set [17]. Node S periodically sends probe packets to acquire the information from relay nodes. Each node randomly decides whether to be a relay node, and sends the response to node S. Node S maintains a table for relaying nodes. If there are more than two nodes in the table, node S will stop sending probe packets. This scheme can reduce the broadcasting redundancy and avoid the NP problem which is essential in other conventional CDS (connected dominating set) algorithms.

C. Underlying broadcasting protocols

Recently, many scholars have begun to study the broadcasting algorithms suitable to MAC or physical layer. Zhang and Shin [18] proposed a scheme named carrier sensing multiple access/collision resolution (CSMA/CR), which can be applied to solve the collision in wireless ad hoc networks. Upon receiving a packet, the node transmits the packet directly without sensing the channel or delay. CSMA/CR performs collision resolution and recovers the packet by a symbol–level iterative decoding. Thus, higher reachability and lower latency is achieved.

D. Position based algorithms

Liu et al. [19] proposed a space-covered broadcast (SCB) algorithm which does not need any neighbor information to mitigate the broadcast storm. With the location obtained by GPS, SCB utilizes the minimal number of forwarding nodes to cover a network by optimizing the spatial distribution of the forwarding nodes.

E. Energy based algorithms

While nodes in wireless ad hoc networks usually run on battery with limited power. Related studies show that data transmission consume more energy than data receiving. Thus, it is necessary to propose an energy efficient broadcasting algorithm to increase the lifetime of ad hoc networks. Many scholars have studied broadcast by taking energy consumption and broadcasting storm suppression into consideration. In [11], the author proposed an algorithm based on residual energy and distance threshold (SED). According to its own residual energy and neighbors' information, the receiving nodes dynamically adjust the retransmission probability PI. The waiting time for a retransmission is determined by PI. Based on different retransmission probability, SED can balance the nodes' energy and improve the network lifetime.

In [20], to maximize the network lifetime, a Minimum Energy-consumption Broadcast Scheme (MEBS) is proposed based on modified version of Efficient Minimum CDS algorithm (EMCDS). Simulation results show that MEBS can help improve the network lifetime by effectively balancing the energy among nodes in a network.

In conclusion, broadcasting protocols with satisfactory performance should have fewer contentions and collisions, fewer redundant retransmissions, lower reliable reachability, low latency and overhead, as well as wide range of applications. In this paper, we propose a broadcast scheme called as Distance and Cooperation Based Broadcast (DCBB). In DCBB, every node selects four nodes at most to forward the packet at different time point according to the distribution of nodes. It reduces the channel contention and increases the broadcasting reliability. Meanwhile, it does not need any GPS to obtain the distance between nodes.

3 The DCBB Algorithm

The objective of DCBB is to mitigate the broadcast redundancy and improve broadcast reliability. Each node in the network periodically sends HELLO packets to exchange neighbor information. According to the distance to all neighbors, a node determines a distance threshold. Let d be the distance between a receiving node and an immediate upstream node. A neighbor node that receives a broadcast packet will not forward it to its own neighbors if d is less than the distance threshold. The node will be a candidate for broadcast transmitting if d is larger than the threshold and closed to $2/3R$ (R is the radius of a node's transmission range). Four candidates at most will be selected as the forwarding nodes to forward the broadcast packet received for the first time in distinct time slot if the combinations of their coverage can cover more next-hop nodes. In the light of research experience, the nodes whose distance to the sender are closed to $2/3R$ will receive packets more reliably and they can also get larger extra coverage.

However, nodes whose distances to the sender are closed to R will not be the candidates for broadcast transmitting because signal amplitude they received is lower and not reliable in the reality. Having taken the above factors into consideration, DCBB can achieve higher coverage and lower collision by the time division forwarding.

A. Obtaining the distance between neighbors

Distances between neighbors are obtained by measuring the signal power of a transmitter and a receiver. There are many models to measure the signal power, such as free space propagation model, two ray propagation model, etc. In this paper, we assume that the wireless channel model is free space propagation mode. Then,

$$P_r(d) = \frac{P_t G_t G_r \lambda^2}{(4\pi)^2 d^2 L} \tag{1}$$

P_t, P_r denote the transmitting power and the receiving power, respectively. d is the distance between a transmitter and its corresponding immediate receiver. G_r is the transmitting antenna gain and G_r is the receiving antenna gain. L is the loss factor and has no relation with the system ($L \geq 1$). A is the wavelength (m). From the Eq. (1), d is obtained as:

$$d = \frac{\lambda}{2\pi} * \sqrt{\frac{P_t G_t G_r}{L P_r(d)}} \tag{2}$$

B. Determining the distance threshold

Every node periodically sends HELLO packets each other. Node S determines its distance to all neighbors according to the amplitude of the signal it received from its neighbors. On the basis of these distances, node S determines a distance threshold D_{th}.

If all neighbors are uniformly distributed, D_{th} is set to be the average of all neighbors' distances. If nodes are unevenly distributed, it will not only need to determine the average distance $aver(d)$, but also set a specific value r ($r = R/5$, for example). For nodes whose d is less than r (those nodes in A1 as shown in Fig. 1) will not retransmit the broadcasting packet because the additional coverages of these nodes are small and cause high redundancy. The final value of D_{th} is determined by the value of average distance $aver(d)$ and r. If $aver(d)$ is smaller than r, D_{th} is set to $aver(d)$. And if $aver(d)$ is larger than r, D_{th} is set to r. That is:

If $aver(d) \leq r$, then $D_{th} = aver(d)$;
If $aver(d) \geq r$, then $D_{th} = r$.

Here are two special situation of nodes' distribution:

- When node S has only one neighbor H, there is no need to determine the threshold. H will definitely be the retransmitted node.

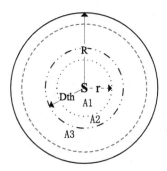

Fig. 1. Areas for different coverage

- When all neighbors of node S are closely distributed around node S, which means node S has to select the relay nodes among these neighbors although the retransmitted coverage they gain are very small.

In both cases, the distance threshold can be determined in accordance with the conditions we described above. In other cases, such as the uneven distribution, the threshold can also be determined. Namely, no matter how many neighbors there are, no matter how they are distributed, a node can determine a distance threshold and relay nodes according to the above approach.

C. Determining the forwarding nodes

We determine the forwarding nodes according to the following rules: usually nodes within the distance threshold will not retransmit, and nodes outside the threshold will be candidates to forward the packet with high probability. If there are more qualified candidates than required and all of these candidates retransmit the packet, it will result in collision at the receiving nodes, which is one form of unreliability. Therefore, to avoid collision, we select four nodes at most to forward the packet in a cooperative way in our protocol. These nodes start to forward at different time point.

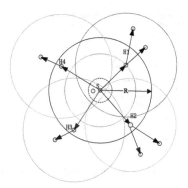

Fig. 2. Determining the forwarding nodes

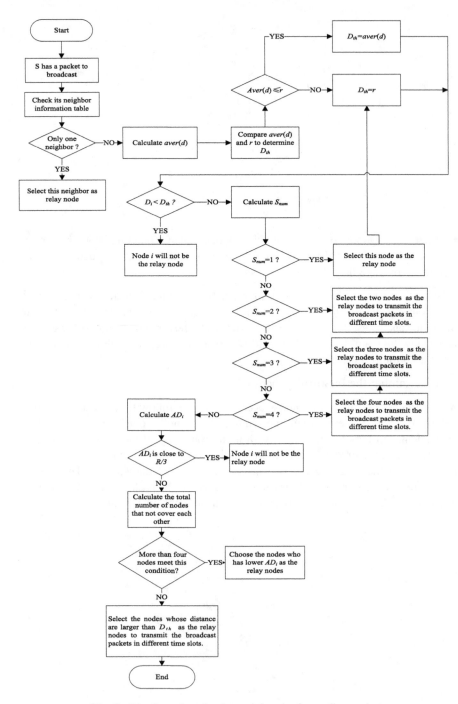

Fig. 3. The flow chart for determining the forwarding nodes

For example, in Fig. 1, nodes in A2 will not forward the broadcasting packet, while nodes in A3 will be the candidates to forward the packet. Among these candidates, four nodes whose distances d from S are closed to 2/3R will be selected to forward the broadcast packet in distinct time slots. There might be more than four candidates close to 2/3R, the criteria to select the forwarding nodes is as follows: firstly, calculate the absolute values between d of these candidates and 2/3R. The less the absolute value is, the closer it is to 2/3R, and the higher possibility it is to transmit the packet. Secondly, node S should do the best to make that the four forwarding nodes are not in each other's coverage. This way can extend the coverage, reduce the broadcast redundancy and improve the reliability. As shown in the Fig. 2, node S is the source node, and *H1*, *H2*, *H3*, *H4* are next-hop nodes to forward the packet in a cooperation manner and they do not cover each other.

Figure 3 is the flow chart for determining the forwarding nodes. Let D_i be the distance between the sending node and the neighbor i, S_{num} be he number of neighbors whose distance is larger than D_{th}, and AD_i represent the absolute difference between D_i and 2/3R. In the flow chart, It can be seen that the occasions of less than four neighbor nodes is taken into consideration as well.

4   Simulation Results and Analysis

We conducted the simulation to test the performance of DCBB. DP is an algorithm which adjusts forwarding probability dynamically based on the number of neighbors [16]. Both DP and DCBB are based on neighbor information, so we selected DP as the reference.

The simulation settings are as follows. The area is a 1.0 km*1.0 km square field with 20, 40, 80 and 100 nodes randomly uniformly deployed. The MAC protocol of each node is IEEE802.11 DCF, and the bandwidth of wireless interface is 11 Mb/s. The transmission range of a node is set to R = 250 m. And there is one source node in the networks which generates broadcast packets. The Data flow sent by the source is in constant bit rate, and it generates 5 packets per second. The size of each packet is set to 64bytes.

The following performance metrics are used for evaluation and comparison: (1) Retransmitted ratio is defined as the ratio of the number of forwarding nodes over the total number of nodes in the network. (2) Reachability is the proportion of nodes in the entire network which can receive a broadcast packet. (3) Average maximum end-to-end delay is the average maximum delay for a broadcasting packet. We record the start time of a broadcast packet as well as the time when the broadcast packet reaches a destination node. The difference between these two values is the end-to-end delay of broadcast.

Figure 4 shows the retransmitted ratio versus different number of nodes in a network. As shown in the figure, retransmitted ratio of DCBB is significantly lower than that of DP because DCBB suggests that few nodes are involved to forward the broadcasting packet. In order to save energy of nodes and prolong the lifetime, it is important for networks to reduce the retransmitted ratio. By reducing the number of forwarding nodes, DCBB can decrease the redundancy and improve broadcast efficiency efficiently.

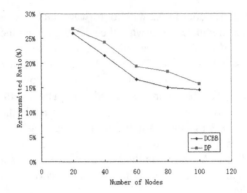

Fig. 4. Retransmitted ratio VS. Number of Nodes

Figure 5 indicates the reachability versus different number of nodes in a network. We can see that the reachability for DP decreases rapidly and is significantly lower than DCBB when the number of nodes in the network is larger than 40. Considering the additional coverage, DCBB selects four relay nodes at most to retransmit the broadcasting packet. Moreover, to ensure the reachability, the relay nodes will forward the packet at different time slots. However, the relay nodes in DP will retransmit the broadcasting packet at the same time, which lead to collision and unreliable broadcast. The simulation results are consistent with the theoretical analysis.

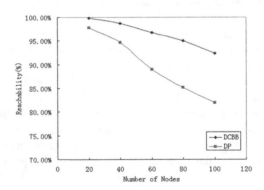

Fig. 5. Reachability VS. Number of Nodes

Figure 6 shows the average maximum end-to-end delay of networks. In DCBB, each forwarding nodes will select a delay time randomly to avoid contending the channel if they transmit the broadcasting packet at the same time. As indicated in the figure, the value of average maximum end-to-end delay of DCBB is a little greater than that of DP. That is because DCBB will select a random waiting time before retransmit the packet to avoid collision. But the delay of DCBB is still very small and does not make a sense to the overall delay of applications.

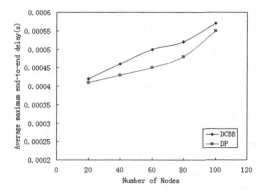

Fig. 6. Average maximum end-to-end delay VS. Number of Nodes

5   Conclusions

In this paper, we propose a distance and cooperation based broadcasting algorithm suitable for wireless ad hoc networks. Theoretical analysis and simulation results show that higher reachability, lower retransmitted ratio and reasonable end-to-end delay have been obtained by DCBB. Therefore, DCBB has achieved the goal of reducing redundancy and the broadcast traffic to a network. It increases the efficiency of broadcast. In general, the algorithm we proposed is applicable to the densely distributed network environment. Through time-division forwarding scheme, every node can reduce channel contending and improve the network utilization effectively. For future work, we wish to apply DCBB to the AODV routing protocol to further demonstrate its performance in the practical scenario.

Acknowledgment. This research was supported partially by the Project of Zhejiang Qianjiang Talent (2010R10007), partially by Zhejiang Provincial Natural Science Foundation of China (Y1090232) and partially by the Graduate Technology Innovation Project of Zhejiang Gong-shang University (1120XJ1511124).

References

1. Lou, W., Wu, J.: On reducing broadcast redundancy in ad hoc wireless networks. IEEE Trans. Mob. Comput. **1**(2), 111–122 (2002)
2. Williams, B., Camp, T.: Comparison of broadcasting techniques for mobile ad hoc networks. In: The 3rd ACM International Symposium on Mobile Ad Hoc Networking & Computing, Switzerland, pp. 194–205 (2002)
3. Ni, S.Y., Tseng, Y.C.Y., Chen, S., Sheu, J.P.: The broadcast storm problem in a mobile ad hoc network. Wireless Netw. **8**(2), 153–167 (2002)
4. Khabbazian, M., Blake, I.F., Bhargava, V.K.: Local broadcast algorithms in wireless ad hoc networks: reducing the number of transmissions. IEEE Trans. Mob. Comput. **11**(3), 402–413 (2012)

5. Lipman, J., Boustead, P., Chicharo, J.: Reliable optimised flooding in ad hoc networks. In: The IEEE 6th Circuits and Systems Symposium, China, pp. 521–524 (2004)

6. Wu, J., Dai, F.: Broadcasting in ad hoc networks based on self-pruning. Int. J. Found. Comput. Sci. **14**(2), 201–210 (2003)

7. Sasson, Y., Cavin, D., Schiper, A.: Probabilistic broadcast for flooding in wireless mobile Ad hoc networks. In: The IEEE Wireless Communications and Networking Conference, New Orleans, pp. 1124–1130 (2003)

8. Mohammed, A., Ould-Khaoua, M., Mackenzie, L.: An efficient counter-based broadcast scheme for mobile ad hoc networks. In: Wolter, K. (ed.) EPEW 2007. LNCS, vol. 4748, pp. 275–283. Springer, Heidelberg (2007). doi:10.1007/978-3-540-75211-0_20

9. Kim, D., Toh, C.K., Cano, J.C., Manzoni, P.: A bounding algorithm for the broadcast storm problem in mobile ad hoc networks. In: IEEE Wireless Communications and Networking Conference, USA, pp. 1131–1136 (2003)

10. Lipman, J., Liu, H., Stojmenovic, I.: Broadcast in ad hoc networks. Comput. Commun. Netw., 121–142 (2009)

11. Yuan, Q.J.: Based on residual energy and distance threshold broadcasting algorithm in ad hoc network. Dalian University of Technology, Dalian (2008). (in Chinese)

12. Lou, W., Wu, J.: A reliable broadcast algorithm with selected acknowledgements in mobile ad hoc networks. In: Global Telecommunications Conference, USA, pp. 3536–3541 (2003)

13. Vollset, E., Ezhilchelvan, P.: A survey of reliable broadcast protocols for mobile ad-hoc networks. Technical report CS-TR-792, University of Newcastle upon Tyne, pp. 1–7 (2003)

14. Wang, S.H., Chan, M.C., Hou, T.H.: Zone-based controlled flooding in mobile ad hoc networks. In: 2005 International Conference on Wireless Networks, Communications and Mobile Computing, Hawaii, pp. 421–426 (2005)

15. Khabbazian, M., Bhargava, V.K.: Efficient broadcasting in mobile ad hoc networks. IEEE Trans. Mob. Comput. **8**(2), 231–245 (2009)

16. Hanashi, A.M., Siddique, A., Awan, I., Woodward, M.: Performance evaluation of dynamic probabilistic broadcasting for flooding in mobile ad hoc networks. Simul. Model. Pract. Theory **17**(2), 364–375 (2009)

17. Leu, S., Chang, R.-S.: Simple algorithm for solving broadcast storm in mobile ad hoc networks. IET Commun. **5**(16), 2356–2363 (2011)

18. Zhang, X., Shin, K.G.: Chorus: collision resolution for efficient wireless broadcast. In: IEEE INFOCOM, USA, pp. 1–9 (2010)

19. Liu, J., Li, L., Jing, X.: Space-covers broadcast algorithm without neighbor information in multi-hop wireless networks. J. Electron. Inf. Technol. **32**(10), 2435–2436 (2010). (in Chinese)

20. Xiong, N., Huang, X., Chen, H., Wan, Z.: Energy efficient algorithm for broadcasting in ad hoc wireless sensor networks. Sensors **13**(4), 492–4936 (2013)

Author Index

Printed in the United States
By Bookmasters

Printed in the United States
By Bookmasters